Endangered Languages in India

Edited by
Kamalini Sengupta

INTACH

ENDANGERED LANGUAGES IN INDIA

ISBN: 978-81-7305-468-6

Published by:
INTACH
The Indian National Trust for Art and Cultural Heritage
71, Lodhi Estate, New Delhi - 110003

First Hardback Edition: **2014**

Distributed by:
Aryan Books International
Pooja Apartments, 4B, Ansari Road, New Delhi-110 002 (India)
Tel.: 23287589, 23255799; Fax: 91-11-23270385
E-mail: aryanbooks@gmail.com
www.aryanbooks.com

CONTENTS

Acknowledgements

INTACH is grateful to the India International Centre for providing the venue for the Seminar, Dr. Kapila Vatsyayan, Chairperson, Asia Project, IIC, and Dr Kavita Sharma, Director IIC for their support, all of which facilitated its success.

We would like to thank our other sponsors, as follows:
Professor Rajesh Sachdeva, Director-in-charge, and Dr G.D.P. Shastry, Reader-cum-Research Officer, Head, Centre for Tribal and Endangered Languages, Central Institute of Indian Languages; Shri Agrahar Krishnamurthy, Secretary, Sahitya Akademi; Professor R Govindan, Vice Chancellor, National University of Educational Planning and Administration; the UK INTACH Trust; and Jet Airways. Without their support it would not have been possible to include such a number of scholars and specialists from all parts of India and abroad.

Apart from introductory talks by Chairman, INTACH, Shri S.K. Misra and Kamalini Sengupta, Director ICH, the Inaugural Session on the 22nd October was enlightened by excellent talks by Professor S.S.Noor, Vice Chairman of the Sahitya Akademi and eminent Punjabi literateur, Dr. Kapila Vatsyayan, Chairperson, Asia Project, and Keynote speaker Mr Christopher Moseley who introduced and gave a detailed view of the UNESCO Atlas on the World's Languages in Danger, while Shri Yogendra Narayan, Member Secretary, INTACH made some comments and gave a vote of thanks at the end. We thank them all for their invaluable input.

We would particularly like to express our gratitude to His Excellency Professor Piotr Klodkowski, Polish Ambassador in India, for his presentation at the Valedictory Session on the 23rd October, and for sponsoring the visit and participation of Dr. Tomasz Wicherkiewicz in the seminar.

For their invalable intellectual input I would particularly like to thank Professor Anvita Abbi, Chairperson, Centre for Linguistics, School of Languages, Jawaharlal Nehru University, and Professor Udaya Narayan Singh, earlier Director of the Central Institute for Indian Languages and presently Tagore Professor, Visva-Bharati,

Santiniketan. Without their expert and unstinting input, advice and hard work, the seminar would not have been possible.

We would like to thank the following for so ably chairing the various sessions of the Seminar as follows:

Professor Peter Austin – who also gave the plenary talk, Professor Udaya Narayan Singh, Christopher Moseley, Professor Anvita Abbi, Dr Lotika Varadarajan and Dr. Rajesh Sachdeva.

Lastly, we would like to acknowledge the hard work of those members of INTACH who so kindly cooperated with the Intangible Cultural Heritage Division for the resounding success of the Seminar.

Preface

S.K. Misra - Chairman, INTACH

The Seminar on Endangered Languages organized by the Intangible Cultural Heritage Division of INTACH included distinguished participation from India as well as other countries. Mr Christopher Moseley is the editor in chief of UNESCO's latest Atlas of the World's Languages in Danger and delivered the keynote address, Professor Peter Austin specializes in endangered languages at the School of African and Oriental Studies at London University and gave the plenary address, Dr. Christopher Reid is a specialist in Australian Aboriginal languages, Dr. Jean Robert Opgenort is an expert on the Himalayan Languages and is from Leiden University in the Netherlands, Dr Tomasz Wicherkiewicz is from Adam Mickiewicz University, Poland, and holds the Chair of Oriental Studies in the Department for Language Policy & Minority Studies. We were also fortunate that the Ambassador of Poland, Professor Piotr Klodokowski delivered a talk at the Valedictory Session. Among the Indian scholars were represented the top universities and institutions, including Visvabharati University at Santiniketan, Jawaharlal Nehru University in Delhi, Delhi University, Telugu University, Hyderabad University, Dravidian University, the Bhasha Centre in Ahmedabad, Jadavpur University, Rajiv Gandhi University in Itanagar, NCERT, CIIL, etc. The outcome is the production of some satisfying and worthwhile recommendations which are being published in this volume.

INTACH was founded 25 years ago, in 1984. The focus then was on built heritage, natural heritage and material heritage - or the restoration and conservation of art objects, paintings, manuscripts etc. Intangible heritage, on the other hand, is the mainspring of all forms of cultural heritage, and we realized it was time to create a new division. ICH division is now over one year old. The division, at the initiative of Kamalini Sengupta has tackled different areas such as traditional medicine, witchcraft, craft traditions, music traditions etc.

In some communities the numbers are small, and the difficulties of revival insurmountable, but one can at least record and document for community members to be able to access at a later stage, and for scholars and researchers. There are also problems of lack of financial and technical resources. Areas of prioritization will have to be identified, and in following the recommendations we can perhaps think of regionwise pilot projects.

The selection of the language of education is obviously a key area, and one of the practical problems is that education is a state subject. It will not be easy to ensure that all states fall in line, and there will be a need for the Central Government to lay down guidelines after discussions for a uniform policy. Other problems are that most endangered languages have no script or written literature. The community would have to be involved in the acceptance of a script. The level at which the mother tongue will be introduced and used is another aspect which has been discussed. It is also recognized that some major languages are crowding out these languages. Political and religious considerations have also to be taken into account as well as opportunities of employment of those speakers.

This was the first major seminar held by the ICH division. The subject is a complicated and difficult one, and it will not be an easy task to tackle the challenges and problems that face the communities speaking endangered languages. However, it has been possible to discuss many of these issues at the Seminar and I am hopeful that INTACH will be able to act as a catalyst in getting some of the recommendations implemented with systematic follow up.

Introduction

Kamalini Sengupta - Director, Intangible Cultural Heritage Division, INTACH

INTACH's Intangible Cultural Heritage division organized the international seminar on Endangered Languages in India, an area it has decided to prioritize, in order to clarify and understand some of the complex issues involved, before launching and formulating its future programme.

The world has only since the last twenty years or so, ie since the 1990s, turned its attention towards the dangerous trend of language loss and language death. Some of the figures bear repetition:

- By the end of the century about 50% of the languages in the world will be extinct, from which eminent linguist, David Crystal, has calculated that worldwide, about one language dies every fortnight.
- 4% of the world speaks 96% of the existing languages, which if looked at from the obverse side, indicates that 96% of the world, ie the vast majority, speaks just 4% of the languages. These languages, therefore, assume enormous importance. They represent the mainstream, are overwhelmingly powerful, and draw all the resources and status to themselves. They hold the key to crucial aspects of the human endeavour, including livelihood, prestige, influence, creative wealth, new knowledge and growth. They also lead to monolingualism in society and education in large regional swathes, and in the case of English, worldwide. In many cases, these languages have been dubbed 'killer' languages because they swamp and drown the smaller languages.

Why should this trouble us or the world? Why not allow the natural or man-made death of languages wherever it occurs? This is a question asked by many who are unaware of the many millions who speak the smaller languages. (It should be noted that 'smaller' in this case, indicates the number of speakers and not the richness or complexity of the language.)

We have understood that language loss includes the loss of almost the entire culture carried within that language – including song, poetry, lore, history, customs, as well as traditional and valuable knowledge systems, philosophy and wisdom, not to speak of the very identity and cultural ethos of the speaker community. When a language dies, that is, when no language knower is left, when no documentation, recording, film, or written word remains, then the loss is indeed very great. This loss is not only to that community, but to the world at large. It is also distressing, that such language speakers are often sidelined by insensitive educational systems which cause them damaging loss of self esteem, pride and identity.

In India, which was the area under study at the Seminar, about 2-3% of the people speak Tibeto-Burman and Munda languages from the Himalayan and north eastern hilly areas and Jharkhand respectively, where almost all the local languages are in various stages of attrition. There are many other areas of the country which suffer from greater or lesser degrees of such attrition. One estimate (see *Language Endangerment in Central India* by Dr. Ramakrishna Reddy, page 73) is that, including the above, a total of 'less than 8% or so' of Indians are from endangered language communities. This comes to around a staggering 80 million souls. Even if we discount the rest of India and look only at the 20-30 million who are known to be Tibeto-Burman and Munda speakers, we cannot ignore such numbers. While also working on balancing the hegemony of the big powerful languages such as English or Hindi, the place of the 'smaller' languages in early school systems must surely also be carefully and seriously addressed.

Global research in cognitive studies indicates that early learning is decidedly beneficial if it is in the mother tongue rather than another language. '... it is axiomatic that the best medium for teaching a child is his mother tongue' (J Cummins - Review of educational research, 1979 sagepub.com) In India, as is well known, this other language would be either English (the most sought after and the choice for most elite schools), Hindi or a mainstream state language such as Bengali, Tamil, Gujarati etc. Fluency in reading and writing in the mother tongue would then greatly ease the learning of another language, through enhanced cognitive skills, at a later stage, according to such studies. Indeed bi-lingual or tri-lingual education, imparted in well regulated stages, is strongly indicated. 'The development of skills in a second language is a function of skills already developed in the first language.' (James Cummins, Canadian Modern Language Review) This holds meaning for the Indian situation where there has been much bandying about of three-language formulas. Indeed, Professor Anvita Abbi is of the view that even four-language formulas are recommended. This formulation obviously means starting at a very young age, ie at the primary level or Class 1. If this pattern is not followed, especially in societies which do not have a traditional writing system, and are therefore basically illiterate, ie for first generation literates, or even among poorer communities, the children will find it difficult to decode the lessons imparted to them; certainly, they will find themselves at an unfair disadvantage vis a vis children from more fortunate backgrounds. In worst case scenarios a child can miss out altogether on the lessons imparted at school, and emerge with almost no education or even proper literacy. MLE (Multi-lingual education) with an MT (mother tongue) starter at the very earliest stage, is, therefore, an essential consideration which should be urgently addressed by the educational and language policy makers of the country.

Many well meaning states and educational systems are, however, launching into precipitate English medium instruction at the youngest level to cater to the rush for mainstreaming and success in the job market. This trend should be very carefully and indeed, swiftly reversed, though it may be difficult in the face of the aspirations and mindsets of the majority. It must be clearly demonstrated that English or the desired mainstream language, will come with greater success at a later stage. 'Students perform much better if they learn fluent reading and basic concepts in their own mother tongue. This is particularly important when the official language of instruction has complex spelling rules (for example English, French Portuguese). Governments must be helped to overcome the logistical and political obstacles associated with teaching in local languages, including both teacher and parental resistance.' (*Efficient Learning for the Poor- Insights from the Frontier of Cognitive Neuroscience, Helen Abadzi, World Bank.)*

We have gained a mass of useful and helpful pointers, and hopefully some clarity, in this complex subject at the seminar and made some headway in understanding a large number of issues. The work, studies, analyses and examples given, not only from India, but from key areas around the world, including Australia and Europe, will help to give us a perspective and vision of avenues of possible progress.

A major conclusion is that there is no coverall formula or solution, but that each region, each language or group of languages will have to be studied individually and balanced against national and other considerations to find viable solutions; but this should not gainsay the fact that all successful programmes or 'best practices' should form a useful base or starting point, or be adapted and even replicated.

It was recognized that it would be impractical to revive some languages that are moribund or already dead. Here, the better course would be to work on research and documentation, such as grammars, lexicons, stories, music, lore and knowledge still remembered.

An example of path breaking work of this nature has been done by Professor Anvita Abbi with the Great Andamanese community. She has lived in the field area for prolonged periods, become a close friend of the community of approximately 50 persons and made an interactive on line dictionary, a grammar, documented lore and songs, and produced a letter book; all these activities aroused great interest within and without the community, and the letter book is now in use in several schools.

The seminar also appreciated the plenary talk by Professor Peter Austin of SOAS (School of Oriental and African Studies of London University) which described his remarkable work in the revival of Gamilaraay-Yuwaalaraay, an Aboriginal language of North Central New South Wales in Australia, which was considered 'dead'. He and his colleagues introduced a slew of measures, including the creation of interactive materials and the popularization of songs in the language, apart from dictionaries, text books and other well thought out and creative materials. Such activity, however, should not be lightly undertaken, but should have clear goals and commitment.

The aims of the seminar were:

1. Spreading awareness of the existence and dangers of loss of endangered languages
2. Exchanging views and information among specialists, academics and scholars on the present situation, and pin pointing the problems

These first two aims certainly found a start at the Seminar. It was widely attended by people from educational institutions, interested public, scholars, activists and reported in the press and on television. The attendance by large numbers of students across the board was very encouraging. And of course, many of the specialists felt it had been a very useful exercise to interact with fellow specialists and exchange views and discuss problems.

3. Ascertaining the place of minority and regional languages in education and society, and
4. Recommending viable solutions on a future course with emphasis on education, the younger generation and continuity.

The last two items have also been addressed to a great extent, though obviously various details and aspects of the work will be an ongoing process, and there will have to be frequent reviews and sustained and focused activity. The case of Andhra Pradesh is an encouraging example of a state government's concern and involvement in tackling the problem with measures put into practice at the ground level, as indicated in the presentation by Dr M. Sreenathan; this certainly bears close study and possible replication. Dr Nicholas Reid has given a detailed account of the steps that have been taken for reviving endangered languages of the Aboriginal communities again, in Australia; these can be studied for best practice indicators. Other speakers have also given accounts of methodologies thus enabling us to compile what I hope will be a valuable document for reference and consultation in a variety of scenarios.

The seminar has given us an important indication of the seriousness with which endangered languages and linguistic rights are now regarded worldwide. So we learn that there is equal concern in Europe and that, as Dr. Thomasz Wicherkiewicz has said, apart from the European Bureau for Lesser Used Languages, a body of long standing and the Foundation for Endangered Languages in London etc., the European Union has ratified a Charter for Regional and Minority Languages. One of the aims of this charter 'is the creation of societies in which cultural and linguistic difference is a source of stability, rather than the opposite'.

We greatly appreciate the encouraging participation of scholars not only from the field of linguistics, but from the fields of political science, literature, ethnology, aesthetics, the arts, and education, and those with commitment, concern and vision who will surely encourage achievable and sustainable remedial activities in this key problem area.

At the end of this book, we have set down the recommendations worked out as a result of this seminar. Professor Udaya Narayan Singh made a tremendous contribution with his Valedictory Address on the 23rd October, where he summed up the presentations of the speakers, and culled a string of useful recommendations. We have added a few more of our own, where we feel INTACH can interact with some of the nodal Indian organizations such as the Central Institute of Indian Languages and in other sectors under the Human Resource Development Ministry which also looks after education. INTACH's work can also achieve greater strength from its countrywide spread of 150 plus dedicated and active convenors.

However, there is no doubt that the road ahead will be a long and hard one.

Inaugural Session

Prof. S.S. Noor - Vice Chairman, Sahitya Akademi

Professor Noor remarked on the significance of the discussion to be held at the Seminar about problems of endangered languages and mentioned that after two months there was to be a significant conclave of 200 linguists in Patiala. He felt that these days, there are many discussions on these problems, especially after David Crystal said that in the next 50 years, out of 6000 languages, 50% would die. One must try to save them. A UNESCO research paper on language vitality and endangerment discussed how to judge this endangerment with the following points: Language communication from one generation to the next; availability of written documents and material; policy and will of the state; attitude of speakers to their languages; learning; and medium of education. He felt that we must be conscious that we are responsible for this problem. Studies are necessary. For example, Adity Mukherjea has studied that in Delhi Punjabis and Bengalis are responsible for the next generation losing interest in their own languages and speaking English or Hindi. UNESCO's study in language vitality and endangerment stresses the need of primary education in the mother tongue. But a survey in Punjab illustrates that in about 3000 primary schools the education is not in Punjabi and that most public schools ignore Punjabi as a subject. The loss of interest in Punjabi is also there because the material of different subjects is not available in Punjabi. Nevertheless, universities and institutions are struggling to create this material. It is the same with most languages. Material was earlier available in English, and now in Hindi. Science and social sciences are mostly in English. English and Hindi have all the power. They are crushing other Indian languages, though Tamil, Bengali, Kannada etc are also developing. A pluralist society must maintain diversity of languages and cultures. Globalization is also advocating that English is the only global language which one must know for international careers. English is the language of globalization, but not the language of localization. These local languages must be saved and linguistic fascism must be fought. Only India understands this diversity, through the aesthetics of Kalidas, Kabir and Nanak in the original languages. Translations cannot convey the beauty of the original. Several studies have been made about endangerment. There is a warning: Where have all the speakers gone? Professor Noor hoped the scholars would discuss all these problems.

Keynote Address

Christopher Moseley - School of Slavonic and East European Studies, University College, London

Endangered Languages of India and the UNESCO Atlas of Languages in Danger – Mapping a Complex Mosaic

I have been invited to speak to you as the general editor of an Atlas of the world's endangered languages, so I make no claim to any special expertise of my own on the subject of the endangered languages of India. The Atlas that I want to introduce to you today is in fact the third edition of this volume – and at last we can say it is a pretty comprehensive one. The previous two editions made no claim to covering the entire globe; rather they concentrated on the situation in certain continents. India is in fact one of the countries that is being represented for the first time in this edition. So I think a word of explanation is needed as to how this project came about in the first place.

The United Nations Educational, Scientific and Cultural Organization has now existed for sixty years, and in that time its areas of concern have shifted slightly. India as a nation has existed for about the same length of time. The concept of 'language endangerment' as a field of study is much younger than that; it is a field that has burgeoned really only in the past twenty years. The idea that the diversity of the world's languages needed to be protected, needed intervention, is younger than the idea that species of flora and fauna need safeguarding, in fact. Nowadays the organization has a whole important section devoted to Intangible Heritage, and it is under that section that the idea of this atlas was fostered. It is in keeping with its aims of ensuring mother-tongue based multilingual education; cultural diversity and inter-cultural dialogue; and free and pluralistic mass media.

How does UNESCO define language endangerment? What situation does a language have to be in, to gain a place in this Atlas? The simple definition of endangerment is: A language is endangered when children no longer learn it. But to define endangerment more closely, a number of factors have to be considered:

- Absolute number of speakers
- Intergenerational language transmission

- Proportion of speakers within the total population
- Community members' attitudes toward their own language
- Availability of materials for language education and literacy
- Shifts in domains of language use
- Response to new domains and media
- Type and quality of documentation
- Governmental and institutional language attitudes and policies, including official status and use

UNESCO is also concerned about linguistic rights as human rights, and there are now a number of widely ratified standard-setting instruments that ensure the right to education in one's mother tongue, the right to publish in the language of one's choice, equitable access to state funding and so on. Some of them are binding, like the International Convention of Civil and Political Rights, and some are non-binding declarations, like the International Declaration in the Rights of Indigenous Peoples.

The organs of the United Nations can only operate through getting international agreements, and by carrying out the programmes of action that are enshrined in these conventions and agreements. As far as endangered languages are concerned, it engages in programmes of awareness-raising, capacity-building, and monitoring status and trends. And that is where this Atlas comes in – for it grew out of one of the articles in the 1992 Convention on Biological Diversity. The primary aim of this Atlas, then, is to provide indicators on the status and trends of linguistic diversity and numbers of speakers of indigenous languages.

This Atlas was first published in 1996, under the general editorship of Stephen Wurm, Professor at the Australian National University. It listed 600 languages which were considered endangered, with 53 pages of text and 12 maps. The second edition, in 2001, was also edited by Professor Wurm, completed just before he died. For both of these editions, he gathered around him an international team of experts, who described the regional situations in texts to accompany each map, and plotted the positions of the endangered languages using a colour-coded system which we still use, basically, in this third edition, and which I will explain shortly. In the second edition the number of languages listed was increased to 800, and there were 90 pages of text and 14 maps. But it was still not complete and comprehensive.

Thanks to some generous funding from the Government of Norway, it was possible to expand the project in several ways for this edition. Firstly, it is appearing for the first time in two forms: a digital, on-line edition that is accessible through the UNESCO web-site, and a printed edition. In fact the printed edition has yet to appear. The digital version was launched in Paris in February this year, to coincide with International Mother Tongue Day. There are both advantages and disadvantages in the print version being delayed. One important advantage is that now that it is accessible to all users, any faults or errors of omission or commission can be rectified for the print version. The disadvantage is that the accompanying text, which goes a long way to explaining the situation on the maps, is not yet freely available to the users. The scope of the Atlas is now greatly extended, to include 2,500 languages – which is probably more than a third of all the languages in the world. Since languages are constantly dying at the rate of at least one every few weeks, naturally we had to decide to include some recently extinct ones among these, so approximately 230 of the languages have been extinct since 1950; in other words, the lifetime of UNESCO, or two generations of language-losers.

The mapping itself has changed profoundly since the last edition. Previously, the printed maps were simply flat outline maps in a single colour, drawn to the appropriate scale for the region being shown but with no topographical detail and few indicators of towns or other landmarks. The new maps are based on Google technology, and this we have in common with, say, the *World Atlas of Syntactic Structures* edited by Martin Haspelmath. It is still not overloaded with geographical detail, because it is important not to distract the user from seeking the location of a language. But the amount of topographical detail, the opportunity to zoom in and out of different scales, all help the user to easily get their bearings.

And of course what is very important is that users have a chance to give their feedback. Some of this feedback will lead to changes in the information provided about the languages in the Atlas. Some of the changes will be incorporated in the printed version of the Atlas, which is currently expected in December this year, but all of it will contribute to the continuous improvement of the Atlas.

When I refer to 'us', I mean of course the team of regional editors who contributed to this project, as well as their consultants and contributors. The world was divided up into regions, more or less continental in scope, and the editors for each section worked on the maps and provided the text. The project had a Web editor in Paris at UNESCO headquarters, the very hard-working Hugues Sicard, who allowed password access to each editor to plot the position of each language on their own map, and provide the accompanying information. The languages were then indexed and grouped by country in alphabetical order, so that the user can scroll down a list for each country to locate a particular language. The information was checked against the ISO codes – and in some cases our regional experts had to disagree with the codes given, either because they applied too widely to a group of separate languages or too narrowly to misidentified languages or dialects, so we are also contributing corrections to the official code list. New codes are needed in some cases; some old codes need to be reassigned.

Another important point about the mapping of languages in this Atlas is that languages are shown by points, not by polygons. Each language point is of a single standard size. The reason is obvious – very small points could easily be lost; very large points, measured by numbers of speakers, would crowd out the smaller points. Also, since we are not mapping stable or unthreatened languages at all, we cannot use polygons – shapes representing the actual area where a language is spoken – because they would border onto nothing. They would raise more questions than they would answer. So therefore we faced the challenge of placing the standard point in the most central location for each language. If the speakers are scattered over a wide area, this presents a further problem, and if there are other languages in between, naturally we do have to use several points. But we have tried to be sparing with these. Such a policy has to be applied judiciously if the speakers are nomadic, for instance – in such a case all we can do is provide a minimum number of representative points. These points themselves, you will notice, are in a range of colours, and these colours indicate the degree of endangerment. The degrees are described on one of the Web pages: Safe - Vulnerable - Definitely Endangered – Severely Endangered – Critically Endangered – Extinct. There has been much discussion about these terms, and they have changed slightly since the last edition. What is most controversial is the last term, Extinct. There are of course languages whose last native speaker has died, maybe even several generations ago, and yet there are second-language speakers who are consciously reviving the language, as they claim it as part of their ancestry. We are considering adding a special category for 'revived' or 'revitalised' languages.

For the preparation of this edition, since we were virtually starting from scratch with mapping India, and the surrounding subcontinent, we needed to call on different kinds of expertise. The subcontinent, especially if we include Pakistan, Nepal, Sri Lanka, Bangladesh, Bhutan and so on, consists of several large and widely different language families; no single expert could be expected to cover it all. In addition to two European scholars, Stuart Blackburn from the School of Oriental and African Studies in London, and Jean-Robert Opgenort, from the University of Leiden, we also needed someone within India to perform a co-ordinating role and check on the current status of endangered languages. The obvious choice was to turn to the Central Institute of Indian Languages in Mysore, and its former director, Dr. Udaya Narayana Singh, to perform this role, and we ended up with a very successful collaboration. I had been lucky enough myself to visit the Institute some years ago, in 2006, when Dr.Singh and his colleagues were the hosts of the annual conference of the Foundation for Endangered Languages. And here I want to pay a special tribute to the memory of the dynamic organizer of that conference, Elangaiyan, who worked tirelessly and selflessly to make that conference a success, and who sadly died two years ago. It was Elangaiyan who made me realise the enormous contribution the Institute has made to the preservation of the language diversity of India.

Perhaps I should explain a little about my own background in mapping the world's languages, and how I came to be involved in this project. From 1987 until 1993 I was involved in preparing the Atlas of the World's Languages for the British publisher Routledge. The joint general editor on the project with me was Professor Ron Asher of the University of Edinburgh, who is now a retired emeritus professor of Linguistics there, and whose field of expertise involves two of the major languages of south India, Tamil and Malayalam. Naturally he was the author in charge of mapping India and southern Asia for the Atlas. Since then we have worked together another six years to produce a second edition, which appeared in 2007, with much improved cartography, and indeed our own cartographic editor, which made a great difference. Mapping languages is not as simple a task as might at first appear, and it requires training and skills that few if any trained linguists have. I mention all this because the demands of that atlas were quite different to the demands of this one. Most obviously, we had to use polygons to represent the true areas inhabited by speakers, not just points on an otherwise blank background. Then there is the question of multilingualism and mixed speech communities; one language area does not necessarily form a border neatly onto another one. Then we had to consider how best to show that languages are related to each other, or unrelated, so we had to introduce a system of colour coding, with as much contrast as possible between families on any one map, and as much subtle shading of a colour to show differences between languages (yet not so subtle as to confuse the reader). We had to make sure that the scale of every page was right, so that we could fit in as many languages as possible within a given country or continuous geographical area, and still leave room for a Key – a colour chart with a numbered list of languages, each number corresponding to a numbered area on a map. Then we had to consider what to leave out - town names? Topographical features? Population density indicators? We decided not to clutter the maps with too much detail, but rather to include topographical features only on world maps on the end-papers of the book, and to show mixed speech communities in urban areas by a series of pie-charts within the text. Names of towns and rivers were included only if they marked important linguistic centres or boundaries. Yet none of these challenges prepared me for the different challenges of editing an atlas like this one for UNESCO. The Routledge Atlas tried to be all-inclusive; this Atlas is selective and is designed to highlight a particular problem.

In highlighting the problem, we need to back up our claims with statistical data. Census data is available for language use in most countries of the world. It varies in reliability. Nor can we merely copy the data from *Ethnologue.* In each case our regional editors sought the latest available figures. In the case of India, the census data raise a lot of complex questions. Therefore a lot of cross-checking was necessary from a number of different sources. Within the region, the problems of collecting data vary from country to country. Taking India and the Himalayan Chain together, the situation presents one of the most complex mosaics in the world. And for this edition, the expansion of data was the most dramatic of any region: starting from just 17 languages in the previous edition, virtually exclusive to Nepal, the region now shows nearly three hundred. One hundred and eighty of these alone are Tibeto-Burman languages clustered along the Himalayan Chain, down to the borders of Bangladesh and Burma. The other, more scattered, languages under threat include some Dravidian, Austroasiatic, Daic and Indo-Aryan examples. I have a complete alphabetical list of these languages with me, and it makes interesting reading.

What about the degree of endangerment of languages of the region? Stuart Blackburn and Jean-Robert Opgenort, the editors for this region, calculate that over a hundred are 'unsafe', nearly as many are 'definitively endangered', a couple of dozen are 'severely endangered', about forty are 'critically endangered' and ten have been included that are recently extinct. Within India alone, the number of endangered languages is about 170. As you would expect, the 'tribal' languages of the northeast and central east are the hardest hit. The states of Arunachal Pradesh and Nagaland contain a high proportion of the threatened Tibeto-Burman group.

Of the Austroasiatic languages of the east and the Nicobar Islands, about two dozen are included.

What are the factors specific to India that are killing off these languages? India has layers of language hierarchy – so do many other countries, of course, but in India the layers are built into the institutional fabric of the state. So, lack of official support is that much more clear-cut in India than elsewhere in the world. Not only are languages not transmitted at home to children, but those that are declining are not taught in schools and lack state support. As my regional editors, say, 'In India, where languages and scripts underpin regional identities and political power, these unofficial and unscripted languages are at a distinct disadvantage.'

Official status in India means inclusion in the 8th Schedule of the Constitution. Since the original 14 languages were included in 1950, eight more have been added. These include two languages under threat: Manipuri (Meithei) and Bodo in Assam. State governments in India determine the medium of instruction in schools, and although some endangered languages are approved for teaching, few are actually heard in the classroom. True, in the small northeastern states there are threatened languages that do have official status within the state – Kokborok in Tripura, Mizo in Mizoram, Garo and Khasi in Meghalaya. But in Nagaland and Arunachal Pradesh, with a high density of minority languages and no clear majority, none have official status, just English in Nagaland and Hindi in Arunachal Pradesh. In this latter state, the situation is exacerbated by a large influx of recent immigrants speaking mostly Hindi, Bengali or Assamese.

One of the aspects of language that this Atlas does not measure is literacy. It is not an easy factor to chart in an Atlas – for a start because a distinction would have to be made between mother-tongue literacy and later-acquired second-language literacy. The Indian census questions, for instance, make no such distinction. Mapping literacy rates is a goal to be pursued for future editions, maybe: but it is an acute problem for India's smaller languages, particularly. Many of them lack a viable script. Probably nowhere else in the world is this issue more complex than in India, because of the wide variety of possible scripts, each with their cultural and religious associations. In the smaller northeastern languages, a script may appear through missionary activity. But the amount of readable material will be small, and literacy in a larger language will inevitably take precedence in schools. Judging by the census results alone, the literacy rates for these northeastern states are fairly impressive, but for the mother-tongue they would actually be negligible.

In the course of this conference, I'm sure we will be touching many times on some of the issues I have raised in this address. Some of my own eminent contributors will also be addressing you. This Atlas is just one way of monitoring the situation for India's and the world's threatened languages. In the number and variety of its languages, India is just about unrivalled in the world, as a single country. We're celebrating a rich storehouse of human culture here, some of which is under threat of extinction, and I would urge you too, to contribute any feedback you would like to present to the Atlas if you feel you have something to add, amend or correct, and ensure that you bring that fragile diversity represented in this country to the world's attention.

Dr. Kapila Vatsyayan - Chairperson, Asia Project, India International Centre

Long-term colleague Shri S. K. Misra, Chairman of INTACH, eminent poet, writer and Vice-President of the Sahitya Akademi Professor S. S. Noor, Professor Christopher Moseley of the University College, London University, Smt. Kamalini Sengupta, Director, Intangible Cultural Heritage Division of INTACH, distinguished delegates, among whom are many friends, from India and abroad.

Thank you for inviting me to address you. As I said immediately after the remarks of Shri S. K. Misra, Professor Noor and Kamalini's introduction, there is little I have to say. The subject is so complex that understandably I am diffident, almost hesitant. This diffidence and hesitancy have increased after listening to Professor Christopher Mosley's presentation of the UNESCO's Atlas of the World's Languages in Danger. I can thus only underline some aspects of the subject in the hope that they may have some relevance for the participants to this conference, many of whom are specialists in the field and have been engaged in their particular spheres for some time.

Allow me first and foremost to congratulate INTACH for having identified this subject and for organizing the conference competently. I would like to specially mention the dedication and energy of Smt. Kamalini Sengupta who has brought together a very distinguished group of scholars. Perhaps it is necessary to reiterate that INTACH has identified the subject keeping in view UNESCO's endeavour to place the issue of endangered languages within the ambit of Intangible Cultural Heritage.

UNESCO's programme of Intangible Cultural Heritage comprises many forms of cultural heritage which have a fluidity as also tenacity. Also, UNESCO has been sensitive to the fact that the entire package of Intangible Cultural Heritage has a direct relationship with issues of environment, bio-diversity and cultural diversity. Besides, there is an intrinsic relationship with the social science sector of UNESCO. It has been my privilege to participate in many of these discussions in different forums of UNESCO, epecially in the last five years as member of the UNESCO Executive Board.

Altogether each of the constituents of Intangible Cultural Heritage cannot be dissociated from the concern of the world community in regard to sustainable development. Some of the participants present here will recall the very important and extensive thematic debate in UNESCO in October 2008 on 'Protecting indigenous and endangered languages and the role of languages in promoting EFA in the context of sustainable development'. The consolidated record of the thematic debate circulated in December 2008 is indicative of the extensiveness as also the urgency with which the issue has to be addressed.

As is obvious, there can be no intangible heritage in the absence of that primary capacity of the human to articulate through sound and the spoken word. Is it not true that most, if not all, forms identified as Intangible Cultural Heritage – from different parts of the world, ranging from the Gagaku in Japan to Vedic chants in India and many, many others – are the gifts of the human through this faculty? In the Indian context, *Nada* is equated to the universal being Brahman: the primordial word is *shruti*. In other cultures too, the 'word' is primary. This unique capacity of the human for articulating through speech, stored memory, of perception of phenomena has been responsible for the formation of societies. Thus, language, epecially the oral articulated word, has been the cause and effect of social cohesion, epecially in those societies which are today termed as 'tribal societies'. Furthermore, language is directly related to the environment, to the flora and the fauna, the cosmology evolved by societies. Language is that medium which allows the human to communicate with the primal elements, to create specific cosmologies. It is the basic instrumentality of social cohesion.

Bio-diversity, cultural diversity and linguistic diversity are all parts of a whole. The shrinking of bio-diversity and cultural diversity impacts on linguistic diversity, and the shrinking of linguistic diversity means loss of the capacity of articulation of a worldview, of a system of values and, more, the understanding and comprehension of the environment and ability to communicate. If we place these interlocked issues in the context of our conference, it will be immediately clear that the subject of endangered languages cannot be dissociated from issues of cultural identity and imbalances between the developed and the developing world. It will be clear that the subject of language thus has enormous proportions.

Obviously, not all these issues can be addressed in this conference, despite its very well thought out aims of spreading awareness of the challenges in the loss of endangered languages, exchanging views and information in regard to linguistic streams, creating wider awareness of the challenges humanity faces if a large group of languages are lost, and attempting to ascertain the place of these languages in education.

If we address ourselves to the primacy of language for the human species and its role in relating the human to his or her natural environment, and its capacity to store knowledge of the environment through a highly systematised structure or oral communication, then it will be clear that the loss of language or the shrinking of linguistic diversity will tantamount to the loss of many important vital knowledge systems of the world.

The conferences in different parts of the world over the last decade have drawn attention to the relationship of language and bio-diversity, language and world views, language and identity, and, most of all, language and the knowledge systems threatened to extinction. This is as true of the communities in the North as in the South. Scholars have drawn attention to the fact, and rightly so, that within nation-states worldwide, the tension is between what is considered global and what is considered local. It is the prioritised languages on account of socio-political considerations, now also economic, which are pressurising the vulnerable cohesive communities to lose their lifestyle as also their language, i.e., speech, but, more, their language of thought. The world community will be poorer; the loss will be irreparable. What are the answers?

Understandably this conference will address not only the linguistic streams, but also the role of major languages within a cultural area which are prioritised. All these discussions will only make us even more sensitive to not only the challenges but the urgency of finding solutions.

I have not had the occasion to read the abstracts carefully, but even a glance convinces me of the richness of the content. My own effort at creating a Thesaurus of five primal elements in some of the indigenous languages of India brought out that the so-called standard languages (written languages) do not measure up to the richness of vocabulary in the indigenous languages, e.g. Water.

Finally, Professor Christopher Moseley's presentation was as illuminating as it was disturbing. India appears to be the country where the largest number of languages are threatened. The data presented and the methods of collecting that data have also been elucidated. Perhaps this data requires very concentrated and serious discussion at the level of linguists, anthropologists, social scientists, educationists and policy makers.

Plenary Talk

Prof. Peter Austin - Endangered Languages Academic Programme, Department of Linguistics, SOAS, University of London,U.K.

Documentation and Revitalization of Eastern Australian Languages

1. Introduction[1]

This paper is an overview of the documentation and revitalization of Aboriginal languages spoken in eastern Australia, and presents a case study of one language, namely Gamilaraay-Yuwaalaraay spoken in north-western New South Wales. We begin with some background about the settlement of Australia and the documentation of its indigenous languages, and then move on to the case study in some detail. The paper concludes with some ideas about what might be learned from the Australian experience by researchers and communities elsewhere who are interested in documenting and revitalizing their own languages.

2. Historical Background

Australia was settled as a penal colony by the British and others commencing at Sydney Cove in 1788. Settlement extended south with the formation of separate colonies in Tasmania (1825), South Australia (1836) and Victoria (1851), joined later by Queensland (1859), and Western Australia (1890). In 1901 a united federal nation of Australia was established, composed of six states and one territory (a further Capital Territory was added in 1911, and the Northern Territory gained responsible government in 1978).

The history of relations between the colonists and indigenous people in eastern Australia was one of land appropriation, killings (including explicit policies of

1 I am grateful to a large number of Gamilaraay and Yuwaalaraay people for sharing with me knowledge of their language, culture and history. Thanks are also due to John Giacon and David Nathan for collaborative work on the language, and for helpful comments and feedback on my research. I am grateful to INTACH, and the Director of its Intangible Heritage Section Kamalini Sengupta, for the opportunity to visit India in November 2009 and participate in the seminar where the original version of this paper was presented. All errors and omissions are my own.

extermination carried out, for example, in Tasmania), and herding remaining groups onto 'missions'. From the late 19th century until 1970 so-called 'mixed-blood' children were removed from their parents and placed in dormitories or given to white families to bring up (these Aboriginal people are now referred to as the 'Stolen Generations' or 'Stolen Children', see Australian Human Rights Commission 1997). It was not until 1967 that Aboriginal people became citizens of Australia and achieved a degree of equality with the majority population.

There have been major social and cultural changes in Australia since 1972 which saw the election of a Labor socialist government led by Prime Minister Gough Whitlam. This government introduced bilingual education and Aboriginal land rights, among other reforms. However the 1980's and 1990's saw reversals of these developments under the Liberal conservative government led by Prime Minister John Howard (see below). In November 2007 a Labour government led by Prime Minister Kevin Rudd took office and undertook a range of measures to redress the indigenous situation, including making a public apology for past wrongs (see below).

3. The Indigenous Context

Australia has been continuously occupied by Aboriginal and Torres Strait Islander people for at least 60,000 years (Horton 1994). It is estimated that at the time of first contact with British settlers in the 18th and 19th centuries there were 600 indigenous groups living throughout Australia, each with its own land, customs, history, and way of speaking. Population estimates are difficult to make due to the impact of disease brought by the colonists, but the pre-contact population may have been of the order of one million people (Australian Bureau of Statistics 2008). Linguists estimate that the 600 groups spoke roughly 250 different languages (Dixon 2002:5, Walsh 1997). The languages can be classified into two major genetic groupings: Pama-Nyungan (occupying the southern three quarters of the continent) and non-Pama-Nyungan (roughly 25 different groups, most probably separate language families, spoken in the 'Top End' of the Northern Territory and Western Australia). It is not clear if all the indigenous languages of Australia are ultimately related (Bowern and Koch 2004, Evans 2005).

Traditionally each language showed a number of different speech styles (avoidance, ritual, and song styles being commonly distinguished) and there was widespread multilingualism through exogamous marriage, with children growing up speaking several languages (Dixon 2002:4).

Today only 10% of the original indigenous languages are spoken fluently as first or second languages. Approximately 40% of the languages are moribund (having a few older speakers) or extinct (50%). In the 2006 national census, 55,695 people, or about 12% of the indigenous Australian population, said that an indigenous language was their primary household means of communication (Australian Bureau of Statistics 2008). Only 12 languages (5% of the original) remain strong in the sense that they are being learned as first languages by children and are in widespread use in their communities. All the strong languages are located in the centre and north of Australia. Note that some strong languages have gained speakers by replacing other smaller indigenous languages.

4. Political Developments in Last 25 Years

Bilingual education in several Aboriginal languages was established by the Federal government in the Northern Territory in 1972, and extended later to other states. In 1988 the bicentennial of British colonisation prompted national discussion about Australian identity and history, and relations with the indigenous peoples. In 1992 the Federal court 'Mabo decision' recognised Aboriginal and Torres Strait Islander's prior occupation and ownership of land and overturned the fiction of '*terra nullius*' that had been the legal framework for the occupation of the continent. In the same year, the Prime Minister, Paul Keating declared at Botany Bay in New South Wales "[w]e took the traditional lands and smashed the original way of life. We brought the diseases. The alcohol. We committed the murders. We took the children from their mothers. We practised discrimination and exclusion. It was our ignorance and our prejudice."

Between 1995 and 2007 a conservative federal government led by Prime Minister John Howard reversed a number of the developments of previous governments in bilingual education and indigenous rights. The low point of government-indigenous relations came in June 2007 with the Federal 'intervention' under which remote indigenous communities lost control and self-management of their affairs, with forced medical examinations of children and changes in access to government benefits. Some communities were occupied by army troops. The 'intervention' began to be wound up back in November 2007 when a Labour government led by Prime Minister Kevin Rudd took office. One of his early actions (on 12th February 2008) was to make a public apology in the national parliament for past treatment of Aboriginal and Torres Strait Islander people.

5. Language Developments

A remarkable feature from 1992 onwards was the establishment across the country of local Aboriginal Language Centres that are owned and run by indigenous people (eg. Kimberley Language Centre, Katherine Language Centre, Wangka Maya Language Centre being early instances). The Institute for Aboriginal Development was set up in 1969 in Alice Springs, central Australia, to teach indigenous languages to service providers such as doctors, nurses, and teachers, to provide interpreting in Aboriginal languages, and to publish books and dictionaries of indigenous languages.

A notable feature of the past 10 years has been an enormous growth in the use of indigenous languages in popular music (through bands such a Yothu Yindi), and on the World Wide Web (see Nathan 2010 for a listing). There are a number of indigenous radio and television broadcasters (such as by the Central Australian Aboriginal Media Association), although it is not possible to determine precisely what percentage of the broadcast content is in indigenous languages.

There has also been significant language documentation work on Aboriginal and Torres Strait Islander languages beginning in the early 1970's and including in particular in recent years research by indigenous scholars on indigenous knowledge systems related to heritage and the environment (the Federation of Aboriginal and Torres Strait Islander Languages, an indigenous professional organisation, has been responsible for sponsorship of some of this work – see http://www.fatsil.org.au/).

6. A Case Study – South-Eastern Australia

In 1788 it is estimated that approximately 70 languages were spoken in the area now occupied by New South Wales, the Australian Capital Territory and Victoria (Wafer and Lissarrague 2008:4, Dixon 2002). There are early records of the languages beginning in 1788 with the Sydney language. By 1900 most of the languages in this area were moribund, and by 1950 many were extinct or reduced to a handful of last speakers. Modern linguistic research began in New South Wales in 1955 (with the data collection of Stephen Wurm) and in Victoria in 1965 (with salvage materials collected by Luise Hercus). The years 1971 to 1980 saw documentation of much of the remaining language knowledge, most of which has now been lost with the deaths of the last speakers and semi-speakers.

6.1 Gamilaraay-Yuwaalaraay

The Gamilaraay language (and the closely related Yuwaalaraay dialect) was traditionally spoken over a vast area of north-central New South Wales when Europeans began colonising Australia. Gamilaraay territory (see map below and Ash et al 2003:1) extended west of the Great Dividing Range, apparently from as far south as the town of Murrurundi, to the areas now including Tamworth, Narrabri, Moree, Boggabilla, Mungindi, Collarenebri, Walgett and Gunnedah.

Map: Location of Gamilaraay-Yuwaalaraay

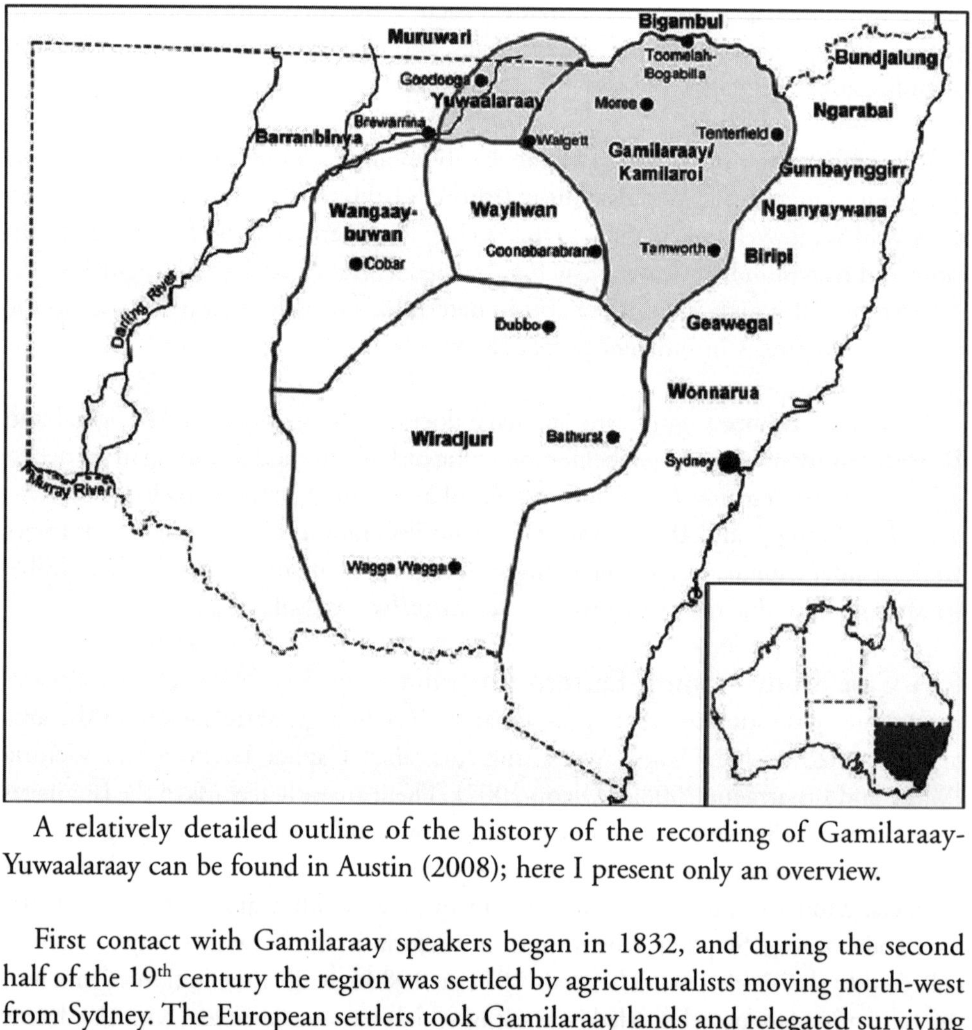

A relatively detailed outline of the history of the recording of Gamilaraay-Yuwaalaraay can be found in Austin (2008); here I present only an overview.

First contact with Gamilaraay speakers began in 1832, and during the second half of the 19th century the region was settled by agriculturalists moving north-west from Sydney. The European settlers took Gamilaraay lands and relegated surviving populations to 'mission' settlements, or to life on the fringes of white society. There are quite a number of missionary and amateur writings dating from this period (Austin 2008, Wafer and Lissarrague 2008:226-237) but they are generally of rather low quality. By the 1930's when the anthropologists Laves and Tindale collected some materials (see Austin and Tindale 1986) Gamilaraay and Yuwaalaraay had become private languages of old people. By 1949 anthropologist Reay could find no speakers of the language (Reay 1949). In 1971 R.M.W. Dixon located some rememberers who could recall vocabulary their parents had used in their youth (Dixon 1984); between 1972 and 1975 I recorded all that these rememberers and others seem to have known, amounting to around 250 words and a few fixed phrases (like *yuulngin ngay ginyi thalaa thuwarr* 'I am hungry, where is the bread?'). In 1976 Corinne Williams worked with the last two reasonably fluent semi-speakers of Yuwaalaraay (see Williams 1980, Austin et al 1980), collecting a vocabulary of 1,500 words and basic grammatical information. By 1990 it appeared that the language was effectively 'dead'.

In 1992 and 1993 I published two small dictionaries (Austin 1992, 1993) containing all of the material that Dixon, Wurm and I had been able to collect, together with some 'reconstitutions' of vocabulary based on older amateur sources. In 1996 David Nathan and I published a version of the larger 1993 dictionary on the internet (Austin and Nathan 1996); this was the first fully hypertext bilingual dictionary published on the web and continues to be consulted even 14 years later. Further work was carried out by John Giacon, transcribing and analysing Williams' tapes (and other materials) resulting in 2003 in a major reference dictionary (Ash et al 2003).

6.2 Language Revival

Interest in reviving Gamilaraay-Yuwaalaraay began in 1998 among Aboriginal groups and school teachers in Walgett, Moree, Boggabilla and Tamworth. There was no centre of activity as such, but rather grass-roots actions building on existing family and education networks. Several workshops and conferences were held, and a newsletter *Yaama Maliyaa* (Hello Friend) was published. In 2000 the New South Wales State Education Department was lobbied to approve the introduction of the language into schools to meet the compulsory Language Other Than English (LOTE) requirement.

Two years later Betts and Giacon (2002) published some introductory language teaching materials, followed in 2003 by a song book with accompanying CD (Yuwaalaraay and Gamilaraay Language Programme 2003). In June 2003 the State government introduced school language programmes that were properly funded, with production of good quality textbooks and teacher materials (in January 2004 the State government granted $500,000 for indigenous language programmes). Three years later Chandler and Giacon (2006) developed a resource book for teachers, and in the same year a picture dictionary for primary school children appeared (Yuwaalaraay and Gamilaraay Language Programme 2006). Giacon began evening classes with school teachers to prepare them to teach the language and by 2006 had introduced a course at the University of Sydney on Gamilaraay-Yuwaalaraay.

In 2006, there were 41 New South Wales Government schools offering programmes in 10 languages (Bundjalung, Dharawal-Dhurga, Dharug, Gamilaraay-Yuwaalaraay, Gumbaynggirr, Ngiyampaa, Dunghutti, Wadi-wadi, Wangkumarra and Wiradjuri). Local Language Centres to support these official moves were established in several places across the state (eg. Muurrbaay Aboriginal Language and Culture Co-operative which published the major reference work of Wafer and Lissarrague 2008). The Department of Aboriginal Affairs established The Aboriginal Languages Research and Resource Centre in Sydney providing resources and guidance, and grants for revitalization work (see http://www.alrrc.nsw.gov.au/).

The State Department of Education website also provides support materials for teachers (see http://www.curriculumsupport.education.nsw.gov.au/secondary/languages/languages/aboriginal/index.htm), and a range of resource materials, dictionaries, school books and CD-ROMs are now available.

One of the most impressive products for Gamilaraay-Yuwaalaraay revitalization was released in 2009, namely Giacon and Nathan's *Gayarragi winangali* (Search and Listen) a free interactive multimedia resource that contains:

- a searchable Gamilaraay Yuwaalaraay Dictionary with over 2,600 entries, all including audio
- 957 spoken sentences from traditional speakers, all transcribed, and hyperlinked to the dictionary
- 30 songs and 14 stories, all transcribed, and hyperlinked to the dictionary
- games, including crosswords and memory/matching games
- other language resources as pdf and text files

These materials are now in use in a number of schools across north-west New South Wales and the language is being taught to several hundred children. Initial indications are that genuine language learning is being achieved.

6.3 Outcomes

There have been a number of outcomes from this language revival and language teaching. The most important of these are positive and affirming messages being given to children and parents about language learning, especially the learning of indigenous languages.

The use of the Gamilaraay-Yuwaalaraay language has become iconic as a badge of group membership. In addition, it is now common for all major events in the region to begin with a 'welcome to country' speech in the language (note for example that the *Yanay to Gamilaraay Festival* (http://www.y2g.com.au/about) held in Moree 21st to 27th September 2009 highlighted language as an important identity and cultural marker).

There is increasing use of modern media and communications channels to promote both this language and others in New South Wales. Thus, for example, it is possible to find language materials, songs etc. on YouTube in Gamilaraay-Yuwaalaraay as well as Gumbaynggir and Wiradjuri (see for example, http://www.youtube.com view_play_list?p=B3D7224317cdc1a6&search_query=wiradjuri+language).

It is quite clear that the goal of these materials and in school language teaching is not productive conversational language use but rather language awareness and the development of positive attitudes, with some learning of formulaic expressions in the traditional languages.

7. Conclusions – What Can We Learn About Revitalization from Eastern Australia?

Languages are historical entities that exist in particular social and political environments, but perhaps it is possible for us to identify some wider lessons from the experiences of language documentation and revitalization in eastern Australia. These might include:

1. Revitalization relies on the existence of solid documentary materials such as tape recordings, dictionaries, grammars and text collections. Without the data and analysis assembled by Williams, Giacon, Nathan and myself it would be extremely difficult to develop revitalization materials and language lessons for Gamilaraay-Yuwaalaraay.
2. Even so-called 'dead' languages can be revitalized, provided there are sufficient materials and energy and commitment to use them.
3. Revitalization projects need clear goals and clear understandings about their functions. In the case of Gamilaraay-Yuwaalaraay there was clarity about the politics and ideology, namely that language is closely connected to identity and serves iconic functions of signalling group membership, even if only in the form of one or two word expressions.
4. There is a need for both local grass-roots activity and government recognition and support (and the resources that governments can provide).
5. Collaboration between linguists, teachers, indigenous specialists and local custodians of knowledge can lead to significant concrete outcomes

(including non-linguistic outcomes like increased self-esteem and other social goods).

It is to be hoped that the recent successes seen in eastern Australia can serve as a beacon for other indigenous communities interested in supporting and revitalizing their languages.

References

- Ash, Anna, John Giacon, and Amanda Lissarrague, 2003, *Gamilaraay, Yuwaalaraay & Yuwaalayaay dictionary*. Alice Springs: IAD Press.
- Austin, Peter, 1992, *A dictionary of Gamilaraay, northern New South Wales*. Melbourne: La Trobe University.
- Austin, Peter, 1993, *A reference dictionary of Gamilaraay, northern New South Wales*. Melbourne: La Trobe University.
- Austin, Peter K., 2008, 'The Gamilaraay (Kamilaroi) Language, northern New South Wales — A Brief History of Research' in William McGregor (ed.) *Encountering Aboriginal languages: studies in the history of Australian linguistics*, 37-58. Canberra: Pacific Linguistics.
- Austin, Peter, and David Nathan, 1996, *Kamilaroi/Gamilaraay web dictionary*. At http://coombs.anu.edu/WWWVLPages/AborigPages/LANG/GAMDICT/GAMDICT.HTM.
- Austin, Peter, and Norman B. Tindale, 1986, Emu and brolga, a Kamilaroi myth. *Aboriginal History* 9:8–21.
- Austin, Peter, Corinne Williams, and Stephen A. Wurm, 1980, The linguistic situation in north central New South Wales. In Bruce Rigsby and Peter Sutton, eds *Papers in Australian linguistics No. 13: Contributions of Australian linguistics*, 167–180. Canberra: Pacific Linguistics.
- Australian Bureau of Statistics, 2008, *1301.0 - Year Book Australia.* http://bit.ly/91hFku [accessed 2010-01-04]
- Australian Human Rights Commission, 1997, *Bringing them home: The 'Stolen Children' report.* Canberra: Government Printer.
- Betts, Marianne, and John Giacon, 2002, *Yaama Maliyaa*. Tamworth: Narnia Bookstore.
- Bowern, Claire, and Harold Koch (eds.), 2004 *Australian languages: Classification and the Comparative Method*. Amsterdam: John Benjamins. Current Issues in Linguistic Theory vol 249.

- Chandler, Karan and John Giacon, 2006, *Dhiirrala Gamilaraay! Teach Gamilaraay! A resource book for teachers of Gamilaraay*. Armidale: Catholic Schools Office.
- Dixon, Bob, 1984, *Searching for Aboriginal languages: memoirs of a field worker*. St Lucia: University of Queensland Press.
- Dixon, R.M.W., 2002, *Australian Languages*. Cambridge: Cambridge University Press.
- Evans, Nicholas, 2005, Australian Languages reconsidered: a review of Dixon 2002. *Oceanic Linguistics* 44.1, 242-286.
- Giacon, Gianbattista (John), 2001, Creating new words in Gamilaraay and Yuwaalaraay. BA Honours thesis, School of Languages, Cultures and Linguistics, University of New England.
- Giacon, John and David Nathan, 2009, *Gayarragi winangali*. Interactive multimedia. [downloadable from http://lah.soas.ac.uk/projects/]
- Horton, David, (ed.), 1994, *The encyclopedia of Aboriginal Australia*, Vols 1 & 2. Canberra: Aboriginal Studies Press.
- Nathan, David, 2010, *Aboriginal Languages of Australia*, http://www.dnathan.com/VL/austLang.htm [accessed 2010-01-04]
- Reay, Marie, 1949, A half-caste Aboriginal community in north-western New South Wales. *Oceania* 15: 296–323.
- Wafer, Jim and Amanda Lissarrague, 2008, *A handbook of Aboriginal languages of New South Wales and the Australian Capital Territory*. Nambucca Heads: Muurrbay Aboriginal Language and Culture Co-operative.
- Walsh, Michael, 1997 How many Australian languages were there? In Darrell Tryon and Michael Walsh (eds.) *Boundary Rider: Essays in Honour of Geoffrey O'Grady* , 393-412. Canberra: Pacific Linguistics, C-136.
- Williams, Corinne, 1980, *A grammar of Yuwaalaraay*. Canberra: Pacific Linguistics B-74.
- Yuwaalaraay and Gamilaraay Language Programme, 2003, *Yugal: Gamilaraay and Yuwaalaraay songs*. Tamworth: Coolabah Publishing.
- Yuwaalaraay and Gamilaraay Language Programme, 2006, *Gaay Garay Dhadhin Gamilaraay and Yuwaalaraay Picture Dictionary*. Alice Springs: IAD Press.

Map: Location of Gamilaraay-Yuwaalaraay

Session 1

Overview of Endangered Languages in India: Pinpointing the Problems

The Sense of Danger: An Overview of Endangered Languages in India[1]

Prof. Udaya Narayana Singh – Tagore Professor, Visva-Bharati, Santiniketan
Earlier, Director, Central Institute of Indian Languages, Mysore

1. The Objectives

This paper aims at demonstrating that in the context of languages of India facing a threat of extinction, there are two kinds of barriers that are at work, bringing in a division among those that are 'achiever languages' and those that are 'endangered languages'. One of them is a 'Socio-cultural barrier' (resulting mainly from ethnic affiliations and inter-ethnic relationships as well as from societal and cultural practices) and another – 'Physical barrier' (especially the hills and the mountains as well as wide rivers and desert) – both of which have been important in creating a kind of seclusion for certain languages that are moving towards endangerment over a period of time. While seclusion poses one kind of danger, living together could result in a silent killing of less functional languages because of our 'assimilationist' tendencies. Even though there are constitutional provisions for all language communities, the real life situation is far from satisfactory. It is, therefore, not surprising to find India topping the list of endangered languages in the world in the latest UNESCO count.

India accounts for 2.4% of the world's land surface with a densely populated space where 16% of the world's population lives (*India: A Country Study* by James Heitzman and Robert L. Worden eds. Federal Research Division; 1995; Also, *The Library of Congress: Country Studies*; Federal Research Division, U.S. Library of Congress)[2].

[1] Paper presented at the International Seminar on Endangered Languages in India (INTACH with IIC, Sahitya Akademi, CIIL, NUEPA, and JNU (22nd-23rd October 2009).

[2] See: http://lcweb2.loc.gov/frd/cs/intoc.html

1961 census reports mentioned a total of 1,652 'mother tongues,' out of which 184 had more than 10,000 speakers[3]. The encyclopaedic *People of India* series of the Anthropological Survey of India[4], identified 75 'major languages' out of a total of 325 languages used in Indian households. Some other accounts show India[5] as a home for 398 languages - 387 of which are living languages. India thus writes in many languages and speaks in many more voices.

As a nation-state, 'India' (or, *Bhârat* as it has been known in our Cultural History) has emerged as a unique cultural space that has 'absorbed' numerous religious and philosophical thoughts, different practices of life as well as a countless number of speech varieties. And yet, communication has never broken down in this sub-continent. India has been a picture perfect example – a mix of comprehension, compassion and conviction - a singular country with plural expression. All this was possible because language always mattered to us. For instance, the technical theme of *Phonetics*, the science of speech sounds was *ShikSaa* (literally, 'education') in ancient India, without which no education could be complete. Besides, in all ages, we had authors who wrote in many languages.

It is estimated that there are about 700-1,000 languages spoken in the South Asian region, belonging to at least four major language families - Indo-Aryan (most of which belonged to one sub-branch of Indo-European), Tibeto-Burman, Dravidian and Austro-Asiatic. Multilingualism is not a new phenomenon in the Indian context. Even Sir George Grierson's twelve-volume *Linguistic Survey of India* (1903-1923) – had identified 179 languages and 544 dialects. One of the early Census reports also showed 188 languages and 49 dialects (1921 census). Each speech community in India has a number of languages in its repertoire – used for different functions. The base language(s) would be in the inner fringe – and so are the basic elements of grammar. What is acquired through acculturization and socialization are in the relatively outer fringes. Thus, while planning for either state intervention in policy planning vis-à-vis our languages and cultures, or in drafting our Constitution, the founding fathers had emphasized both mother tongues as base languages and the regional/link languages. Language has been like a 'peelable' entity for India, with multiple layers.

2. The Distribution

At this point, it may be ideal to introduce the linguistic complexity with respect to

---

[3] *The 1981 census reported 112 mother tongues with more than 10,000 plus speakers*

[4] *People of India Project/edited by K.S. Singh. 1992, 72 volumes; New Delhi: Anthropological Survey of India.*

[5] *http://www.ethnologue.com/show_country.asp?name=India*

language diversity in India and the following facts about India may be worth noting:

- 1,576 *rationalized* mother-tongues (2001 Census);
- 1,796 other mother-tongues;
- 122 languages (with 10,000 plus speakers)
- 22 languages in the Indian Constitution, cover 96% of our population.
- 20 *Austric* & 98 *Sino-Tibetan* languages make up another 2%.
- Highest literary award in 24 languages
- Magazines & Newspapers in 101 languages
- Radio programmes in 146 speech varieties
- 50 languages with literary vitality (1989 estimate)

Gut.	DEV	GUJ	PUN	BEN	ORI	TEL	KAN	TAM	MAL	SINH	URD	SIND
k	क	ક	ਕ	ক	କ	క	ಕ	க	ക	ක	ک	ڪ
kh	ख	ખ	ਖ	খ	ଖ	ఖ	ಖ	–	ഖ	ඛ	کھ	ک
g	ग	ગ	ਗ	গ	ଗ	గ	ಗ	–	ഗ	ග	گ	گ
gh	घ	ઘ	ਘ	ঘ	ଘ	ఘ	ಘ	–	ഘ	ඝ	گھ	گھ
ṅ	ङ	ઙ	ਙ	ঙ	ଙ	ఙ	ಙ	ங	ങ	ඞ	ں	ڱ

Fig 1: Major writing Systems of India

- Earlier about 69, but now 33 languages used in schools; '04
- 14 major writing systems, but about 25 in all – many yet to be connected to the UNICODE consortium activities. Above is a sample of India's major scripts.

The extent of linguistic variation is so complex that a single language like Hindi has over 49 speech varieties.

Genealogically, it is the Tibeto-Burman and the Austric groups that seem to be in the danger zone more than the smaller languages within the Indo-Aryan and Dravidian fold. This, however, cannot be a sweeping statement, because more than the 'language family', it is the distance and seclusion that have played an important role here. As historical facts show, there has been a great deal of admixture of ethnic and linguistic groups in the eastern part of India, and it is these small groups of mother tongues that are more severely threatened. But let us look into the details of language families in this region first.

Languages spoken in the South Asian region belong to at least four major language families: Indo-European (most of which, i.e. 74.24% belong to its sub-branch Indo-Aryan, IA), Dravidian (with 23.86% speakers), Austro-Asiatic (1.16%), and Sino-Tibetan (0.62%)[6]. The Wikipedia figures (Wikipedia, the Free Encyclopaedia[7]) are slightly different though: 72% Indo-Aryan, 25% Dravidian, and 3% people speaking Tibeto-Burman, Austro-Asiatic and other languages. But since the former figures are generally endorsed by both Census reports and Ethnologue, we could stand by the same. The biggest chunk of languages and mother tongues belong to the Indo-Aryan sub-family of Indo-European languages. The immediate predecessor of Indo-Aryan happens to be Indo-Iranian, the oldest specimens of which are available in the Zend-Avesta. Among the modern Indo-Aryan languages, Hindi (especially, the western variety) is a Midland Indo-Aryan language, spoken in the Gangetic plain and around it, on three sides, are Punjabi, Gujarati, Rajasthani. The Eastern Hindi varieties are spoken in Avadh and to its south. In the outer layer of the midlands, we get languages such as Kashmiri, Lahnda, Sindhi, Gujarati, Marathi, in the northern and the western region, and Oriya, Maithili, Bengali and Assamese in the east.

Among Dravidian languages, besides the four internationally known languages spread in many parts of the world, namely, Tamil, Malayalam, Kannada, and Telugu, there are 26 Dravidian languages by the current count, of which 25 are spoken in India and one (Brahui) in Baluchistan on the Pakistan-Afghanistan border. Spoken by more than 300 million people in south Asia, the antiquity of Dravidian languages is largely due to the rich grammatical and linguistico-literary tradition of Classical Tamil[8] and other classical stages of Kannada and Telugu.

The Austric family of languages is divided into two branches, Austroasiatic and Austronesian, the latter formerly called Malayo-Polynesian. They are spoken in India, Southeast Asia, and the Pacific Islands. The Austroasiatic branch has the Munda languages in India, spoken in the eastern and southern parts of India. The well-known Munda languages include the following: Santali, Mundri, Bhumij, Birhar, Ho, Tri, Korku, Khari, Juang, and Savara, etc. The Munda speakers are found mostly in the hills and jungles, while the plains and valleys have some pockets inhabited by people speaking these languages.

---

[6] *http://www.ethnologue.com/show_country.asp?name=India*

[7] *See: http://en.wikipedia.org/wiki/Demographics_of_India*

[8] *Annamalai, E. Review of Bh.Krishnamurti's 'The Dravidian Languages'; In Frontline, Volume 20 - Issue 22, October 25 - November, 07, 2003*

The Tibeto-Burman family is a part of Sino-Tibetan languages, spread over a large area - from Tibet in the north to Burma in the south, and from Ladakh in Kashmir in the west to the Chinese provinces of Sichuan and Yunnan in the east. Lepcha, Sikkimese, Garo, Bodo, Manipuri, and Naga are some of the better-known Tibeto-Burman languages. Besides a few that are close to Tibetan, Bodo and Tipra sub-groups are now well-known, and so are the Naga languages. The Kuki-Chin languages as well as Lushai and Manipuri fall somewhere in between these extreme sub-families. Several smaller languages that cannot easily be fitted into any of the above large families such as Burushaski in the North-West are language isolates. Then there are separate families[9] like Andamanese which would include quite a few diverse languages in the Andamans, and one could possibly also add six odd languages spoken in 22 odd Nicobar islands.

Thus, as is evident from this discussion, language families in India roughly coincide with the broad geographic divisions of the sub-continent. Indo-Aryan speakers are spread over northern and central regions, whereas the twenty-odd Dravidian groups are mostly located in the Southern peninsula. The Austro-Asiatic languages are spoken mainly in the East and Central India, whereas the Tibeto-Burman communities live in the northern Himalayan region (like Himachal Pradesh) as well as in the seven north-eastern States.

In the socio-cultural space called *'Bharat'* or 'India', what happened through the ages was the following: Every time a new element was introduced (from the Aryan influx to the hostile Turks and the Moghuls, leave alone the British merchants) in this cultural space, all concerned speech communities – the hosts as well as the external groups "finally settled down for a peaceful commingling and cultural as well as racial fusion with their predecessors in the land"..."after an initial period of hostile contact in some cases". In the political entity called India, there is no doubt "there have been occasional clashes of interests and ideals or of attitudes which are ultimately based on or linked up with the desire to wield power and control pelf – on the political and economic factors." All the late-comers (such as the Indo-Mongoloids, or the Turks or the Perso-Arabic groups) fell into this pattern established through 3,000 years of contact and convergence. This kind of convergence has given rise to what has been called the '*Sprachbund*' or '*Linguistic Area*' as in M.B.Emeneau's 1958 work – 'India as a linguistic area'. This means that 'assimilation' – rather than 'aggressive conflict' has been a natural trend in the South Asian region.

---

[9] *Mallikarjun, B. 2002. Mother tongues of India according to the 1961 census.* Languages of India, *Vol 5. August no.*

3. Where is the danger?

We will assume here that the latest *UNESCO Atlas of the World's Languages in Danger* (2009), released on Feb 19th 2009 (on the eve of the International Mother-tongue Day – 21st February) presents a tentatively more-or-less accurate and expanded data-set of 2,500 endangered languages – ranked on the basis of five different levels of vitality: unsafe, definitely endangered, severely endangered, critically endangered and extinct. The report is extremely worrisome because it finds that "more than 200 have become extinct during the last three generations, 538 are critically endangered, 502 severely endangered, 632 definitely endangered and 607 unsafe" (http://portal.unesco.org/en/ev.php-url_id=44605&url do=do topic&url _section =201.html).

Although—with the exception of the Andaman & Nicobar Islands—a greater number of nearly extinct languages are located in other countries, it is still painful to note that "199 languages have fewer than ten speakers and 178 others have 10 to 50."

To give an over-all picture of the endangered languages in India, one finds that some of these 196 languages listed in the *Atlas* are spread across different states, and hence the total of all zones as given below would add up to 239. As is predictable, 67.36% of these are located in the eastern region, with another 18.41% in the Himalayan region in the north. If we take up their location with respect to the Himalayan belt, we find 70.29% of them tucked into this region. This only proves the thesis proposed here that the mountains offer a seclusion and barriers where the outer world with more widespread and commercially viable languages is able to reach last. Consider the following distribution of 239 threatened linguistic zones where it is possible to place these 196 languages:

North	[48]	The Himalayas – 44 ; The Rest – 4 (Chattisgarh– 3; Himachal – 19; Jammu & Kashmir – 12; Madhya Pradesh – 11; Uttarakhand – 13; and Uttar Pradesh – 1)
West	[04]	(Maharashtra – 4)
South	[26]	(AP – 11; Karnataka – 6; Kerala – 2; Tamil Nadu – 7)
East	[161]	The Himalayas –124; The Rest – 41 (Andaman & Nicobar Islands – 9; Arunachal – 36; Assam – 24; Bihar – 5; Jharkhand – 10; Manipur – 28; Meghalaya – 5; Mizoram – 6; Nagaland – 21, and Orissa – 17)

Even if one looks into the southern region, in both Andhra Pradesh and Tamil Nadu-Karnataka zone, these languages are located on the hills and in the areas surrounded by dense forests.

Consider the following map of language endangerment in India:

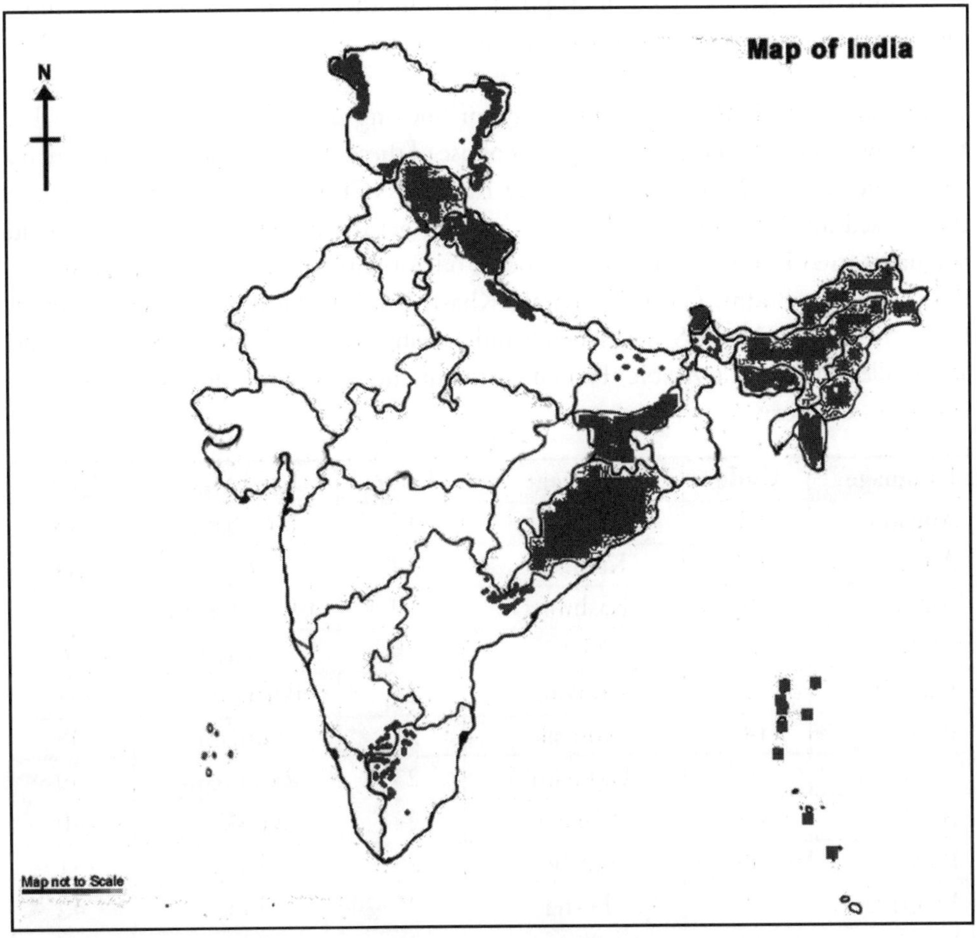

Fig 2: Plotting the Endangered languages in India

4. Possibilities

Language planners and socio-linguists would of course take objection to this apparently primitive explanation such as the one proposed here based on 'barriers' and 'distances', but to my mind, the greatest impact of modern technology and the opening up of the universe of media and communication has been felt here. Since physical mobility had been minimal in these regions, the ideal situation would have been towards retention of these mother tongues (MTs). But the glitz and glamour of the other India or the outer world have reached or begun reaching these corners only in the last decade with the explosion of both communication and media (television and radio) technology and their outreach. Hence, the impact – such as unconscious or planned decisions in favour of dropping one's mother tongue and adopting a more functional language instead - has also been greater.

My conjecture is that this 'shift away' or 'moving out' of MT has been further helped by yet another factor, namely, lack of use of these languages as media of primary education. As the 7th Education Survey Report (NCERT) shows, of the 'language codes' used for different MTs already in use, we get the following picture of 47 odd languages used in our school system today, out of which only 18, i.e. Angami, Ao, Bhoti, Bhutia, Bodhi, Garo, Kakbarak, Khasi, Konyak, Ladakhi, Lepcha, Limbu, Lotha, Mizo, Nicobaree, Sema, Tibetan and Zeliang are outside the 8th Schedule, and are smaller MTs, while Arabic, French, German and Portuguese are in the "foreign" languages category.

Language	Code	Language	Code	Language	Code
Angami	01	Kakbarak	17	Nicobaree	33
Ao	02	Kannada	18	Oriya	34
Arabic	03	Kashmiri	19	Oriya(lower)	35
Assamese	04	Khasi	20	Persian	36
Bengali	05	Konkani	21	Portuguese	37
Bhoti	06	Konyak	22	Punjabi	38
Bhutia	07	Laddakhi	23	Rajasthani	39
Bodhi	08	Lepcha	24	Sanskrit	40
Bodo	09	Limbo	25	Sema	41
Dogri	10	Lotha	26	Sindhi	42
English	11	Malayalam	27	Tamil	43
French	12	Manipuri	28	Telugu	44
Garo	13	Marathi	29	Tibetan	45
Gujarati	14	Maithili	30	Urdu	46
German	15	Mizo	31	Zeliang	47
Hindi	16	Nepali	32	Other language	48

Table 1: Languages in our Schools

The claim is not that their introduction in the school system would automatically make them functionally vibrant. For instance, among these, once again, ten of them, i.e. Angami, Ao, Kakbarak, Konyak, Khasi, Ladakhi, Lepcha, Limbu, Mizo, and Sema also figure in the endangered languages list. However, it is true that the new generation speakers of these languages would usually go by the utility value, or as McConnel and Mahapatra said, by 'language vitality score' (including their availability in the newspaper/magazine/radio domain etc. There are 37.75 million land-line telephones and 362.3 million cell-phones (2009 figures), 2.207 million net providers (2008) with 80 million internet users (2007 figures) and 562 television stations beaming 24 hours in Indian languages (Cf. https://www.cia.gov/library/publications/the-world-factbook/geos/in.html) .

5. How to Overcome the Possible Barriers?

With a population size of 1,166,079,217 (July 2009 est.) where 31% were in the 0-14 age-group, and only 5.3% above 65, and only 2.5% annual rate of urbanization (by 2005-10 estimate) to add to 29% urbans, there is a terrible speed at which changes happen in India (http://www.theodora.com/wfbcurrent/india/india_people.html). There is no doubt that the demographic profile of India has changed and is changing very fast. Over one-third of Indians are younger than 15 years of age, by 2000 estimates.[10] Further, more than 70% of the population lives in more than 550,000 odd villages.[11] Notice that 37.7% Indians are now in 0-14 age-group (by 1996 figure), but this will drop down to 27.7% by 2016. In comparison, most Indians (55.6%) today belong to the 15-59 age-group[12] – the population of which will dramatically go up by 2016 - pushing the people in older age groups[13]. Add the fact that the figure of 'Internally displaced people' (due to construction of large dams, political turmoil, insurgencies etc) in India is significantly large.

All these indicate that if an inclusive language policy based on multilingualism and pluro-culturalism is not in place, a young and changing/moving country such as India will feel adverse repercussions later when we become a country with many more old people. The matter will get further complicated with many other questions, beginning from the issue of dominance of larger languages and LWCs (or, 'Languages for Wider Communication') to empowerment of smaller languages as well as to the interplay of market forces and language loyalty.

---

[10] *the details of which are: 0-14 years: 34% (male 175,228,164; female 165,190,951); 15-64 years: 62% (male 324,699,562; female 301,821,383); and 65 years plus: 4% (male 23,925,371; female 23,138,386)*

[11] *See: http://www.indianngos.com/issue/population/statistics; Courtesy: www.unicef.org*

[12] *http://www.indianngos.com/issue/population/statistics/statistics5.html*

[13] *Calculated from the Report of the Technical Group on Population Projections*

A few more points about India: It is administratively organized into 35 states and union territories (unless we further divide ourselves into yet newer states for which negotiations are on at the moment). Each of these units has under it, divisions or units at several sub-levels. At the first level, there are districts (612 in number) – further sub-divided into sub-districts (5,564)[14]. Nearly 26.1% of the total population live in the urban areas which have shown a phenomenal population explosion - from 28.85 million in 1901 to 159.46 million in 1981 and 217 million in 1991[15]. Currently, there are 51 cities, 384 urban agglomerates and 5,161 towns (2,843 in 1951) in India. A total of 138 million people, or 16 percent, lived in only 299 urban agglomerates (Census 1991). Only 24 metropolitan cities account for 51 percent of India's total population, with Bombay and Calcutta leading at 12.6 million and 10.9 million, respectively. With greater urbanites, one might think the chances of homogenization would be better but that has not happened in India.

Although states in India are organized according to languages (where each state has its own official language), each state has also numerous other language communities who may be speakers of one major language or the other migrating from other states. Further, at any given time, about 15% of Indians are on the move to other places. Therefore, the attempt was to tackle this by creating facilities for out of state groups to open, maintain and nurture their own educational institutions with other than state languages. In addition, a large number of *Kendriya Vidyalayas* or Central Schools (that would use both English and Hindi as media of instruction) and *Navodaya Vidyalayas* funded and managed by the federal government have been of great help. Similarly, each state was to have a Central University that would cater to the linguistic needs of the out of state and migrant population as well as aspirants from other states. It goes without saying that the states in India have excellent universities and colleges, that give preference to state languages, as well as state-level secondary examination boards that manage and affiliate all state-run and many private schools following the state's linguistic policies and syllabi. At the same time, the states also allow private schools to be set up in states, but seek affiliation from the CBSE (Central Board of Secondary Education) and/or ICSE (Indian Council of Secondary Education) that offer an all-India pattern.

After India gained independence in 1947, it was suggested that the newly independent nation should have a federal system, composed of a limited number of states. The basis of their formation was to be linguistic - a region with one major

[14] *http://www.censusindia.net/results/admin.html*

[15] *http://www.cpcb-ecocities.com/e1622/e1628/e2110/index_eng.html*

language would make up one state. In order to overcome the political barriers, Jawaharlal Nehru, the first Prime Minister of India, appointed the States Reorganization Commission (SRC) in August 1953 with Justice Fazal Ali, K.M. Panikkar and Hridaynath Kunzru as members. After the Commission submitted its report, the States Reorganization Act was passed by parliament in November 1956, and it provided for reducing 27 states to 14 states and 6 centrally administered territories. Although there was no one-to-one match, the Indian Constitution (in its 8th Schedule) recognized 14 languages to start with. Later, one out-of-state language – Sindhi - was added to the list of 8th Schedule languages, because unlike Bengali speakers and Punjabi speakers, Sindhi speakers migrating from Pakistan had no particular state to claim as their own.

In 1956, some states were created from parts of others to unite members of a language group, as the whole approach was to be based on the linguistic principle. But even before the act was passed, there was already strong agitation for bifurcation of the Bombay state into two large states – one each for Gujarati and Marathi speech communities. Since the SRC did not agree to that, language riots followed in both Bombay and Ahmedabad. Finally in 1960, Bombay was divided into two new states, Gujarat and Maharashtra. Once again, in November 1966, two states were formed of one earlier state, Punjab. One remained the state of Punjab, where the majority spoke Punjabi with Sikhs as the dominant religious group, and the other entity, with a predominantly Hindu population, was known as Haryana, where the majority spoke a variety of Hindi (often known as 'Haryanavi'). Similarly, Karnataka state (focusing on Kannada as its principal language) as well as the state of Andhra Pradesh (with Telugu as its principal language) also came up. Now we have 35 states and union territories with 22 Constitutional languages, which are all "National languages". The list does not include English, though Hindi and English are the official languages of the Union of India. Each state has its own official and associate official language. And yet, the demand and passion for creating still newer states have not died down, with the Telangana and Andhra issue coming up so prominently, besides the demand for a Gorkhaland.

On a different note, although earlier we only had Assam and the NEFA (or, the North-Eastern Frontier Areas), north-eastern India now has seven different states, nick-named as the 'seven sisters'. These states are spread over an area of over 255,088 sq. km., which is 7.7% of India's territory[16], but which houses the largest number of linguistic groups, most of them speaking Tibeto-Burman languages. In fact, ever

[16] *http://www.satp.org/satporgtp/publication/faultlines/volume12/Article3.htm; esp. Sahni, Ajai. 'Survey of Conflicts and Resolutions in India's North-East'. [Institute for Conflict Management (ICM)].*

since the British gained the charge of governance of Assam in 1838, the plan was to isolate the tribal linguistic groups here, and accordingly, in 1873, through the promulgation of the Bengal Eastern Frontier Regulation, the NEFA was created. Except Assam, which itself had a chequered history, all other north-eastern states of today were created at different periods of time. In 1972, Meghalaya (with mostly Khasi and Garo speakers) was carved out of Assam through a peaceful process. Tripura, too, with Tipra or Kokborok languages (spoken by 19 Scheduled Tribes besides Bangla and Manipuri, out of which Bangla speakers account for 40% of its population)[17] had become a state in 1972. But much before that, Nagaland became a self-governing state within India (in 1960), although the state was officially inaugurated in 1963[18]. This 16,579 sq. km area has between 12 to 14 Naga languages. One of the latest states to be included was Sikkim (inhabited by speakers of Lepcha, Bhutia, Nepali, Limbu), which was an independent kingdom till 1975 before it merged with India. After the memorandum of settlement between Government of India and the Mizo National Front was signed in 1986, Mizoram became an official state with Mizo and English as official languages in February 1987. At the same time, Arunachal Pradesh[19] was set up– on 20th February 1987. The major lingua-ethnic groups include: Adi, Nyishi *(including* Bangru and Puroik), Apatani, Bugun, Galo, Hrusso, Koro, Meyor, Monpa, Tagin, Mishmi *(including Idu-Mishmi, Taroan and Kamman),* Sajolang, Sartang, Tai Khamti, Yobin, Singpho and Tangshang *(including* a number of smaller groups from the *Changlang district as well as Nocte, Wanchoo and Tutsa from the Tirap district).*

Now, to give one instance of attempts to disturb the linguistic-ethnic composition of the region, take the case of migration because of which as against the 355,320 Muslim population of the Assam Valley (as per 1911 census), the number had grown almost three-times to 1,305,902 by 1941. It is not surprising, therefore, that violence against the speakers of 'Other tongues' has erupted here repeatedly in 1979, 1987, 1989, 1990 and 1992[20], and the region is disturbed linguistically even now. The violence has its roots in the large-scale immigration from Bangla-speaking Muslims from East Bengal/ now Bangladesh during the last century. Among the north-eastern states, Manipur is one of the oldest, as it achieved full statehood status in 1972. Although Manipuri speakers are the majority, about 30% are speakers of Naga and Kuki, with a number of other very small speech groups. Since 1972, under the North Eastern Council Act, 1971, a North Eastern Council (NEC) has been established (with representation from

---

[17] *http://www.economywatch.com/stateprofiles/tripura/profile.htm*

[18] *www.economywatch.com/stateprofiles/nagaland/profile.htm*

[19] *http://arunachalpradesh.nic.in/*

[20] *http://www.hvk.org/articles/1002/113.html*

all seven north-eastern states at the highest level) to act as an advisory body in respect of the balanced socio-economic development of the region[21].

As one can see, the Indian state has had to make many changes in its political and constitutional structures to solve the political issues connected with languages. As mentioned already, when the Constituent Assembly adopted the Constitution of India on November 26, 1949, there were 14 languages listed in the Eighth Schedule of the Indian Constitution. They were (in the order of number of speakers): *Hindi, Telugu, Bengali, Marathi, Tamil, Urdu, Gujarati, Kannada, Malayalam, Oriya, Punjabi, Kashmiri, Assamese* and *Sanskrit*. There have been three amendments to the Eighth Schedule during the last 55 years, results of which have been as follows.

Sindhi was included through the Constitution Amendment Bill No 21 in 1967, *Konkani, Manipuri* and *Nepali* (or, *Gorkhali*) through Amendment Bill No. 71 in 1992, and *Maithili, Santali, Bodo,* and *Dogri* through Amendment Bill No. 100 in 2003. Thus, currently, there are 22 languages in the Eighth Schedule. Table 4 as given here lists these languages together with the number of speakers of each of these languages (as in Census 1991):

Sr. No.	Languages	Speakers	Percentage
1.	Assamese	1,31,68,484	1.33%
2.	Bengali	8,33,69,769	8.39%
3.	Bodo	13,50,478	0.14%
4.	Dogri	22,82,589	0.23%
5.	Gujarati	4,60,91,617	4.64%
6.	Hindi	42,20,48,642	42.49%
7.	Kannada	3,79,24,011	3.82%
8.	Kashmiri	55,27,698	0.56%
9.	Konkani	24,89,015	0.25%
10.	Malayalam	3,30,66,392	3.33%
11.	Manipuri	14,66,705	0.15%
12.	Marathi	7,19,36,894	7.24%

[21] http://necouncil.nic.in/about_m.htm

Sr. No.	Languages	Speakers	Percentage
13.	Maithili	1,21,79,122	1.26%
15.	Oriya	3,30,17,446	3.32%
16.	Punjabi	2,91,02,477	2.93%
17.	Sanskrit	14,135	0.01%
18.	Santali	64,69,600	0.65%
19.	Sindhi	25,35,485	0.26%
20.	Tamil	6,07,93,814	6.12%
21.	Telugu	7,40,02,856	7.45%
22.	Urdu	5,15,36,111	5.19%

Table 2. Scheduled Languages in the Indian Constitution and their Speakers

Multilingualism being the rule, rather than the exception in India, it is not surprising that cultural habits, rituals, and belief-systems show an equal extent of plurality. Religion, caste, and various social issues usually dominate the politics here.

In terms of religion, even though the Hindus account for 83% of the population, the country has 14% or 120 million Muslims, 2.4% Christians, 2% Sikhs, 0.7% Buddhists, 0.5% Jains, and 0.4% others (http://www.goski.com/1india.htm). The Census 2001 has given details of the decadal growth rate of different religious groups in India which is worth reproducing here, and one could see that the rate of decline is alarming among the Sikhs, whereas Christianity seems to be on the rise.

As for the caste system in India, it reflects occupational and religiously defined hierarchies in this region. Traditionally, there are four broad categories of castes (*varnas*), including a category of outcastes, earlier called 'untouchables' but now commonly referred to as 'dalits', and special constitutional provisions have been made for these castes, generally known as the 'Scheduled Castes'. Similarly, there is also a separate list of 'Scheduled Tribes'. The Scheduled Caste (SC) and Scheduled Tribe (ST) population in India according to 1991 census are 13,82,23,277 and 6,77,58,380 respectively, constituting 16.33% and 8.01% of India's total population

[22] *http://gbpihed.nic.in/envis/HTML/monograph2/SC-STPopulation.html*

respectively[22]. It may be noted that the proportion of SC and ST population has increased considerably from 15.8% and 7.8% respectively in 1981. It is these tribes that are likely to speak the smaller languages of India.

During the debate in India's Constituent Assembly, Jaipal Singh had proposed that out of the 176 *Adivasi* (or Tribal) languages (as in 1949), Mundari (with its 400000 speakers), Gondi (with 320000 speakers) and Oraon (with 110000 speakers) should be included in the 8th Schedule of the Constitution, because they were important and were spoken by more people than some of the languages already included. He selected only three out of many tribal languages so as not to overburden the Schedule, and he felt that they would "enrich the *rashtrabhasha* [national language] of the country" (CAD[23], p. 1439). Some others like Naziruddin Ahmad argued for Rajasthani and Hindustani to be included in the list (CAD, p. 1482), and Shyama Prasad Mookerjee for Sanskrit (CAD, p. 1391). But finally, only 14 languages were included. Notice that in 1951, besides these 14 languages, there were 23 major tribal languages and 24 other minority languages in several other official documents, including the Census, each of which was spoken by over 100,000 speakers. Therefore, these were pushed to the "minor" languages category, although demographically, they should have been counted as stable. Even if these efforts were to succeed, this constitutional provision could only be one solution to the issue at hand.

As for the Government of India, many constitutional provisions were made to arrest the decay of stable languages and for the protection of the rights of linguistic minorities. The Schedules (8th, 5th and 6th) and Articles 224 (provision for linguistic and other minorities), 350B (special officers for linguistic minorities), Articles, 330, 332 through 334 (special representation was made for the STs in the Parliament & and State legislative assemblies), and Articles 16 and 338 (for separate State-level and National Commissions under the Ministry of Tribal Welfare) were some examples. In addition, Article 350 allows the minority communities to express their grievances in their own languages and a special provision under Article 350A allows the smaller communities to demand educational opportunities in their mother tongue.

There are and can be other administrative actions that could help ease the

---

[23] *CAD: Constituent Assembly Debates; see: http://parliamentofindia.nic.in/ls/debates/debates.htm*

tension of many languages losing the ground under their feet, as it were. For instance, the Government of India has taken some positive steps such as the following, although one could always argue that these are not enough:

- Grant-in-Aid scheme under Article 275(1);
- Protection of Civil Rights Act, 1955
- The Scheduled Castes, Scheduled Tribes (Prevention of Atrocities) Act 1989;
- 43 Special Multi-purpose Tribal Blocks (SMPTBs; 2nd 5-Yr Plan);
- Under the 4th Plan, projects set up in Andhra Pradesh, Bihar, Madhya Pradesh and Orissa.
- Later, a separate Tribal Development Agency was established
- Under the 5th Plan, a Tribal Sub Plan (TSP) for direct benefit of STs was launched;
- In 1987, the TRIFED or Tribal Cooperative Marketing Development Federation was set up;
- National Forest Policy and Forest (Conservation) Act 1980 are being looked at afresh to prevent land alienation from tribals to non-tribals.

Many of these policy initiatives did not get translated into equally forceful action for various reasons, resulting in linguistic debasement in some parts of the country. Since nations are "imagined communities", to quote Benedict Anderson, this imagination is expected to tie us up together territorially (in terms of shared space), economically (common goals and failures), politically (sense of participation in decision-making and with common rights and duties), culturally (through practices that are profane – beyond religious beliefs and biases) and historically (sharing the same myths, memories and texts). And, they are bound together by speech and communication, because languages should act as bridges and not as barriers. They are a privileged means to access 'the other'.

6. Concluding Remarks

Those engaged in containing or reversing the trend of the growing number of endangered languages need to understand that – as I mentioned in the conclusive remarks of the talk ('India Speaks, India Writes: To Plan Languages is to Plan Societies') given at the Global Seminar on the International Year of Languages organized by the UNESCO and UNDP at the United Nations on Dec 17-18-2008 – language planning must be extended to help to build civil societies based on acceptance of diversity of cultures and languages. This is because no matter what provisions are made on paper, the danger to such ideal systems come from three kinds of tensions:

(i) The first is a constant tension between '*being*' and '*becoming*.' It is not only one's numerical strength (or weakness), nor a biological danger in terms of reproductivity that could threaten languages. Even larger languages can disappear, if they decide to change their natural '*being*' of bilinguality to '*becoming*' members of a larger linguistic entity. This could happen for various reasons, ranging from higher education, better job prospects, or more social prestige. In a multi-cultural milieu, it is natural *being* bilingual. But in the process of *becoming* a bilingual, a large scale conversion may take place. This may result in language shift leading to language loss.

(ii) The second danger comes also because of the 'perception' of one's language universe. The members of a smaller linguistic group will often have to negotiate with some of these questions: How do you see yourself, and how do others look at you? Which of these two evaluations do you accept and why? How deep is your commitment to your 'own' tags of identity? This type of tension in smaller linguistic groups was pointed out long ago by Dell Hymes in his paper 'Two Types of Linguistic Relativity'. Many small speech groups survive the onslaught of the forces of globalization, whereas many larger groups accept a negative evaluation and give up their own tags.

(iii) The third type of tension comes from how a speech group tries to *'include'* or *'exclude'* other speech groups that may be genetically, genealogically, and culturally related to their own group. Whether the group in question tries to divorce from the larger identity to create a space for its own language or tries to forge an identity with the other to create a new and larger identity. *'Split'* and *'Merger'* are part of the political game language continents often play, and this dynamics is often difficult for an observer from outside to understand. However, this urge to be like the rest of 'others', or the itch to forge one's own destiny quite often grows out of particular historical moments, or as counter-moves against a perceived move by others.

That multilingualism and pluro-culturalism have been highly respected in India in all ages is clear from many documents and much evidence. In fact, even while talking about ancient Indian literature – which many of us confuse with only history of Sanskrit literature, we find scholars like Winternitz commenting that *"The history of Indian literature...not only stretches across great periods of time and an enormous area, but is also one which is composed in many languages"*. But there is no denying the fact that the country has also been a field of linguistic tension. Such tensions involving smaller languages can be seen even now. For example, even though 80% of all Indians - nearly 750 million (1995 estimates) – speak one or other among the recognized Indian languages, and even when Hindi is understood by close to 60%, there are still many other languages with a long literary history, grammatical and lexicographical tradition and rich literary heritage, and they are still in use in all modern means of communication. Smaller languages often do not enter into this game that bigger linguistic groups play, because they are engaged in a battle of survival in the first place. Civil society must take some concrete action to protect and promote this intangible heritage.

Where Have All the Speakers Gone?

A Case of Depleting Populations, Depleting Languages, and Loss of Biocultural Diversity in the Andaman Islands

Prof. Anvita Abbi-Chairperson, Centre for Linguistics, School of Language, Literature and Culture Studies (JNU), Delhi

1. Introduction

As languages are repositories of human history, human civilization and migration, the depleting indigenous language speaking populations of hunters and gatherers in the Andaman Islands signifies the loss of a large scale knowledge base. The paper presents the case of Great Andamanese, a moribund language which is on the verge of extinction. The contact between the Great Andamanese people and food producing communities has led to loss of old cultural practices as well as diminishing indigenous vocabulary pertaining to specific hunting activities, local flora and fauna, medicinal plants and their uses, boat-building and diverse gathering activities. The author proposes 'Reverse Education' among several other measures to save this loss.

2. Wealth of Biodiversity

The richness of a country can not only be measured in terms of its Gross National Product or the quantum of reserves in its banks, but also by the diversity and multiplicity of its languages and cultures. Countries with a large number of languages and dialects, distinct language families representing a long diachronic evolution of languages that have coexisted for centuries, giving rise to sustainable and adaptable societies, are the real indicators of the richness of a country. The language ecology of the country shows us how languages develop, spread, interact, and decline as part of socio-cultural, political and environmental processes. Scientists have now proved (Maffi 2000, 2001) that:

1. Linguistic diversity and biological diversity are inseparable; and
2. The strongest eco systems are those which are the most diverse. This is because

diversity contains the potential for adaptation. Uniformity can endanger a species by providing inflexibility and non-adaptability (*Skutnabb-Kangas 2000*).

Today about 6,500 languages are spoken world-wide, and maybe there are equally as many sign languages. Almost half of them are endangered. A quarter of these languages have fewer than 1,000 speakers, and many of them are already moribund (no longer learned by children). With more than 500 tribal languages of India which are still spoken but are threatened under the dominance of the Eighth Schedule which lists the recognized languages in India, we are facing the enormous responsibility of guarding this wealth of the country for posterity. We can not talk of linguistic rights unless we facilitate the speakers of these languages to use them for education. An important issue before us is to realize that depleting language use leads to depletion of the knowledge-base of society, as it is language alone that records and preserves intellectual knowledge. Linguists believe that languages carry evidence of earlier environment, habitat and practices which may or may not be in the memory of the community. Loss of language thus, translates into loss of biodiversity and comprehension of ancient world knowledge.

The fundamental question that we can ask ourselves is: when a language is on the verge of extinction what dies along with the language? Is it the history, culture, ecological base, knowledge of biodiversity, ethno-linguistic practices, or the identity of the community, or, all of these? Most definitely, it is all of these which are extinguished along with the extinction of the language. Languages are the witness of the diverse and varying ways the human cognitive faculties perceive the world. Each language has unique lexical stock and unique signification. Various manifestations of language are ecological and archeological signatures of the communities that maintain close ties to their environments. Hence language death signifies the closure of the link with its ancient heritage. As we move on we will see how language death, in this case the Great Andamanese language, has resulted in loss of language ecology and the knowledge-base of one of the most ancient civilizations of the world. However, before we proceed we must try to comprehend the notions that linguists strongly believe in, which serve as the basis for a language revolution to save dying languages.

3. Linguists' Beliefs

Linguists believe that:

1. The loss of languages, cultural practices and indigenous ecological knowledge all reflect the breakdown in the relationship between humans and their environment. Therefore, when seeking solutions for the sustainability of both

human communities and the environment, one must recognize the link between cultural diversity and biological diversity (*Maffi 2000*).

2. The challenge of maintaining, restoring, and perpetuating the diversity of life on earth is one of supporting and promoting diversity in nature, culture, belief, and languages.

3. These diversities are seen as intimately related to and profoundly shaping each other over the whole history of human presence and activities on earth.

4. Language is a window to society. Cultural beliefs, values, knowledge, and behavior in relation to the environment are expressed in language. If the inter-generational transfer of heritage language is absent, the loss of language leads to loss of beliefs, values, and knowledge.

5. Loss of environment also leads to loss of language. Removal of the indigenous environmental base of the various tribal societies forces them to forget their language as it no longer serves the purpose of transferring the indigenous knowledge base. 'This complex web of connections is pervasive throughout the globe, although at present it may remain more easily recognizable in indigenous, minority, or local communities that maintain close ties to their environments' (*Skutnabb Kangas 2000*).

4. Great Andamanese[1]

Great Andamanese is a generic term used for the amalgam of ten different but closely related varieties of the same language once spoken in the entire set of the Andaman Islands, located in the Bay of Bengal. Andamanese had been considered the fifth language family of India (*Manoharan 1985*) which had Jarawa, Onge, Sentinelese and Great Andamanese in its fold. However, a recent study undertaken by the author of this paper (2003, 2005, 2006, 2008) gives enough indication to suggest Great Andamanese as a separate sixth family (or perhaps the very first one to exist in this region) as it differs from the other languages of the Andaman Islands in substantial historical and typological ways. Andamanese tribes in general, according to geneticists (*Thangaraj et al. 2005:996*), are among the oldest tribes, with a history

[1] *The current study is based on first-hand data collection by the author and her team members Abhishek Avatans and Bidisha Som from the Great Andamanese then living in the post Tsunami tribal reserve of Adi Basera in Port Blair and Strait Island, a small island situated 53 nautical miles away to the east of Port Blair. Extensive fieldwork was conducted by the author by making several visits to the Island (five since 2005. The language has shrunk subsequently each year with the loss of speakers), in the project Vanishing Voices of the Great Andamanese, supported by the Hans Rausing Endangered Language Fund, SOAS, University of London, U.K.*

that dates back to 70,000 years before present when the first migration of humans took place out of Africa. Till about three hundred years ago, the Great Andamanese tribes were spread all over the Andaman Islands, divided into ten different subgroups (map 1)

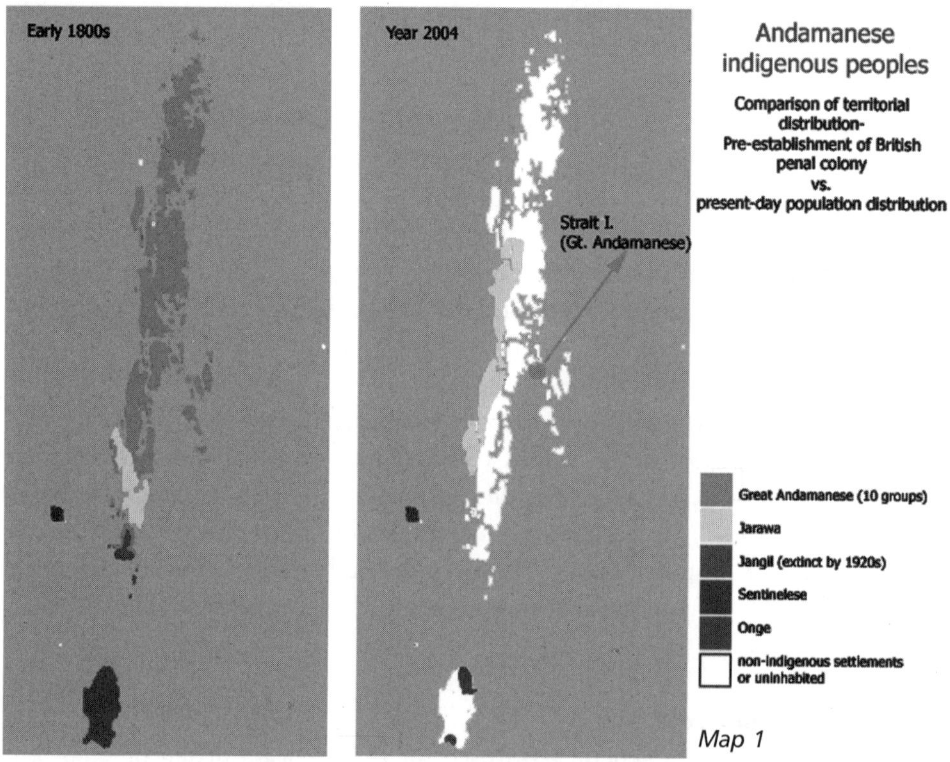

Map 1

What remains of the entire group is a mixed group of people comprising 51 members, who are descendents of different sub-groups. Once a diverse tribe with 10 different sub-tribes speaking equally different language varieties, the Great Andamanese people today are an endangered population of 51 with only 5 heritage speakers left, who are descendants of four different sub-tribes speaking mutually intelligible varieties of the Great Andamanese language (Sare, Bo, Khora, and Jeru). Not only has their number dwindled by an alarming proportion, but the heritage language has virtually been wiped out. Of the 5 remaining speakers, no one speaks the language fluently. At best, they can converse among themselves within a restricted domain. The community uses a variety of Hindi called Andamani Hindi for intra-tribal communication as well as for communicating with non-tribal people living in the Andaman Islands. A drastic shift in the mode of subsistence and lifestyle patterns has taken them away from their language as well as the cultural symbolism and semantic-pragmatic ontological constructs specific to their language. The Great Andamanese are no longer a hunter-gatherer tribe. As a result, their verbal repertoire shows a lack of information in the areas of their cultural heritage that was part of their life not very long ago (*Som 2005*). Loss of different registers of the language and the erosion of the art of narration can also be related to this fact.

5. The Nature of Language and Culture

Great Andamanese is a moribund language which has ceased to be passed on from one generation to the other. What follows is an account of the sociolinguistic situation of the Great Andamanese people, when there were 7 speakers. All 7 speakers were well over forty years of age and were not 'fluent speakers' as understood in normal parlance. It must be noted here that 'fluency' has to be redefined with respect to the Great Andamanese. The term 'fluent speaker' of any language generally refers to a person using the language spontaneously and continuously for any duration of time in all domains and contexts. However, this is not the case with Great Andamanese. The use of the 'heritage language' is sporadic and not spontaneous. It needed a great amount of coaxing to make two of the 'best speakers' converse in their own language, and within no time they started taking recourse to Hindi. The only occasion where a member of the tribe would spontaneously use the 'heritage language' with another, was to exclude a perceived 'outsider' from the conversation. So it can be said that the language at this stage is best used as a 'secret code' rather than as a standard mode of communication. Even in this kind of usage, these were usually short exchanges of words and phrases and not lengthy conversations. And this too was the case with the 'best speakers' of the language. The continuum of language competence among the Great Andamanese that we discuss below should be understood against this background. In this paper we use the term 'best speaker' for speakers with the competence level 5 and speakers at the level 4 are termed 'semi-speakers'. The term 'best speakers' is used for those who were found best among the few members who still use the language though not very fluently and not in all domains.

Apart from loss of language the Great Andamanese also suffer from loss of cultural heritage, loss of ancient practices and rituals, as well as loss of the genre or art of narration. The few persons who speak the language now do not remember any native stories or folk tales. Story telling as an activity does not exist any more. Neither can the mothers, nor the old people of the community narrate stories to their children. The loss of mother tongue thus has very serious implications, and the present generation of Great Andamanese have never heard a story from their elders, either in their heritage language or in Andamani Hindi. A thorough investigation of the linguistic behavior of the Great Andamanese presents a bleak picture and points to a future when they will totally lose their language and culture, and, hence, their symbols of identity.

6. Population Figures, Language and Education

As already mentioned, the present study was conducted when there were 51 Great Andamanese members in all with 7 speakers. Among these the number of children was 20 under the age of ten years; 13 in the age-range of 20-30; 10 in the age range of 30-80; and 13 infants, i.e. up till the age of 5.

Among the Great Andamanese conglomerate of sub-tribes, the largest input is from the Jeru tribe. Inter-marriages among the various tribes have led to the mixed Great Andamanese language. In this variety, one can easily see traces of other languages such as Khora, Sare, Jeru, Pujjikar and Bo. The linguistic system of present Great Andamanese appears to be close to Koineization. In spite of the representations of these language varieties, the preferred heritage language is returned as Jeru/Jero. It is commonly understood that the Great Andamanese should be identified with 'Jero' as it is considered prestigious to speak Jero when outsiders are present[2]. Interestingly, speakers associate themselves with the father's tongue and not with the mother's tongue.

A group of Great Andamanese

[2] *A similar situation exists in the nine states of the Hindi belt where if asked, each person claims to be a mother tongue speaker of Hindi and does not mention heritage languages such as Braj, Bagri, Kumaoni etc.*

Language Competence

An analysis of the language competence of the present day Great Andamanese people reflects the health of the language. As seen, among the 51 members, 13 are below the age of 5. Our analysis is of the population that is above this age group for obvious reasons. The fluency level of the remaining 38 members was judged on a scale of competence ranging from 0-5 as per the graph given below.

Key to Competency Levels

0 = no knowledge of the language
1 = neither speaks nor understands, recognizes only a few words
2 = low level of understanding, do not speak
3 = phrase level awareness, but do not speak
4 = semi-speakers
5 = best speakers

This scale of competence is used in the following graphs as well as in the analysis of the comparative competence level of the Great Andamanese speakers.

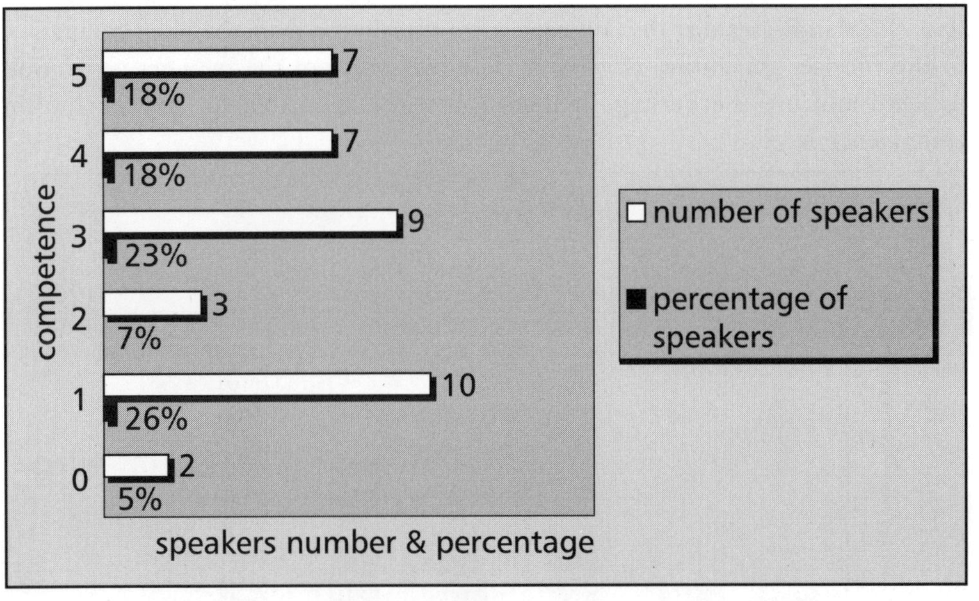

Figure 1: Percentage and number of speakers on the scale of competence

We can see that the number of 'best speakers' and 'semi-speakers' is the same, and adds up to 36% of the community. The number of speakers in the highest competence group, i.e. level 5, is just 7 (unfortunately two speakers died in 2009). This means that 14 members of the community, which in quantitative terms is rather small, can speak the language in some domains and registers. Our figure shows the highest number of people, i.e. ten in all, is in the group denoted by the number 1, signifying that part of the society which has very low or negligible understanding of the language. These speakers possess passive knowledge of only some words of the language without ever being able to use them. The second highest category is occupied by the number 3 in the graph, representing the group with phrase level understanding but not speaking the language. As no two speakers speak the same variety of the language, though they all claim to be speaking Jero, comprehensibility of each other's speech is rather low. For instance, the oldest member of the tribe is an 80 year old woman, whose mother tongue is Bo. Her speech is not intelligible to other member of the community. They somehow 'make out' what she says.

It is noteworthy that the best speakers are all above the age of forty. The mean age of the semi-speakers is thirty five. It is then clear that the level of competence goes down with diminishing age, the oldest having the best and the young generation the least knowledge; this shows a gradual process of language erosion (Fig 2) and indicates that the language is not transferred from the older generation to the younger generation effectively. The reluctance of the younger generation to learn and use the heritage language is also responsible for this decline in competence level.

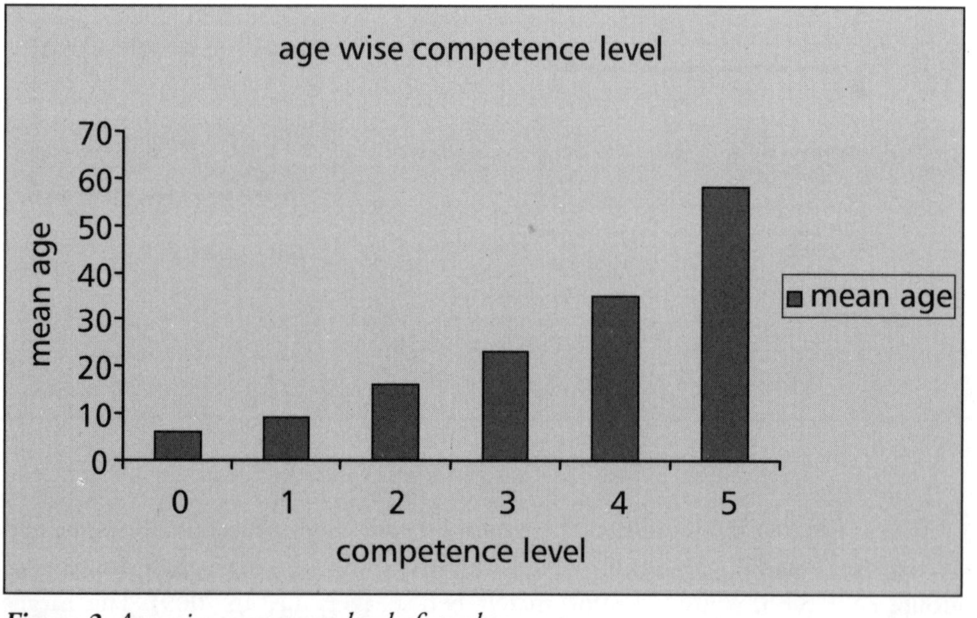

Figure 2. Age-wise competence level of speakers

The following Fig 3 sums up the situation of language competence among the Great Andamanese with respect to the age of the speakers and their number in the community. The members with the highest competence also have the highest mean age, and their number is very small. The members with low competence have a low mean age and their number is considerably higher than the previous group, indicating the moribund status of the language. Competence level is positively related to the age factor. The higher the age group, the higher the proficiency and the lower the age group, the lower the proficiency in Great Andamanese.

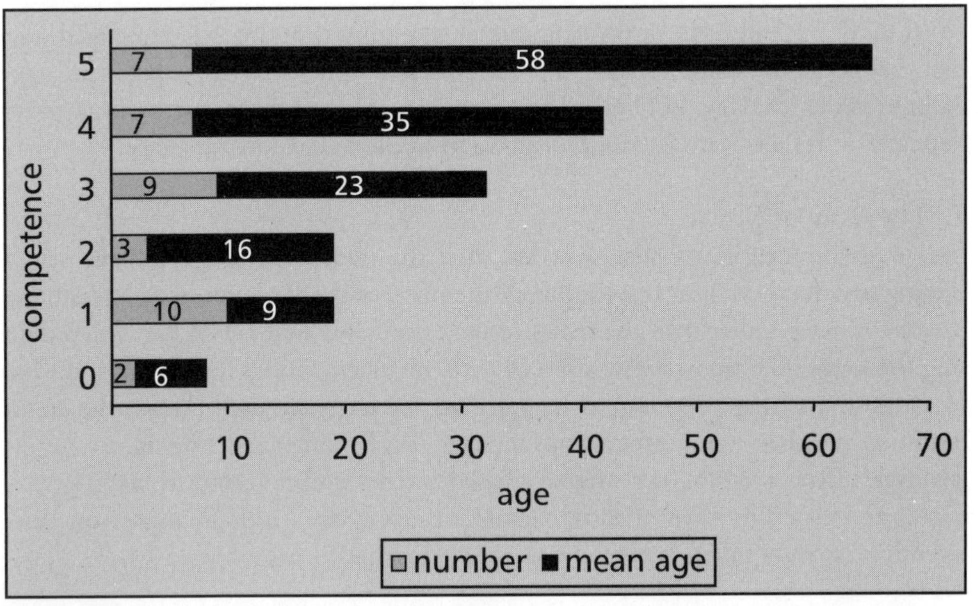

Figure 3. *The number and mean age of speakers on the competence scale*

Language Use

It is clear by now that the Great Andamanese are no longer monolingual in their heritage language. The few members of the tribe (above the age of forty) who can speak the indigenous language are bilinguals, i.e. they speak both Hindi and the heritage language. The members who are below forty are monolinguals in Hindi which they use as a *lingua franca*. Some members of the younger generation, especially teenagers, also speak a few words of English and other Indian languages, such as Bangla and Tamil. This kind of linguistic mosaic in the background of the language of communication among the tribe members decides who uses what with whom and when. In the intra-community usage, cases where only Jeru is used are rather rare. If at all, this situation is witnessed only when the language is used as a secret code among the oldest members of the tribe. Another important observation is that very few registers were used in the heritage language. For instance, none among the so called best speakers could narrate an incident or a story[3]. Hindi shares space with Jeru in most of the conversations, with Hindi being the matrix language and the heritage language being limited to a few words and phrases. There was a not a single instance of longer than phrase-long communication in the heritage language. Children and young adults used Hindi in most domains. Old members of the tribe used Hindi to communicate with young and old alike. The use of Jeru was almost negligible. Conversation between elders was bilingual, a mixture of Jeru and Hindi.

Of the 7 'best speakers' of the language, it was noticed during our prolonged stay, that they could not communicate in their respective varieties of languages in all areas without taking recourse to Hindi. Their non-homogeneous linguistic heritage could have led to this awkward situation of non-use of the indigenous language.

7. The Role of Music

It must be mentioned here, however, that the traditional songs and the art of singing have not been lost. It is the female members of the community who retain the treasure of song rather than the males (only a negligible number of the latter could sing the songs); the women sang a few of the remembered songs for us. Thus, the life of songs in a heritage language is longer than the language itself. While the art of narration perishes in the process of language death, songs and singing are not as adversely affected. Music is a memory based activity and narration is language-use based, and this difference in their cognitive process has a serious impact on their retention, as exemplified here in the Great Andamanese case.

8. Vanishing Population, Depleting Domains of Use and Vanishing Language

The case of the Great Andamanese language is a complex one because of the dwindling population, low competence in the heritage language and linguistic variations among the few remaining speakers.

It will be relevant to consider the Great Andamanese language according to the Vitality Index of Language as framed by UNESCO. According to UNESCO directives, there are six major evaluative factors for language vitality, which should be used in conjunction with each other. We have added one more without which the true picture for vitality cannot be assessed, i.e., the competency level of the existing speakers in

[3] *The exception was Nao Jr, our main speaker, (died in February 2009) who did narrate folk tales in Hindi after much prodding. It took him, at times, many days to complete a story as he had never narrated one in his life and had heard them from his elders only when he was a child. Other old members of the community reported loss of memory regarding folk tales. It was a very sad state of affairs as a couple of speakers wanted to oblige but could not.*

the heritage language. Evaluating Great Andamanese along these sets of factors we get the following results:

Table 1 Major Evaluative Factors for Language Vitality Assessment	
Language Vitality Factors	**Great Andamanese**
1. Intergenerational Language transmission	Nil
2. Absolute Number of Speakers	05
3. Proportion of Speakers within the Total Population	10%
4. Shifts in Domains of Language Use	Total
5. Response to New Domains and Media	NA
6. Materials for Language Education and Literacy.	NA
7. Competency Level in the Heritage Level	Low

As we have observed, factors five and six are not relevant for the assessment and as far as the first four factors are concerned we can, without any doubt, claim that the language is not thriving at all. It is on the brink of extinction. The seventh factor is most important in the vanishing language case as it reflects the gradual death of the language concerned.

The UNESCO scale of safe versus unsafe languages also gives us a strong assessment of the Great Andamanese language as unsafe and critically endangered.

Table 2. Degree of Endangerment		
Degree of Endangerment	**Grade**	**Proportion of Speakers within the Total Reference Population**
Safe	5	All speak the language.
Unsafe	4	Nearly all speak the language.
Definitely endangered	3	A majority speak the language.
Severely endangered	2	A minority speak the language.
Critically endangered	1	Very few speak the language.
Extinct	0	None speak the language.

We cannot but agree with Blair, H & S. Fredeen, when they say 'The profile of language death generally includes evidence of fewer and fewer speakers, a reduction in the use of language, more association with speakers of the more prestigious language, an increase in the need for bilingualism and in the number of bilinguals, less and less acquisition of the mother tongue, and an increase in the age of the fluent speakers, who eventually die leaving less proficient speakers. (*Blair, H and S. Fredeen, 1995*). Added to these factors is the one which characterizes the low competence even among those who claim to speak the language. By these parameters Great Andamanese is a classic example of a dying and moribund language.

9. Great Loss of Knowledge-base

If languages are repositories of human history, human civilization and migration, then a depleting indigenous language speaking population of hunters and gatherers in the Andaman Islands signifies loss of a large scale knowledge-base. As already mentioned, the contact with food producing communities has led to loss of knowledge of a number of old cultural practices. This author believes that languages carry evidence of the earlier environment, habitat and practices which are no longer in the memory of the community. Hence language death signifies the closure of the link with its ancient heritage.

One or two examples from the language will explain how the loss of language implies the loss of knowledge and subsequently how tampering with ecology also leads to loss of language and hence the knowledge-base. The Great Andamanese were familiar with varieties of crabs each with a distinct name. The following list of thirteen types of crabs is no longer identifiable by the younger generation. Consider:

Keo 'edible large crab'; *taurotarakar* 'kind of sand crab'; *phong* 'large crab'; *roxo* 'kind of crab'; *kol* 'small edible crab'; *kaurob* 'very tiny non edible crab'; *keyatto* 'small edible crab'; *kal* 'small sea variety crab'; *kae* 'black crab found near volcano in Barren Island'; *le* 'kind of crab which now extinct'; *khurum* 'medium sized red edible crab'; *munu* 'kind of crab'; *korai* 'kind of crab with a shell' etc.

Similarly, a variety of leaves and their uses and names known to the elderly people of the community are lost to the younger generation. Consider a few examples from our list of flora:

Ondech 'used for wrapping meat before steaming'; *farako* 'used for making thread' *en* 'used for fishing - when these leaves are strewn on water fish become senseless and float up; '*en* bushes no longer exist on the Island as they were washed away by the Tsunami in 2004'; *choro* 'the juice of this is consumed to cure malaria and other kinds of high fever' etc.

The deep ecological knowledge of hunter-gatherer societies is gradually being wiped out by loss of ecological balance on the one hand and loss of language on the other. For instance, a kind of sea fish by the name of *moroy,* which is believed to follow the movement of the sun is no longer known to the people. A very telling example of loss of vocabulary from kinship terms, is one which was used till 30 years ago - *ropuch.* The word refers to a person who has lost his/her sibling. None of the languages I have worked on so far has any word designating this concept. Words for a person who loses his or her parents such as 'orphan' or the one who loses her husband such as 'widow' are common in every language, but never do we find a word for a person who loses his/her brother or sister.

10. What Should We Do?

Because language is the link to knowledge of ecosystems, when languages are revived and passed on to youth, specific nuances of ecological knowledge are also passed on. We should thus, focus on the revitalization of indigenous languages as a key to biodiversity conservation and knowledge. However, revitalization may not work in the case of societies such as the Great Andamanese where the will to revitalize is absent and the majority of the population has shifted to the dominant language of the region. In such cases an attempt must be made to document the language so as to save the knowledge-base. Endangerment is a big issue in the present century. If we cannot revive the languages we at least can document them, write descriptive grammars of them, compile comprehensive, preferably interactive dictionaries with sounds and pictures, recording narrations, discourses and songs. It has been observed that the language documentation-exercise alone serves as a motivating factor for language revival.

We have already made such an exercise and a page from our dictionary in the appendix will explain how one can store this knowledge in a multilingual situation so that it can be used by all and especially by the locals.

Dictionary preparing should not only be a linguistic exercise involving morphology and phonology, or to describe semantic and pragmatic nuances, or to illustrate how to use a word, but can also serve as a historical documentation of the life a tribe must once have lived and experienced. Our dictionary is a storehouse of Andaman ecology, tribal history, ornithological information, endemic biological life and cultural and mythological information. Dictionaries should always reach the locals, those who supply the data, who spend long hours helping elicit information, the informants or contact persons. Hence it should be prepared in the local language as well. Our dictionary is trilingual, Hindi, English and Great Andamanese in multiple scripts such as Roman, Devanagri and IPA (International Phonetic Alphabet).

We strongly advocate that monolithic global human culture is not good for human communities. However, as observed by many linguists such as Skutnabb Kangas, external forces are dispossessing traditional peoples of their lands, resources, and lifestyles; forcing them to subsist in highly degraded environments; crushing their cultural traditions or ability to maintain them; or coercing them into linguistic assimilation and abandonment of ancestral languages. We should see that no language disappears from this earth against the will of the people and as far as possible, that all languages be transmitted to the relevant younger generation.

11. Linguists Need Help

The task of revitalization and documentation cannot be undertaken alone by linguists. We need help from:

1. Officials who claim to be the custodians of the tribes so that they can generate respect for the heritage languages among the tribes as well as among the non-tribals who interact with the tribal population

2. Society in general, so that indigenous languages and their speakers are shown respect and acceptability

3. Research organizations so as to channel resources in the direction of documentation and revitalization of languages. These organizations can also serve to disseminate information at the national and international levels to generate interest in the knowledge-base of these societies

4. Scientists in Genetics, Biology and Historical geography who can research on the evolution and spread of the human population of a region and thus link up their research with that of the linguists' findings

5. Reverse education (refer to next page).

It is understandable that the Government of India has a mammoth task in hand to educate tribes and bring them into the so called 'mainstream'. Yet one must first ask what good this will do. How far will these exercises aid and sustain linguistic diversity? How far will they help the tribes to improve their socio-economic situation? How far will they aid in bringing fulfilment to their societies?

Unfortunately, as far as the other tribes of the Andaman Islands such as Jarawa and Onge are concerned, they are better left alone (*Abbi 2006*). Damage has already been done in the case of the Great Andamanese. A very significant step could be to generate respect and honor in favour of these tribes and this can be done by the process of reverse education. The knowledge-base that these tribal languages exhibit should be incorporated into the local school curriculum of the Islands. Children of city dwellers should be made aware of the cultural life of their fellow tribes, their cognitive world, and their ancient heritage which has been sustained for thousand of years.

A Jarawa boy after the hunt

12. Conclusion

Moribund languages are characterized by lack of will to learn and teach the heritage language. The language does not get transferred from the older to the younger generation. Depleting population accompanied by low competence level of the language of those who claim to speak it make the language loss faster than expected. In such cases all efforts of individuals, society and government bodies should be to record and document the dying language in all its nuances for enhancement and preservation of the knowledge-base of the country. Reverse education is the only answer to sustain, preserve and bring respect to our heritage. *(See Appendix page 247 for sample page from Dictionary)*

References

- Abbi, A. 2003. *Vanishing Voices of the Languages of the Andaman Islands,* June13, 2003. Paper presented at the Max Planck Institute, Leipzig.
- Abbi, A. 2006. *Endangered Languages of the Andaman Islands.* Muenchen: Lincom GmbH
- Abbi, A, 2008. *Is Great Andamanese genealogically and typologically distinct from Onge and Jarawa?* Language Sciences 31:6 (2009) 791-812.
- Avtans, A & Anvita Abbi. 2006. Language Documentation in Andamans-Highs and Lows. *Vital Voices. Proceedings of the Tenth Foundation for Endangered Languages Conference,* Mysore, India. pp. 73-76.
- Blair, Heather and Shirley Fredeen. 'Do Not Go Gentle into That Good Night. Rage, Rage, against the Dying of the Light'. *Anthropology & Education Quarterly,* Vol. 26, No. 1 (March 1995), pp. 27-49.
- Manoharan, S. 1986. Linguistic Peculiarities of Andamanese Family of Languages. *Indian Linguistics.* 47 (1-4): pp. 25-32.
- Thangaraj, K, Gyaneshwer Chaubey, Toomas Kivisild, Alla G. Reddy, Vijay Kumar Singh, Avinash A. Rasalkar, and Lalji Singh Reconstructing the Origin of Andaman Islanders. *Science* 308, 13 May 2005: pp. 996.
- Maffi, Luisa (ed.) (2001). *On Biocultural Diversity. Linking Language, Knowledge and the Environment.* Washington, D.C.: The Smithsonian Institute Press.
- Maffi, Luisa (2000). Linguistic and biological diversity: the inextricable link. In Phillipson (ed.), 17-22.
- Phillipson, Robert (ed.) (2000). *Rights to language. Equity, power and education.* Mahwah, NJ: Lawrence Erlbaum Associates.
- Som, B. 2005. *Conceptual Structure Vs Lexical Structure- The Case of Great Andamanese.* Linguistic Society of India Platinum Jubilee Conference. Hyderabad. Dec 6-8, 2005.
- Skutnabb-Kangas, Tove (2000). Linguistic genocide in education – or worldwide diversity and Human Rights? Mahwah, New Jersey & London: Lawrence Erlbaum Associates. Republished in a slightly revised version in 2008, New Delhi: Orient Blackswan.

Language Endangerment in Central India

Prof. B. Ramakrishna Reddy - Former Dean, School of Language Development, P. S. Telugu University, Andhra Pradesh

1. Introduction

The situation of indigenous tribal languages of India is unique and precarious at the same time, in that the number of languages ranges between 75% to 80% at the national level, though the number of speakers is less than 8% or so. It shows that a small number of the so-called prestigious major languages dominate over a large number of indigenous speeches. The languages of the latter group are unscheduled (not mentioned in the Constitution with two exceptions), not used as a medium of education, lack political power, and are unutilized in administration and other domains of national life. In spite of all the disadvantages, the past indicates retention of these languages as vehicles of tribal identity, heritage, indigenous knowledge systems, cultural ethos, ritual practices and oral literature. But with the advent of mass media, especially television, radio, cinema and other communication systems, the younger generation of tribal communities is attracted more towards major powerful languages at the cost of their parental home languages. This might lead to language shift and loss in future, at least in the case of certain smaller groups.

Unlike the situation in the Americas and Australia where the European invaders carried out a sort of genocide of the natives, the Indian past has been one of 'live and let live'. The prevailing illiterate bilingualism leading to underlying common core grammar coupled with code switching has been accelerating the retention of minor tribal languages. But this cannot be extended to and expected in future. Thus the simultaneous twin processes of endangerment and retention are the Indian reality. With this background in focus, an attempt is made to investigate the problem of language endangerment in East Central India. An examination of each language in terms of retention, shift, loss and morbidity will be explained in some detail. Certain measures are suggested for revitalization of endangered languages.

2. Language Situation in the Area

A unique characteristic of Central India is its linguistic heterogeneity in accommodating languages of three different genetic families, namely, Munda (of Austroasiatic), Dravidian and Indo-Aryan (of Indo-European). For centuries the speakers of these languages have been living together exchanging cultural and linguistic traits among themselves. The regional major languages like Hindi, Marathi, Oriya and Telugu are in constant interaction with tribal minor languages, imprinting their impact on the latter group. When compared to the tribal communities of the North-East, the Central Indian Adivasi groups are backward on several counts such as economy, education, social upliftment and political consciousness.

East Central India is taken here as consisting of Chattisgarh and parts of Madhya Pradesh, Maharashtra, Jharkhand, Orissa and Andhra Pradesh. It is the tribal minor languages of this region which are prone to disappear due to several non-linguistic reasons. An overview of the geographic distribution and demographic figures of these languages is provided as an essential background to evaluate the levels of their endangerment. Since 1971, the Census of India does not include any language with less than 10,000 speakers, thus ignoring many small languages. Unless otherwise specified, the number of speakers of each language, in the following table, is from that of the Census of India 2001.

Munda (Austro-Asiatic) Languages

Sl.No.	Language (Dialects)	Distribution	No. of Speakers	Contact LWCs	Endangerment level
1.	Bonda/ Remo	Machkund and Khairaput Malkangiri dist., Orissa	2569 (1951) 5895 (POI 1981)	Oriya	Seriously endangered
2.	Didayi/ Gataq/ Gatah	Chitrakonda and Balimela, Malkangiri dist., Orissa	3000 (estimate)	Oriya	Seriously endangered
3.	Gutob/ Gadaba	Pottangi and Semiliguda, Koraput dist., Orissa.	5382 (1961)	Oriya	Seriously endangered
4.	Juang	Keonjhar, Dhenkanal and Mayurbhanj districts, Orissa	23,708	Oriya	Endangered
5.	Kharia	Ranchi and adjacent areas of Jharkhand. Jharsuguda, Sambalpur and Sundargarh districts, Orissa	2,39,608	Hindi Oriya Sadri	Potentially endangered

Sl.No.	Language (Dialects)	Distribution	No. of Speakers	Contact LWCs	Endangerment level
6.	Korku	Amaravathi, Maharashtra. Chindwada, Betuland Hoshangabad, M.P.	5,74,481	Marathi Hindi	Potentially endangered
7.	Mundari (Asuri, Bhumij, Birhor, Korwa, Naguri,Lator, Ho, Hasada, Kora, Munda)	Jharkhand Orissa Madhya Pradesh Bihar	Mundari –10,61,352 Bhumij– 47,443 Ho–10,42,724 Korwa–34,586 Munda–4,69,357 Total- 26,55,462	Hindi Oriya Sadri	Safe to potential endangerment
8.	Parengi/ Gorum	Nandapur and Semiliguda. Koraput dist., Orissa	6702 (1961)	Oriya (Desia dialect)	Moribund
9.	Santali	Jharkhand, Bihar, Orissa and West Bengal	64,69,600	Hindi, Sadri Oriya Bengali	Safe
10.	Savara/ Sora/ Saora (Jora or Malhar)	Ganjam and Gajapati districts, Orissa. Srikakulam and Visakhapatnam districts of AP	2,52,519	Oriya (Desia dialect) Telgu	Potentially endangered

Dravidian Languages

Sl.No.	Language (Dialects)	Distribution	No. of Speakers	Contact LWCs	Endangerment level
1.	Gadaba (Ollari, Kondekor)	Salur of Vizianagaram district, Andhra Pradesh. Pottangi and Semiliguda of Koraput dist., Orissa.	26,262	Oriya (Desia dialect) Telugu	Endangered
2.	Gondi(Abhuj Maria, Bisanhorn Maria, Dorla, Muria, Rajgond, Pardhan and Thoti) Koya is a distinct dialect	Andhra Pradesh, Chattisgarsh, Orissa, Madhya Pradesh and Maharashtra	Gondi 27,13,790 Koya 3,62,070 Total 30,75,860	Telugu Hindi Marathi Oriya	Safe to potential endangerment
3.	Indi-Awe	Kasipur Block of Rayagada dist. and Thumal Rampur of Kalahandi district, Orissa	5000 (estimate)	Oriya	Seriously endangered

Sl.No.	Language (Dialects)	Distribution	No. of Speakers	Contact LWCs	Endangerment level
4.	Kolami	Yeotmal district, Maharashtra and Adilabad district, Andhra Pradesh.	1,21,855	Marathi Telugu	Potentially endangered
5.	Konda/Kubi	Araku valley, Visakhapatnam district, A.P. and Padua, Koraput district, Orissa.	56,262	Telugu Oriya (Adivasi dialect)	Endangered
6.	Kui (Kuttia and Kandh Gowda)	Kondhmal-Phalbani, Baudh and Ganjam districts, Orissa	9,16,222	Oriya	Potentially endangered
7.	Kurux/Oraon (Dhangar Kisan)	Jharkhand, Orissa, Chattisgarh, Bihar and West Bengal	Kurux 17,51,489 Kisan 1,41,088 Total 18,92,577	Hindi Sadri Oriya Bengali	Safe to potentially endangered
8.	Kuvi (Kondh, Jatapu, Samanth, Dongria and Tekriya)	Koraput and Rayagada districts of Orissa. Visakhapatnam and Viziagaram districts of Andhra Pradesh	1,57,928	Oriya(Desia dislect) Telugu	Potentially endangered
9.	Malto	Jharkhand and Orissa	2,24,926	Hindi Sadri Oriya	Potentially endangered
10.	Manda	Thuamal Rampur, Kalahandi district, Orissa	6000 (estimate)	Oriya	Seriously endangered
11.	Nayaki/ Nayakri	Chandrapur district, Maharshtra	3000 (estimate)	Marathi	Moribund
12.	Parji	Jagadalpur area, chattisgarh	51,216	Hindi (Chattisgarhi)	Endangered
13.	Pengo	Nawarangpur district, Orissa	5000 (estimate)	Oriya	Seriously endangersed

Indo – Aryan Languages

Sl.No.	Language (Dialects)	Distribution	No. of Speakers	Contact LWCs	Endangerment level
1.	Halbi	Chattisgarh, Maharashtra, Orissa	5,93,443	Hindi Marathi Oriya	Potentially Endangered

Language Isolate

1.	Nahali	Maharashtra, Madhya Pradesh	3600 (1961)	Marathi Hindi Gondi Korku	Seriously Endangered

It is clear from the above table that there are 10 languages under Munda family, 13 under Dravidian, one under Indo-Aryan and a single language isolate. Each one of these languages is different and distinct from one another on several counts. Some of them are found in only one state, others in two states and still others in more than two states. For example, Bonda, Didayi, Juang, Parengi, Indi-Awe, Kui, Manda, Pengo, Parji and Nayaki are confined to a single state. Gutob, Korku, Savara, Kharia, Gadaba, Kolami, Konda, Kuvi, Malto and Nahali are spread in two states. Mundari, Santali, Gondi, Kurux and Halbi are enumerated from across several states of the region. Accordingly, tribal bilingualism has emerged, depending upon the major regional language(s) with which the tribes are in daily interaction, namely, Hindi, Marathi, Oriya or Telugu.

When we look at the number of speakers of each of the Adivasi languages, it ranges from 3000 (Didayi or Nayiki) to 64,69,600 of Santali. In between the rest of the languages have their place. It may be pointed out here that the number of speakers also matters, to a large extent, in retention and continuation of a language as in the case of Santali, Gondi, Mundari and Kurux.

3. The Status of Tribal versus Regional Languages

Due to certain socio-economic and geo-political factors, the tribal languages do not stand on an equal social pedestal with those of the regional major languages. A detailed comparison of the status of the two groups would indicate the reasons for language shift among the tribal communities towards the other group. Observe the following statements indicating the hierarchical structure between these two groups:

	Tribal Languages	Regional Languages
1.	Non-literary	Literary
2.	Oral (spoken), unwritten	Written
3.	Minor	Major
4.	Undeveloped or Underdeveloped	Developed
5.	Non-Scheduled	Scheduled (in the Constitution)
6.	Dominated	Dominating

	Tribal Languages	Regional Languages
7.	Not used in education, administration, judiciary, legislature or other high levels	Languages of wider communication (LWC)
8.	Undermined and neglected by outsiders	Recognized
9.	Not vehicles of power and prestige	Command power and prestige
10.	Referred to (by outsiders) with derogatory epithets and ridicule	Treated with honour
11.	High incidence of natural illiterate bilingualism (even trilingualism)	Monolingualism in rural areas Tutored bilingualism (mostly) with a few exceptions.
12.	Not used in electronic, audio-visual and print media	Used on radio, cinema, television and print media
13.	No separate exclusive script (with certain exceptions)	By and large a separate writing system
14.	Mostly oral literature	Both oral and written literature
15.	Less number of speakers	Large number of speakers
16.	Limited to intragroup communication	Used for intergroup communication as well
17.	Confined to home and ritual domains	Found in all domains
18.	Provide less economic opportunity	Sources of economic opportunity and upliftment
19.	Preserve indigenous knowledge systems	Absorb wider knowledge systems
20.	Speakers not treated as models	Speakers treated as socio-political and economic models
21.	Low level of literacy	High level of literacy

Most of the above factors have a socio-psychological effect on the speakers of tribal languages, paving the way for language shift and to opting for the major group at the cost of indigenous mother tongues. For example, tribal bilingualism acts like a double edged weapon, in that on the one hand it accelerates retention of the mother tongue along with other language(s) and on the other it leads to language loss. Bilingualism among the tribes ranges from 10% to 70% depending upon the local situation. This bilingualism is preceded by biculturalism in almost all cases. Even trilingualism is noticed among the communities living across borders of linguistic states.

4. Levels of Language Endangerment

To assess the vitality and endangerment of the languages under discussion, the criteria suggested by Moseley (2007) and Grenoble (2006) are taken into consideration with certain modifications to suit the central indian situation. A six-point scale is put forward, tentatively, to indicate the possible stages of endangerment applicable to these languages:

1. Safe: A language used by all generations, in all domains, with a large number of speakers, holding prestige and power, having official recognition as a scheduled language, used as a medium of education and widespread in the region. Only Santali stands as an example.
2. Safe to Potential Endangerment: Large number of speakers, used by all generations, confined to certain domains, no official status, no economic power, used as medium partially at school, but vital as of now. Mundari, Gondi and Kurux can fall under this category.
3. Potentially Endangered: Comparatively less number of speakers, lack of prestige and power, used in home and rituals, not used in education, under pressure from LWCs and partial shift to LWCs. Kharia, Korku, Savara, Kolami, Kui, Kuvi, Malto and Halbi may be cited as examples.
4. Endangered: Limited number of speakers, used in restricted domains as at home, not medium of education, prone to shift towards regional major languages, neither prestige nor power, no economic viability and outside impact generating language loss. Juang, Gadaba, Konda and Parji stand as examples.
5. Seriously endangered: Each language spoken by less than or around 5000 speakers. Wurm's (1993) criterion of 5000 speakers treats these as disappearing; not used in education, limited to home, no social power and prestige and no economic opportunity. Most of these languages are spoken in isolated hilly areas. The advent of media like TV compelling shift and loss. Future is at stake. Bonda, Didei, Gutob, Indi-Awe, Manda, Pengo and Nahali fall under this category.
6. Moribund: Not learnt by younger generation, only aged people speak the language. It is difficult to find a reliable informant (language assistant). Complete shift to major language. Parengi (Gorum) and Nayaki(Nayakri) are the examples.

As of now, there are speakers of most of these languages, but all are prone to endangerment. A new linguistic survey with perspectives of endangerment with intensive and extensive fieldwork is required to state any thing in a more definite way.

Reasons for Retention: Large number of speakers. Literacy in native language. Positive attitude towards mother tongue. Living on hills in isolation. Bilingualism leading to common core grammar and phonology. Indigenous mother tongue (home language) as a marker of group identity in a multilingual, polycultural society, considerable oral literature (i.e. tribal folklore) in the language.

Reasons for endangerment: Younger generation opting for regional major languages, speakers switching over to regional prestigious tongues, the impact of regional media, lack of prestige associated with mother tongues, economic progress through other languages, intergroup interaction in others tongues, language loss with tribal identity, oral literature also transmitted into local *lingua franca*. Displacement of the community due to so-called developmental projects by the Government and private agencies.

5. Languages Do Matter

Why bother about these indigenous tribal languages? Because they are the depositories of,

1) Tribal linguistic heritage and language diversity
2) Intangible cultural heritage
3) Indigenous knowledge systems
4) Ancient wisdom, humaneness, worldview, philosophy of life, equality of persons, respect for nature and human dignity.
5) Tribal ethnicity preserved in language structure e.g. lexicon and grammar.
6) Tribal lore – oral literature in the form of tales, narratives, songs, fables, plays, ballads, epics, proverbs, idioms, charms, riddles, jokes and origin myths.
7) Oral history as conceived by the community.
6. Remedial measures to save tribal languages

The following steps are essential for retention and development of tribal linguistic heritage (*Ramakrishna Reddy, 2009*):

I. Basic original fieldwork and research for documentation and archiving.
II. Descriptive grammars of the languages with phonology, morphology, syntax, semantics and pragmatics, including unique traits of the structure of each language.
III. Preparation of bilingual/trilingual dictionaries from tribal languages to major regional languages(s) and vice versa and pedagogical/comprehensive dictionaries.
IV. Collection of Texts: Tribal lore consisting of folk tales, folk songs, narrations, idioms, proverbs, riddles and special expressions of discourse should be recorded, preserved and stored as linguistic corpus.
V. Translation of tribal (oral) literature to other major Indian languages and English; and translation of important works of major languages into tribal languages should be taken up on priority basis as some of the genres are endangered under the threat of mass media.
VI. Material production – linguists in collaboration with educationists and

psychologists can prepare primers and other text-books in the tribal languages, which can be utilized in schools and adult education programmes.

VII. Literacy development through production of materials in tribal languages with familiar content(s) as lessons. Here the oral literature can be accommodated as part of the reading materials.

VIII. Native speakers of the tribal languages (especially the literate ones) should be involved in the production of books through production-oriented workshops. The methodology of documentation has to be taught to them so that all the languages can be documented by native speakers.

IX. In selecting the languages for investigation and description, priority should be given to the seriously endangered languages as they might disappear in near future.

X. Liberal financial support may be provided by the governments to individual scholars, University departments, NGOs and other organization interested in and capable of conducting research work and production of books on tribal languages. Support to literary societies of the tribal people in the form of funds, books, etc., and also to organize literary festivals in tribal oral literature.

XI. The New linguistic Survey of India envisaged by the CIIL would provide much needed impetus for the maintenance and development of tribal languages, as it will involve original linguistic fieldwork to assess the levels of endangerment.

XII. Pressing need for a comprehensive, in-depth, multidisciplinary approach, to tribal studies leading to preservation of language, literature, culture and indigenous traditional wisdom and knowledge systems.

The lesson is: Record and describe as many languages as possible.

References:

- Census of India. Language atlas of India 1991. Delhi: Controller of Publications (2004).
- Census of India 2001. Scheduled tribe atlas of India. Delhi: Controller of Publications (2004).
- Census of India 2001. Language: India, States and Union Territories. New Delhi: Registrar General, India (Paper 1 of 2007).
- Van Driem, George. 2007. South Asia and the Middle East. In Christopher Moseley ed. (2007a). pp.283-347.
- Gnanasundaram, V. and K. Rangan. 2006. Language endangerment in the Indian context and globalization. Indian Linguistics, 67: 83 – 94.
- Grenoble, L.A. 2006. Endangered languages. In Encyclopaedia of Language and Linguistics (Second edition) ed. Keith Brown. pp. 137-147. Oxford: Elsevier.

- Grenoble, L.A. and L.J. Whaley. eds. 1998. Endangered languages: Language loss and community response. Cambridge: Cambridge University Press.
- Hale, Ken. 1998. On endangered languages and the importance of linguistic diversity. In Grenoble, L.A. and L.J. Whaley. eds. 1998. pp. 192-216.
- Krauss, Michael. 1992. The world's languages in crisis. Language, 68. 4-10.
- Linguistic Survey of India, Special Studies: Orissa. 2002. Kolkata: Registrar General, India, Language Division.
- Moseley, Christoper. ed. 2007a Encyclopedia of the world's endangered languages. London: Routledge.
- Moseley, Christoper. 2007b. General introduction. In Moseley, ed. 2007a, pp. VII- XVI.
- Ramakrishna Reddy, B. 2006. Linguistic heritage of South Indian tribes. International Journal of Dravidian Linguistics, 35. 203-219.
- Ramakrishna Reddy,B. 2007. Tribal linguistics in India with focus on central and southern regions. In Nagaraja, K.S; Bhatt, V.P; Sonal Kulkarni – Joshi and P.M. Pingle, eds. Research Trends in Lexicography, Sanskrit and Linguistics. pp.183-200. Pune: Deccan College.
- Ramakrishna Reddy,B. 2009. Language endangerment and fieldwork on tribal languages and literatures. International Journal of Dravidian Linguistics, 38.1-22.
- UNESCO. Ad Hoc Expert Group on Endangered Languages. 2003, Language vitality and endangerment. Paris: UNESCO.
- Wurm, Stephen A. 1993. Information document. The red book of languages in danger of disappearing. Paris: UNESCO.

Mother Tongues, Inequality and Marginalization: Implications of the Linguistic Double Divide in Indian Society and Education

Prof. Ajit K. Mohanty - Professor of Psychology and Chairman-Zakir Husain Centre for Educational Studies, School of Social Sciences-(JNU) Delhi

1. Introduction

With 3592 mother tongues (Census of India, 2001), India ranks fourth in the world in linguistic diversity. At the same time, India also heads the list of countries in UNESCO *Atlas of the World's Languages in Danger* (2009) with 196 languages shown as being in different degrees of endangerment. This paradox of diversity and loss of languages can be explained either as a 'natural' process of decay of languages or as a contrived and intentional process by some agency. The first explanation assumes that loss of linguistic diversity is a 'natural' involuntary outcome of organic decay of languages and, hence, the larger the number of living languages, the larger the number of languages dying. The second explanation, on the other hand, presupposes enforcement of a host of factors leading to language shift and loss of languages by a set of interrelated agencies. Skutnabb-Kangas (2000) discusses the two views of language shift as paradigms of language death and of language murder, linguicide or linguistic genocide. As Skutnabb-Kangas (2000) points out, language shift does not just happen without any agency or intentionality; it is not a natural process of death of a language with its speakers shifting voluntarily. She argues that disappearance of languages is better understood as a process of language murder enforced by a set of interrelated agencies. State policies of discrimination and homogenization, socially constructed inequalities, unjust and inequitable distribution of power and control over resources among languages and their speakers push some languages to disuse and marginalization. The language death paradigm, on the other hand, views loss of diversity as an inevitable and natural process about which little can be done except documentation of the endangered and dying languages. An 'agentic' perspective to loss of linguistic vitality is both necessary and practical; the conditions of unequal and hierarchical power relations among languages and action for minimizing threats to languages need to be understood and resisted.

This paper analyzes the state practices of discrimination and social and educational neglect in India, which are responsible for marginalization of some languages, language shift and loss of linguistic vitality. Features of Indian multilingualism are discussed to show that, despite several positive forces favoring maintenance of minority languages, languages are subjected to inequality and discrimination. It is argued that multilingualism in India, as in other South Asian countries, is hierarchical in nature characterized by a double divide (*Mohanty, Panda & Pal, In press*). This paper takes a position that language policy and practice in education is a critical determinant of loss of vitality and endangerment of languages. Education has often been considered as a process of planned language change since use of language in education is crucial for vitalization/revitalization of languages.

2. Multilingualism in India: Inequalities and Discrimination

In the 2001 census, the people of India named 6,661 mother tongues. These were classified into 3,592 mother tongues out of which 1,635 rationalized mother tongues were listed and the remaining 1,957 were grouped under the 'Other mother tongues' category. These mother tongues in India are variously classified into 300 to 400 languages, although the census of 2001 arrived at 122 languages (plus the unlisted category of 'other languages') under each of which many languages (mother tongues) were listed. The Constitution of India (VIIIth Schedule) recognizes 22 of these languages as official languages and English as an associate official language. Much more than the number, the complex presence of a large number of languages in routine domains of daily life activities makes multilingualism in India a distinct phenomenon (*Mohanty, 1994, 2006*). People use multiple languages in routine daily life transactions and languages complement each other with a smooth functional allocation into different domains of use. For example, I use my mother tongue Oriya in my home, English in my work place, different varieties of Hindi-Urdu-Punjabi in the market place, Bengali for communication with a domestic help and other Bengali friends, Sanskrit for religious activities and some Kui with the tribal contacts for my research with the Kond community. All these languages (plus a few others used occasionally) complement each other in my life without any conflict. Such complimentary and non-competing relationships between languages is quite typical in India and this makes it possible for languages to be maintained in situations of wide spread contact. Common people perceive the boundaries between languages as quite fluid and their linguistic identities are characterized by plurality. Further, a process of early multilingual socialization (*Mohanty, Panda & Mishra, 1999*) leads to an early awareness of the features of Indian multilingualism and the norms for socially appropriate use of languages. Multilingualism is a positive force in India and it is generally accepted as a necessary aspect of the daily life of people. Our studies in India (*see Mohanty, 1994, 2003a, 2003b of discussion and Mohanty & Perregaux, 1997 for review*) show positive cognitive and social consequences of mother tongue maintenance and multilingualism.

Despite such positive features, Indian languages are hierarchically organized in a 'double divide' (*Mohanty, in press*), as has been pointed out earlier. Languages at the bottom of the hierarchical double divide - more specifically the indigenous tribal minority (ITM) languages - are victims of discrimination and social, economic, political and educational neglect. Some languages have greater access to power and resources while others are disadvantaged and marginalized. Indian multilingualism, therefore, has been described as 'multilingualism of the unequals' (*Mohanty, 2004*).

Linguistic discrimination is rooted in the statutory processes of governance. The constitutional recognition of 22 languages as official languages keeps most of the Indian languages out of the domains of power. Besides these official languages, some of the others are also recognized for specific public purposes such as for promotion of literature and for state level use in limited spheres of governance. Such recognitions are invariably related to the political power of linguistic groups. The constitution of India was amended in December 2003 to recognize Bodo, Dogri, Maithili and Santali as official languages. This followed intense political lobbying and prolonged language movements by the respective language communities. Maithili was earlier grouped under Hindi[1]. Bodo and Santali are the first tribal languages to be recognized as official languages and this recognition was possible due to the assertive language maintenance movements. Many other ITM (Indigenous and Tribal Minority) languages are marginalized, often stigmatized as 'dialects', and weakened; their feeble voices for recognition are silenced in the dynamics of power and politics. Apart from the discriminations and inequalities in the statutory provisions and the process of governance, education is a major basis for institutionalized inequality. The ITM languages are neglected in school and literacy programmes; only a few have any place in school education in India, as will be shown later.

Large-scale social neglect and discrimination are responsible for marginalization of languages and loss of linguistic diversity in the world. Languages fail to develop when they are excluded from domains of power, legal and statutory recognition, trade, commerce and education. Social and educational neglect strips languages of

[1] *Hindi has 48 mother tongues, other than Hindi itself, grouped under it, each with more than one 10,000 speakers. 25 of these mother tongues have at least one million speakers. Bhojpuri, grouped under Hindi, has over 33 million speakers.*

their instrumental vitality and contribute to their weakness. Unfortunately, such weakness of languages is often used to justify further neglect that continues to make them weaker in a vicious circle of language disadvantage (*Mohanty, Mishra, Reddy & Ramesh, 2009: 278-291*). Thus, while many languages co-exist in the multilingual mosaic of India, only a few are privileged; the rest are marginalized and weakened in a hierarchical power relationship. As in South Asia and other parts of the world, English is the dominant language in the linguistic hierarchy of post-colonial India and there are major gaps or linguistic divides in society which can be seen as a double divide between English and major languages and between major languages and the ITM languages.

3. The Linguistic Double Divide

The multilingual societies in South Asia are typically characterized by a linguistic double divide in which English (and, in some cases, a major national language) is at the top of the hierarchy, other major languages in the middle rungs and ITM languages at the bottom.

In such a double divide, the dominant languages in the higher levels push the lower level languages out of significant public domains leading to a progressive domain shrinkage for most languages and yielding to the higher-level languages; the rate of domain loss and marginalization is much higher for the ITM languages at the bottom of the three-tiered hierarchy. Thus, ITM languages are progressively endangered in South Asian countries, which are typically characterized by multilingual social realities and monolingual state practices. In India, while English is the language of power, Hindi and other major languages dominate over the ITM languages in the states. This has led to struggle by some of the ITM language communities (such as Bodo and Santali) for recognition and revitalization of their languages. In Nepal, English and Nepali are the dominant languages for all official and educational functions and nearly 100 other dominated languages are beginning to assert themselves through organized political movements in the new democratic set up of the nation. According to Rahman (1998), out of the three official languages (English, Urdu and Sindhi) in Pakistan, English is the language of power and Urdu is the language of Pakistani nationalism; most of the 72 other languages are struggling for recognition and identity through several ethno-linguistic movements. In Bangladesh, Bengali is the only official language while English remains the language of power and dominance. Over 39 other languages, including many tribal languages, remain marginalized in this three-tiered hierarchy. Similarly, the place of nearly 29 languages of the indigenous communities in Bhutan's language and education policy in relation to Dzongkha, the major state language, and English continues to be debated. A linguistic double divide with English as the language of power and statutory presence of one or more major national language(s) as symbols of national identities along with rhetorically supported indigenous and minority languages is typical of all South Asian countries. Ironically, the position of English as the language of power in South Asian societies is reinforced by internal conflicts between competing linguistic assertions. For example, the conflicts between Hindi and South Indian languages in India and between the speakers of Sinhala and Tamil in Sri Lanka have facilitated the dominant role of English. The Bengali language movement resisting the dominance of Urdu led to the formation of Bangladesh as a separate nation; but internal power dynamics and conflicting interests resulted in a dominant place for English. Similarly, English is promoted in Pakistan as a language of power although Urdu is projected as a symbol of national integration.

The Indian socio-linguistic scenario is affected, on the one hand, by the English-regional-majority-language divide or what Ramanathan (2005a, 2005b) calls the *English-Vernacular divide* and, on the other, by the *Vernacular-Minority/Indigenous Language divide*. This double divide is reflected in the very nature of multilingualism, which according to Annamalai (2001: 35), is "bifocal, existing both at the mass level and the elite level". The distribution of bilingualism with and without English in the multilingual mosaic of India shows the hierarchy across the linguistic double divides. This hierarchy also involves a pecking order in which English relegates Hindi and other major languages (of the states in India) to positions of lesser significance and power while the state majority languages push the other languages, particularly those of the ITM, out of the major domains of use and threaten their survival.

The languages across the double divide – English, vernaculars and ITM languages – show quantum differences in their vitality and access to power and privileges in Indian society. The double divide has far reaching implications, particularly for the languages on the underside of the double divide, the ITM languages, which are cumulatively impoverished due to large scale social neglect and discrimination. The double divide is also negotiated through various collective and individual identity strategies (*Mohanty, In press*). In some cases, collective identity strategies have led to assertive maintenance and revitalization of languages (such as Bodo and Santali) and, in others, individual identity strategies of the speakers of indigenous languages have resulted in passive acceptance of marginalization of their language. Dissociation between instrumental and integrative functions of the dominated languages (Mohanty 2004) is also indicative of the passive acceptance. The dissociation is evident from the dominated language community's endorsement of the major languages for children's education and for use in domains of economic significance and of their own languages for in-group identity and culture. Such divergent identity strategies are also reflected in instances of linguistic identity without language (for example, the Kui[2] linguistic identity of Oriya monolingual Konds) and language without identity (for example, many of the upper class English educated Bhojpuri speakers do not identify with Bhojpuri[3]). The double divide affects the processes of language change, marginalization, shift and maintenance and, hence, the very future of multilingualism in India. The languages across the double divide – English, vernaculars and ITM languages – differ substantially in their ethno-linguistic vitality, access to power and privileges in society and how they are placed in language policy and practice in education in India.

4. Languages in Education: Reflections of the Linguistic Double Divide

Education in India has neglected the ITM languages and several factors have come together to gradually establish English as the major language in education (*Mohanty, 2006, 2008a, b*). Education in children's mother tongue is accepted in principle in the Indian constitution and other policy documents. In 1957, the three-language formula (TLF) floated by the government of India sought to deal with the place of mother tongues, regional languages and Hindi, and English in school education in India. This formula recommended use of regional language or mother tongue as the initial medium of instruction and teaching of Hindi or regional languages and English. The regional language and mother tongue were never clearly distinguished and, as a result, it facilitated imposition of the majority state language as the medium of school education on the minority and tribal language children in forced submersion models of schooling. The TLF was modified on several occasions. "Different versions (of the TLF) were applied depending on how the formula was interpreted in various states and school systems. Despite such variations, English became the most common second language subject in all the states, followed by either Hindi or Sanskrit as the third language subject" (*Mohanty 2006: 274*). Thus, despite several modifications, the TLF failed to balance between English, Hindi, regional languages and mother tongues (of the tribal and minority groups). However, it is quite clear that, in the absence of any language policy in education, English is rapidly gaining in significance in school education directly undermining the role of Hindi and other languages. Further, there is a steady decline in the number of mother tongues in schools in India along with negligible presence of tribal languages. The number of languages used in schools in India either as languages of teaching and as school subjects declined from 81 in 1970 to 41 in 1998. At present, the number of

---

[2] *Kui is the indigenous language of the Kond tribe in Kandhamal District of Orissa. In parts of the district, there has been a shift of Kui in favor of Oriya, the state dominant language. The Oriya monolingual Konds in these parts of Kandhamal still identify with Kui language calling themselves 'Kui people*

[3] *Upper class Bhojpuri speakers often assume a superordinate identity as Hindi speaker s. Srivastava (1989) also noted that migrant Bhojpuri workers in Maharashtra show a language shift towards Hindi.*

languages used as a medium of instruction (MI) is 31 at the primary level (Grades I to V), 25 in Grades VI and VII, 21 in Grades VIII to X, and 18 in higher secondary levels (Grades XI and XII). English has an increasingly dominant presence in all levels of education. Place of tribal languages as MI is negligible with only 3 to 4 languages used regularly as languages of teaching (*Mohanty, 2008b*). Thus, the linguistic double divide has resulted in a privileged position for English in Indian education whereas the ITM children are forced to submersion schooling in a language, which is not their mother tongue. As a result, they struggle to learn the language of the school with no or little proficiency in the same and English, which is twice removed from their social reality. This is a major factor in poor school learning, high push out rate, large-scale school failure, capability deprivation and poverty among the tribal mother tongue speakers in India (*see Mohanty 2008b, for an elaborate discussion*).

It has been shown (*Mohanty, 2008b*) that the language disadvantage of tribal children in forced submersion schools in a majority language medium of teaching leads to subtractive language learning, poor inter-generational transmission of languages, 'wash back' effects (*Heugh et al. 2007*) causing de-emphasis of mother tongues in education and loss of linguistic diversity. The programmes of school education in India have not responded to the challenges of its multilingual ethos; they offer only nominal forms of multilingual education (*Mohanty 2006, 2008b*) since they neither support the weaker languages nor develop adequate multilingual proficiency. As has been pointed out, many languages complement each other in meeting the communicative needs of people and, hence, education must necessarily foster multilingual proficiency in the languages of functional significance – MT, languages for regional and national level communication and international language of wider communication. Thus, education for children in a major language as their MT needs to develop competence in at least two to three languages such as Bengali, Hindi and English. Education for the ITM language communities, on the other hand, must develop proficiency in three to four languages including, for example, a tribal language MT, major languages like Hindi and Bengali, and English as an international language of wider communication.

5. Overcoming the Language Barrier through Multilingual Education

Multilingual education (MLE) involves use of two or more languages as languages of teaching (MI) in subjects other than the languages themselves and it develops high levels of multilingual proficiency and multiliteracy (*Mohanty et al. 2009*). International research and experiences with MLE show that the process of education for development of multilingual proficiency starts with development of proficiency in MT as the language of teaching (MI) for at least six to eight years of schooling and gradually develops other languages through their systematic use as MI (*Mohanty et al. 2009; Skutnabb-Kangas &*

Mohanty 2009). Such programmes of MLE are particularly beneficial for the ITM children who are denied the choice of development of their MT and multilingual proficiency in the current system of education in India forcing them to go through subtractive forms of submersion education in a non-MT language (*Mohanty 2006, 2008b*). In recent years some programmes of MLE have started in India to deal with the problem of language disadvantage of tribal children facing the formidable double divide.

The realization that the language disadvantage of tribal children in dominant language schools is a major factor in their educational failure, has led to sporadic efforts in India to try out various models of mother tongue based education for tribal children (*Mohanty 1989, 2006*). The early attempts were transitional programmes of bilingual education (sometimes called bilingual transfer programmes) to facilitate smooth transition from a tribal MT to the major language of schooling. These programmes lacked any theoretical framework and were dropped without any systematic evaluation. Some states have recently started organized experimental programmes of mother tongue based MLE for tribal children. Andhra Pradesh started such a programme in the year 2004 in 8 tribal MTs for children in 240 schools. Orissa started in 2006 in 10 tribal MTs in 195 schools (*see Mohanty at al. 2009: 278-291, for details*). In these programmes, MT is used as the language of teaching and early literacy instruction for the first 3 to 5 years of primary level schooling. The state majority language (Telugu in Andhra Pradesh and Oriya in Orissa) is introduced in the second year as a language subject for development of oral communicative skills and in the third years for reading and writing skills. The state language is used as a language of teaching from the fourth year and the tribal MT children are to join regular school programmrs in the majority language of the states (Telugu/Oriya) from the sixth year onwards. The script[4] of the state language is used with some modifications, wherever necessary, to write the tribal languages.The teachers in the MLE programmes are from the language community and speak the target tribal language. The programmes follow the common school curriculum of the states and seek to integrate the cultural knowledge system of the tribal language community in developing the textbooks and other curricular materials. A special intervention programme (*Panda & Mohanty, 2009*) called *MLE Plus* (MLE+) is implemented in eight of the government MLE schools in Orissa in two tribal languages – Kui and Saora. The MLE+ programme has a special focus on cultural pedagogy with a culture- and community-based approach to collaborative classroom learning and development of cultural identity among the tribal children. Evaluations of the MLE and MLE+ programmes show positive effects on children's classroom achievement, school

[1] *Tribal languages in India do not have any exclusive script system and are usually written in the script of either the dominant regional language or another major language. But, in recent years, some tribal languages, such as Santali, have developed their own writing system.*

participation, parental satisfaction and community involvement (*Mohanty et al. 2009: 278-291; Panda & Mohanty 2009*). It seems, compared to the traditional programmes of submersion education in the state majority language, the experimental MLE programmes offer better quality education for the tribal children. However, because of the pressure of the linguistic double divide, these programmes not only bring in the state language (L2), English and Hindi quite early into the teaching programme (by the second, third and fifth years, respectively), but also plan to discontinue use of the MT from the sixth year onwards. Such early transition from the MT to major language and English goes against the established research findings in MLE. Research shows that late-exit programmes of MLE, continuing with MT as the language of teaching for at least six to eight years, are more effective than early-exit programmes and that the longer the MT is continued as the language of teaching the better is the development of proficiency in other languages including English (*Skutnabb-Kangas & Mohanty 2009*).

Conclusion

Multilingualism, as in India, is and can be a social and individual resource. However, in reality, because of the built in inequalities, it privileges few and disadvantages many. Multilingualism in India triggers a hierarchical pecking order in which the privileged language of the elites pushes the less privileged languages into domains of limited resource. The less privileged languages, in turn, push the disadvantaged ones into invisibility and marginalization. The inequalities in Indian multilingualism are dehumanizing at a certain level; they lead to capability deprivation and poverty for the marginalized language communities and to loss of linguistic diversity.

This paper has sought to show that Indian multilingualism can be viewed as a system characterized by a double divide between English, the vernaculars or the regional dominant languages and the languages of the indigenous and tribal minorities. The linguistic double divide is embedded in the social macrostructure and, at the same time, it affects the same. For example, the system of private and government schooling in India is organized as following from and leading to the linguistic double divide. This bidirectional relationship between the linguistic double divide and the system as well as the processes of schooling must be appreciated in order to understand how schools in India make and unmake society. The current experimental programmes of mother tongue based MLE in India are attempts at helping tribal children to effectively negotiate the double divide. However, these limited experimental programmes are insufficient and inadequate to deal with the language disadvantage of millions of children in the country and the cumulative effects of such disadvantages on its linguistic diversity. Maintenance of the linguistic diversity and egalitarian positioning of languages in India depends on how effectively the formidable problem of the double divide is addressed.

References

- Annamalai, E. 2001. *Managing multilingualism in India.* New Delhi: Sage.
- Heugh, Kathleen, Benson, Carol, Bogale, Berhanu and Yohannes, Mekonnen Alemu Gebre. 2007. *Final report: Study on medium of instruction in primary schools in Ethiopia.* Ethiopia: Ministry of Education.
- Mohanty, Ajit K. 1989. Psychological consequences of mother tongue maintenance and the language of literacy for linguistic minorities in India. *Psychology and Developing Societies* 2:1, 31-51.
- Mohanty, Ajit K. 1994. *Bilingualism in a multilingual society. Psycho-social and pedagogical implications.* Mysore: Central Institute of Indian Languages.
- Mohanty, Ajit K. 2003a. Multilingualism and multiculturalism: The context of psycholinguistic research in India. In Vindhya, U. (ed.) *Psychology in India: Intersecting crossroads.* New Delhi: Concept, 35 - 53.
- Mohanty, Ajit K. 2003b. Psychology of language acquisition and bilingualism in India: The cultural input. In John W. Berry, Ramesh C. Mishra & Rama C. Tripathi (eds.),. *Psychology in human and social development: Lessons from diverse cultures.* New Delhi: Sage, 86-99.
- Mohanty, Ajit K. 2004. *Multilingualism of the unequals: The 'Killer Language' and anti-predatory strategies of minority mother tongues.* Keynote address, International Conference on Multilingualism, Southern African Applied Linguistics Association, University of the North, South Africa, July 13 – 15.
- Mohanty, Ajit K. 2006. Multilingualism of the Unequals and Predicaments of Education in India: Mother tongue or Other Tongue? In Ofelia García, Tove Skutnabb-Kangas & María E. Torres-Guzmán (eds.), *Imagining multilingual schools: Language in education and glocalization.* Clevedon: Multilingual Matters, 262-283.
- Mohanty, Ajit K. 2008a. Multilingual Education in India. In Jim Cummins & Nancy H. Hornberger (eds.), Vol. 5, *Bilingual Education. Encyclopedia of Language and Education* (2nd edition). New York: Springer, 165-174.
- Mohanty, Ajit K. 2008b. Perpetuating inequality: Language disadvantage and capability deprivation of tribal mother tongue speakers in India'. In Wayne Harbert, Sally McConnell-Ginet, Amanda Miller & John Whitman (eds.), *Language and poverty.* Clevedon, UK: Multilingual Matters, 102-124.
- Mohanty, Ajit K. In press. Languages, inequality and marginalization: Implications of the double divide in Indian multilingualism. *International Journal of Sociology of Language.*

- Mohanty, Ajit K., Mishra, Mahendra Kumar, Reddy, N. Upender & Ramesh, Gumidyala 2009. Overcoming the language barrier for tribal children: MLE in Andhra Pradesh and Orissa, India. In Ajit K. Mohanty, Minati Panda, Robert Phillipson & Tove Skutnabb-Kangas (eds.), *Multilingual education for social justice: Globalising the local.* New Delhi: Orient Longman, 278-291.
- Mohanty, Ajit K., Panda, Minati and Pal, Rashim. In press. Language policy in education and classroom practices in India: Is the teacher a cog in the policy wheel? In Ofelia Garcia & Kate Menken (eds.), *Negotiating language policies: Educators as policy makers.* London: Routledge.
- Mohanty, Ajit K., Panda, Smaranika & Mishra, Babban. 1999. Language socialization in a multilingual society. In T.S. Saraswathi (ed.), *Culture, socialization and human development.* New Delhi: Sage.
- Mohanty, Ajit K. & Perregaux, Christiane. 1997. Language acquisition and bilingualism. In J.W. Berry, P.R. Dasen, and T.S. Saraswathi (eds.), *Handbook of cross-cultural psychology: vol. 2 basic processes and human development.* Boston: Allyn & Bacon, 217-253.
- Panda, Minati & Mohanty, Ajit 2009. Language matters, so does culture: beyond the rhetoric of culture in multilingual education. In Ajit K. Mohanty, Minati Panda, Robert Phillipson & Tove Skutnabb-Kangas (eds.), *Multilingual education for social justice: Globalising the local.* New Delhi: Orient Longman.
- Ramanathan, Vaidehi. 2005a. *The English-Vernacular divide: Postcolonial language politics and practice.* Clevedon: Multilingual Matters,
- Ramanathan, Vaidehi. 2005b. Ambiguities about English: Ideologies and critical practice in vernacular-medium college classrooms in Gujarat, India. *Journal of Language, Identity and Education,* 4(1), 45-65.
- Rahman, Tariq 1998. *Language and politics in Pakistan.* Karachi: Oxford University Press.
- Skutnabb-Kangas, Tove 2000. *Linguistic genocide in education - or worldwide diversity and human rights?* Mahwah, NJ: Lawrence Erlbaum.
- Skutnabb-Kangas, Tove and Mohanty, Ajit K. (2009). *Policy and Strategy for MLE in Nepal. Report by Tove Skutnabb-Kangas and Ajit Mohanty. Consultancy visit 4-14 March 2009.* Sanothimi, Bhaktapur, Nepal: Multilingual Education Programme for All Non-Nepali Speaking Students of Primary Schools of Nepal. Ministry of Education, Department of Education, Inclusive Section. (can be downloaded from http://www.tove-skutnabb-kangas.org/en/articles_for_downloading.html).
- UNESCO 2009. *Atlas of world's languages in danger.* Paris: UNESCO. http://www.unesco.org/culture/en/endangeredlanguages.

Bleeding Languages of South India: Issues and Prospects

Dr. M. Sreenathan - Associate Professor, Department of Dravidian & Computational Linguistics, Dravidian University, Andhra Pradesh

1. Introduction

Endangered languages have achieved the status of a credible and serious research proposition worldwide only in recent decades, and the gravity of the issue is quite evident in the UNESCO *Atlas of the World's Languages in Danger* (2009). UNESCO's diagnosis is clear on the future of smaller languages, and the death of such languages is well predicted. This alarming situation has alerted the world which must now approach the problem with the utmost seriousness. It is not just a matter of the death of a language, but a serious matter of the loss of human knowledge forever as a result of growing globalization, warns the United Nations environment programme.

India is a befitting case for the study of endangered languages. In India 96.56% (2001 Census) of the total population is recorded as speaking scheduled languages, while the remaining 3.44% is recorded as speaking non-scheduled and other languages. The majority of nonscheduled and other languages is represented by tribal mother tongues. These mother tongues are markers of tribal identity but they are officially and socially excluded. The grave under-representation of these languages is a social insult to the linguistic rights of the marginalized. Setting up safe passage for the death of smaller tongues has become a sponsored agenda of the Indian democracy. No nutrition is given to these languages nor enough manure to stop them from perishing. This is the pan Indian ecology of smaller languages.

It is difficult to underline even a couple of safe smaller languages, but it is easy to fit many into the endangerment spectrum. This is distressing to those who are concerned with diversity. What is required therefore is intervention. As a first step, knowing and respecting the other tongue is crucial. India is a veritable store house of tribal languages and the tribal communities represent different stages of the socio-cultural evolution of India. However, to put it squarely, a comprehensive survey of tribal languages in the light of linguistics remains neglected in India. Much of this language pool still has to be systematically investigated and catalogued. The New Linguistic survey of India (NLSI) initiated by CIIL is an effort in that direction; this is certainly an appropriate time to undertake such an exercise. Due to the current sweep of globalization and penetration of market forces deep into hitherto inaccessible regions, the existing rich diversity, including linguistic heritage, is threatened and there is a danger that any further delay might wipe all this out before it gets recorded.

Based on limited field exposure and by assembling available data, together with some contextual analysis, I attempt to present the ethnolinguistic fabric of South India. It is my hope that policymakers may thus understand the social pathology of the minor languages of the region. The attempt is to highlight increasing language loss and its influence on language diversity. This study underlines the urgent need to have a language policy with an emphasis on minor language planning in order to control language decline. It will expose the linguistic ecology that is prevalent in South India – that is, Andhra Pradesh, Karnataka, Tamilnadu, Kerala, Lakshadweep and Pondicherry. It will follow the trend of diminishing linguistic identities. The paper concludes with an end note pinpointing the urgent requirement of mother tongue based education in order to ensure the vitality of minor languages in South India.

South India is home to several dominant languages and many small languages which are socially insulted. The ecology of language, (the socio-economic conditions of a particular social environment in which language is spoken) in general favours some languages, giving them a selective advantage over others, which in turn affects the inherent linguistic diversity. The shift of tribal languages (*Ishtiaq1999*) has quite convincingly established the trend of language decline in tribal India. The magnitude of language shift is critical in Andhra Pradesh (66.24%), Karnataka (74.21%), Kerala (98.31%), TamilNadu (94.90%) and Lakshadweep (82.98%). In the areas where tribals are minorities, the language shift is quite evident.

South India has been attested as a Dravidian homeland. But no state in India is unilingual. Despite the dominance of Dravidian languages, South India has been linguistically a multilingual space and is home to all four major linguistic families of India. The languages that are currently spoken in the region can be divided broadly into 3 groups: the languages of the tribal people who constitute the region's earliest migrants starting several thousand years ago, of the Indo-Aryan speakers who migrated from other areas, and of the well established Dravidian language speakers. There is a wide variation not only among the language groups, but also among the families of languages. Dravidian tribal languages are characterized by the small size of speaker populations and by the absence of dominant languages. However, the speakers are usually bilingual, and can speak or at least understand the languages of neighboring populations; it is believed that this situation has existed for a long time. A clear distinction between in-group and out-group communication and choice of language according to the context of situations is evident.

Except Lakshadweep, the Austro-Asiatic languages are present everywhere, though their numbers are not too significant, except Savara and Gadaba in Andhra Pradesh. The numerical strength of the Tibeto-Burman family is also quite negligible. But the noticeable point is that this family is spreading down to the South from its core area, as is evident from the decadal censuses. It is a point to be addressed. Peripheralization of languages from their core area is one of the reasons for enhanced bilingualism and eventual reduction of smaller tongues. The Indo Aryan spread is visible in south India by the presence of more languages than even Dravidian languages, though tribal languages belonging to the Indo Aryan family are not significant, other than Lambadi and Adivasi Oriya in Andhra Pradesh. Also, the periodical censuses reveal that there has been a strong presence of major Dravidian languages in South India over a significantly long period.

As far as smaller linguistic identities are concerned, each state acts mostly as a space of convergence and of language shift. Interstate migrants are incapable of maintaining their mother tongue identity. This poses problems for language planners. Providing equal opportunities for the maintenance of mother tongue is always a matter of concern. The numerically larger minority populations can sustain their mother tongues provided the opportunities of interaction prevail. The state minority status reports show that dominant minorities can find some space for survival through minority mediums of education. Others have no chance of maintaining their languages. In reality, the educational set up favours the regional languages rather than the minority languages. In fact, no state promotes numerically weak minority languages in education. Such languages have to surrender to the regional language. The multilingual space strengthens the regional dominant *lingua franca* through minority bilingualism and language shift. The three language formula provides the minority language speakers with no choice than to adjust to the prevailing conditions.

2. Tribal Languages of Andhra Pradesh

The 33 scheduled tribes in Andhra Pradesh constitute 6.6% of the total state population. In Andhra Pradesh, most languages are vulnerable but in some areas they are definitely endangered and in others severely endangered or critically endangered. There is no uniformity in language loyalty across regions; it is governed by the immediate ecology. Active bilingualism is noticed among all minor linguistic groups. The level of language loyalty among these groups is governed by the settlement and demographic pattern at the local level. Indo-Aryan migrant languages like Andh are definitely endangered but not Kolami, Kuvi, Konda and Kurru as listed in UNESCO's Atlas. Naikri is extinct in Andhra Pradesh. However, the majority of the tribal communities in the state speak Telugu. Also, there are communities which speak both Telugu and Oriya.

The two tribal languages belonging to the Indo Aryan family are Banjara(Lambadi) and Vaghri in Andhra Pradesh. Banjara is heavily influenced by Telugu. Dommari is critically endangered. Naikpod speakers in Andhra Pradesh have also shifted to Telugu, but their counterparts in Maharashtra speak Naikri.

External features impinge on the language attitudes of a speech community. For instance, let us verify the speaker's strength and concentration of groups in Andhra Pradesh. Some groups are represented by below 500 speakers and some have quite a respectable strength. Their distribution is also important. Many of the groups still maintain core areas. The Parji, Gondi, Koya, Konda, Kuvi, Kui, Kolami, Adivasi Oriya, Lambadi etc have chances of survival since their rural presence is quite high. The Gadaba and Savara are two groups with mixed identities. Their existence in Andhra Pradesh has led to their language being influenced by Telugu, as their counterparts in Orissa are influenced by Oriya. Hence, these languages are counted both in Dravidian and Munda families. Distribution in wider areas and the dominance of non tribal groups even in scheduled areas are directly reducing the chances of maintaining hard core tribal language identity. Meantime, staying in multi tribal villages also necessitates that they maintain certain differences in culture and language. Socially demanded maintenance of language in the home domain is widely seen. Socio-economically, all groups are relatively backward. The main cause of worry is that they do not have autonomy over resources. Bilingualism and a shift to the regional tongue are evident in most areas. Out migration, the majority's attitude towards the tribes and lack of awareness of linguistic rights are negative to the survival of these languages. Also most of these groups have a migrant history and their homeland is originally not in Andhra Pradesh. A sense of historically developed insecurity and unfavourable social ecology enforces them to accept the dominant *lingua franca*, Telugu.

At the local level, they are bound to interact with other linguistic groups in multilingual settings for their sustenance and for official recognition through Telugu. This is evident in their pattern of bilingualism. The provision of literacy and religious contact with non tribals too plays an active role in reducing tribal language use. For instance, Telugu has influenced these communities in ritual practices. In a few languages like Kuvi, Kolami, Lambadi, which have some dictionary and bible resources and which have appeared minimally in radio programmes, generally resource building and extensive use in media and other domains are weak. The communities did not receive mother tongue education support till 2005. Since 2005, officially 8 Tribal mother tongues (Savara, Koya, Gondi, Kolami, Lambada, Konda, Kuvi and Adivasi Oriya) are recognized for primary education.

3. Tribal languages of Karnataka

In Karnataka, the Scheduled tribe population constitutes 6.6%. 49 groups are notified and their major concentration is reported from the districts of Bellary, Raichur, Mysore, Chitradurga, Belgaum, Davanagere and Kolar. The seven districts account for 54 % of the ST population of the state. The remaining 46 % ST populations are distributed in 20 districts.

Despite having many languages in Karnataka, external features like speaker's strength and concentration of groups, distribution pattern, migrant origin and absence of core areas, lack of economic autonomy, bilingualism, out migration, majority's attitude towards the tribes and the lack of awareness on linguistic rights are negative to the survival of these languages. Languages which are identified as dialects of Kannada have more survival chance. The state social ecology is in no way supportive to the maintenance of smaller identities; hence the shift level and endangerment level are high except Kannada related linguistic groups and the nomadic groups which are always in contact with their core areas. A clear regional pattern of endangerment is visible in the state. In some areas Hakkipikki uses more Kannada than Waagri, as is the case with Indo Aryan communities like Chodri. The Karnataka bound languages like Jenukruba, Soliga, Yerava etc are vulnerable yet they are in a better state than migrant languages.

4. Tribal Languages of Kerala

The scheduled tribe population in Kerala is 1.14% of the total population. The State has a total of 35 five government-recognized scheduled tribes in Kerala and they are overwhelmingly rural. But their number is actually between 48 to 54, for all practical purposes. Such discrepancies in the official classification creates problems of identification and tribal groups often lose their original identity and are known to officials by a different name. They helplessly cling to their newly endowed names because they receive the official benefits and recognition only if they possess the name, no matter what their actual nomenclature!

As per the official status, no tribal language has been recognized in Kerala. The literacy rate in the regional tongue of the Kerala tribes is quite high. They speak languages or dialects which are related to Tamil, Kannada, Tulu and Malayalam. The numerically weak speaker strength, and scanty distribution, land alienation, high contact level with non tribals, lack of political support and awareness on linguistic rights, strong intervention of government machinery in schooling and competitive social ecology has ensured a shift to the regional language. Even after all these factors, tribal tongues are distinctively maintained by many groups in the home and community domain. Language shift and endangerment are locally patterned. For instance, Kadar in Wayanadu is shifted while they use Kadar language in Thrissur and Palakkad.

5. Tribal Languages of Tamil Nadu

Scheduled tribes in Tamil Nadu cover 1% of the total population. Thirty six STs have been notified in Tamil Nadu. Of these, Malayali, Irular, Kattunayakan, Kurumans and Kondareddis together constitute 85.3 per cent. Out of 36 communities, 31 are shared with Kerala and some communities with Karnataka. The distribution across states is a problem to these communities. Like that of Kerala, the distinctiveness of languages has been dwindling and shifting towards the main regional language, Tamil. Institutional safety networks do not favourably encourage these languages. The state's linguistic ecology, population strength, Tamil-based literacy, scanty distribution, economic dependency, non tribal influence and so on lead these languages to minimal use and endangerment. The Nilgiri group of languages is also facing endangerment.

6. Discussion

This discussion begins with a note of appreciation on the attempts of UNESCO in spreading critical awareness on language endangerment. As per the latest assessment (2009), India has the largest number of endangered languages. Of these 196 languages, the Dravidian family is represented by 17 languages.

Vulnerable	Definitely endangered	Critically endangered	Severely endangered
Gondi, Irula, Kui, Kurux and Tulu	Kolami Kond,Kurru and Kuvi	Bellari,Koraga, Kota,Kuruba, Naiki,Parji, Pengo and Toda	Nil

The above listing is not parallel to the reality. For instance, the lack of code switching between Tulu and Kannada has facilitated the maintenance of Tulu in the South Kannara district of South India where Tulu is largely spoken (*Malavika Shetty 2003*). No systematic field study on language endangerment based on UNESCO's language vitality and endangerment framework has been attempted in South India, hence the claims are tentative. Another factor is that studying a language in one state and validating it on the endangerment frame is also a faulty proposition in the Indian context. Many languages are shared across states and each state may also have a sizable population (for instance, Koya in Andhra Prdaesh) but in migrant states or districts that particular language may be in a potentially endangered or even moribund stage, while it may be safe or vulnerable in core areas. A micro level survey at settlement level is required for understanding the real endangered status of any language in South India rather than a macro level assessment. The issue of Tulu takes us to yet another important problem that minor languages are facing in India, that is, the peripheralization process.

Outward migration is a common phenomenon in India. The Tibeto-Burman presence in South India is one of the examples. It may be intra-district or inter-district or inter-state, on a permanent or temporary basis. There is free movement from rural to urban areas resulting in the creation of large slums in Indian cities. These urban spaces lead to the convergence of different linguistic identities. But the relationship between urbanization and language is complex. This complexity arises because urbanization engulfs different languages in favour of the dominant tongue, and survival options, such as food and social security, education and health care etc. are directly linked to this. This suggests that urbanization primarily accelerates language attrition. Thus it is recognized as one of the causes of language shift.

While discussing vanishing linguistic diversity in general, Abbi(2004) reports that 'The sense of pride in associating with the dominant regional language is considered as a step towards merging with the mainstream.' Abbi (2004) further observes, 'The inevitable fears of the tribes about being pushed back in society, desires to rise up to the elite and superior languages and amalgamate with the mainstream are the factors discouraging the lower rung language speakers to exercise their linguistic rights'. The social setting of language attrition is clear even in rural areas where development has reached.

Language shift is a culturally, socially and economically related process (*Hoijer, 1948, Fishman 1976, Milroy and Milroy 1985*). This is explained mainly in terms of industrialization, urbanization, political centralization, administrative favour (policy of standard language promotion in media and education) and mass media .The changes in the structure of the economy encourage speakers of small languages to become bilingual. Bilinguals may subsequently abandon their ancestral tongue (*Annamalai, 1990 2001*). The one and a half decade old assessment (*Ishtiaq1990*) on tribal language shift attests to the gravity of language shift among the tribes in India. In other terms, the ideology of development lies in assimilation rather than maintenance of smaller identities. Exertion of language rights of smaller identities is quite often recognized as sectarian revolt. The shrinking trend of linguistic diversity in India is an ongoing reality. As has been described above, there are various contributing processes - displacement of tribes, land alienation, migration, economic dependence, modernization, government policies, urbanization etc.

Many languages can be detected under various stages of endangerment in south India. But such identification is tentative due to two factors:

i) Languages are distributed across states and districts. So a critically endangered language may be at a vulnerable stage in the other state or district
ii) Assessment studies are not made at the micro level, hence the assessment remains tentative. A thorough status survey is needed.

The present status of tribal languages of south India shows similar patterns.

1. Numerical strength determines the viability of the use of mother tongues.
2. The concentration of speech communities in an area determines the survival of their mother tongues.
3. The scanty distribution of speech communities in wider areas affects their language loyalty.
4. Their migrant status leads these communities to shift towards the dominant language.
5. The prevalent social and political ecology is not in favour of smaller language maintenance.
6. Except Andhra Pradesh, no other states give special importance to mother tongue education. (In Andhra Pradesh, The Tribal cultural Research and Training Institute, Dept of Tribal welfare, Govt of Andhra Pradesh has initiated Tribal Mother Tongue (TMT) education. In the first phase, text books for class 1 in eight languages, namely Savara, Koya, Gondi, Kolami, Lambada, Konda, Kuvi and Adivasi Oriya have been prepared and are under implementation. This is aimed at reducing the drop-out rate and create interest in the students, to protect tribal mother tongues and cultures, to make home language and school language similar, improve adult literacy and ensure that education at primary school level

is made easy and enjoyable. The Multilingual education programme of AP State is a gradual transition model, i.e., TMT to the official language of the State, Hindi and English in a gradual manner. 1st class is taught only in TMT, 2nd class in TMT 80% and Telugu 20%, and 3rd class TMT 60% and Telugu 40% and 4th class 40% TMT and 60% Telugu, and in 5th class 20%TMT and 80% Telugu. From 6th onwards 100% Telugu. Since the tribal child's competence in Telugu is not equivalent to that of the MT Telugu child, care has to be taken to teach both the languages simultaneously and curriculum planning was accordingly carried out.

Other states do not have such success stories in TMT education. The lack of choice has made tribal communities and other minorities opt for the regional tongue for their own betterment. As a result of the unfavourable social ecology, the majority of tribal languages are subsumed by the dominant regional languages.

7. Conclusion

1. Mother tongue education is one of the vital options available for both preserving mother tongue and creating interest in education among tribals.
2. Minor languages of south India needs the utmost attention and care in documentation and revitalization, as most of them are under survival pressure characterized by endangerment at different levels.
3. Endangerment assessment cannot be successful until a settlement level linguistic survey is done across states.

References

- Abbi.A, 1995. Language contact and Language Restructuring: A case study of Tribal Languages in central India. small languages and small communities.22. International Journal of the Sociology of Language, 116(1):175-86.
- Abbi, A.2004. *Vanishing Diversities and Submerging Identities -An Indian case*, Retrieved June 20, 2006 Forum Bracelona www.barcelona2004.org/
- Annamalai, E.1990. Dimensions of bilingual education in India. : *New Language Planning Newsletter June- 4*(4), 1-3.
- Annamalai, E. 2000. *Managing Multilingualism in India: Political and Linguistic Manifestation* (Vol.8). New Delhi, India: Sage.
- Census of India 2001. Office of the Registrar General and Census commissioner. India. pdf document. Census of India .Retrieved June 2007. http: // www.censusindia.net (the official website of Census of India).

- Ishtaq.1999.Language shift among the Scheduled Tribes in India: A Geographical Study, NewDelhui. Motilal Banarsidass.
- Singh,K.S and Manoharan,S. 1997. *Language and Scripts*. People of India, Vol.IX. New Delhi: Anthropological Survey of India and Oxford University Press.
- UNESCO (2009): *Atlas of the World's Languages in Danger* (interactive online edition), retrieved April (http://www.unesco.org/culture/ich/index.php?pg=00206 and http://www.unesco. org/culture/ich/UNESCO-EndangeredLanguages-

Session 2

Is Revival Possible or Desirable? Best Practices

A Language Journey

Prof. G. N. Devy - Founder Director, Bhasha Research and Publication Centre, Ahmedabad

During the mid-eighties of the last century, I became vaguely aware that there existed a large number of languages other than the ones recognized by the Eighth Schedule of India's Constitution. This awareness turned into a sense of unease and anxiety when I plotted them on the map of India and, thereby, noticed that practically every language in the central belt of India, the Adivasi belt, had remained unrecognized. Out of my anxiety and with plenty of ignorance, I decided to give up my professorship and to start documenting these languages. Not only did I have no tape-recorder or any really good camera with me, but I did not possess even the basic knowledge either of Linguistics or of Anthropology. I had been merely a student of literature, and all that I had mastered till then was the skill to talk about poetry and literary theory within the confines of a classroom.

Today, two decades later, as I turn back and view the map of intellectual accidents and cultural pitfalls I have crossed, I can count first and foremost a series of periodicals in Adivasi languages that I launched, nearly ten 'scripts' that I put together, a series of bilingual volumes of Adivasi literature, a Museum of Voice, an Academy for the Adivasis, a library with 40,000 titles, mother tongue schools in over a hundred villages, a dozen pictorial glossaries and an active publication centre as well as a well developed theatre. During these years the Bhilli group of languages within which I have been working showed a massive 90% increase while the actual population growth has been just a little over 10%.

Why did I think of taking up any work at all with the adivasis? Was it a romantic fascination for the unknown and the inscrutable? Was it an ideologically charged move into a social sector? Was it a pure academic project of intellectual adventure? Or was it a turning away from the tired urban social-scape? The answer, honestly, I do not know. It all happened to me like a current happens to a stream, restlessness to the waves and greening to a tree. If they do not know how or why, why should I? In 1984 I had planned to set up a school in an adivasi village; but I could not. In 1987-88 I took up relief work in drought hit Savli-villages, but had to give it up. In 1992, I thought I would start traveling through the adivasi villages collecting their songs and stories; but I did not. At last in1996 my body, mind, family and financial condition together gave a go ahead.

I was never alone in the work from the very beginning. Everybody helped me. Former students from the Baroda University came as unpaid volunteers. Others started bringing in monetary contributions. Yet others came forward to acknowledge the ideas and execute them. Many brought new ideas. As for my Adivasi Academy students, I have never ceased to learn from them!

I have not been good at inventing names and so I always chose simple words: 'Bhasha' for the Trust, 'Adivasi Academy' for the institute of experimental learning, 'Dhol' for the magazine of tribal concerns, 'Vacha' for the museum of voice, 'Samveg' for the learning cottage, 'Vikas' for the development-projects-complex, 'Samas' for the forum of like-minded literary persons and simply 'Tribals First' for the first adivasi-managed tribal craft and cultural centre. I thought, the fewer the words the better.

In 1996, I went to Saputara looking for tribal stories. Then some adivasis came forward to share their songs and stories, vibrant with their profound memory. They then wanted to try their hand at the print medium. Now they write books, publish them through Bhasha, edit magazines, write plays, direct and perform them, organize adivasi literary meets. They have now become a powerful movement. Our time together has been short, but their waiting in the past had been long. Nobody had ever much listened to them. I was eager to lend my ears to them. They decided to speak. Bhasha facilitated this adivasi voice.

Though everyday of the last thirteen years has been a new learning experience, the days have not been all joy and excitement. When one works with the adivasis one just cannot escape the pain and misery surrounding their existence. There is, for instance, the incurable genetic mutation causing sickle cell anemia, land alienation due to the stringent forest act, forced migration due to the construction labour market since employment opportunities as well as agricultural irrigation are not sufficiently available;

and, of all, the plight of the nomads mistakenly branded as criminals, a moving story of a grave social injustice.

Had Bhasha Research Centre not turned its attention to these issues I would have felt that my work suffered from a sense of ethical inadequacy. A purely academic study of an adivasi language or a merely aesthetic appreciation of adivasi art may have been attempted in the past; but in our time, if these interests do not go firmly together with the concern for economic empowerment and human rights protection, the project ought to be seen as a deeply flawed one. 'Bhasha' naturally decided to weld together aesthetic and socio-economic concerns. The adivasis themselves have come to realize the need for a comprehensive approach to their life and future, and have come to recognize 'Bhasha' as their friend.

The trust that the adivasis have put in 'Bhasha' is phenomenal. The Gram Vikas Kendras in thirty locations are now working with nearly eleven hundred villages, creating for them micro-credit self help groups, food grain banks, water harvesting cooperatives, non-formal schools, craft training and healthcare. All this work is managed by the adivasi men and women trained at the Tribal Academy of Tejgadh. They know that development does not mean becoming clones of the urban population. They have decided to become self-reliant. In their hearts, the days of subsidy and of a mere subsistent agricultural economy are over. The pride in their own ability to handle their developmental concerns generates a kind of new energy that will inspire them to create new ideas and imaginative expression. Real life concerns cross over into aesthetics in 'Bhasha', as in all truly great aesthetic experiments.

When I started the work, I did not know where the funds would come from. My ideas were somewhat unusual and I did not know how to market them smartly. Somehow, and quite often miraculously, funding support kept coming to us, though never in tune with the requirements and never with any regularity. The precarious existence of 'Bhasha' has now been a habit for everybody associated with it. However, for such ventures and experiments, this is but as expected.

Within months of commencing the work on the fifty volume series, many adivasi writers and scholars approached me with the idea of starting a magazine in their own language, meant for adivasi communities and to be read out rather than for individual reading. 'Bhasha' accepted the idea. The magazine was called 'Dhol' (drum), a term that has a totemic cultural significance for adivasis. We started using the state scripts combined with a moderate use of diacritic marks to represent these languages. The response to the magazine was tremendous. More adivasis approached Bhasha, and asked for versions of *Dhol* in their own languages. Within two years of its launch, *Dhol* started appearing in ten adivasi languages of western India. When the first issue of Chaudhary language *Dhol* was released, it sold seven hundred copies on the first day. This was a record of sorts for a little magazine.

Inspired by the success of the oral magazine, our adivasi collaborators started bringing to 'Bhasha' manuscripts of their autobiographies, poems, essays and even anthropological studies of their communities which they wanted us to publish. Subsequently, in order to highlight the oral nature of adivasi culture, we launched a weekly radio magazine which was relayed throughout the adivasi areas of Gujarat and Maharashtra. All these initiatives together gave birth to a small but focused publishing and book distribution house, which now works under the name 'Purva-prakash', and is the first community owned publishing programme for adivasis and nomadic communities of India. It is not so much a commercial venture as a cultural and literary platform for intellectual concerns and a forum for expression in the people's own languages.

Oral literature, unlike written literature, is not an exclusive verbal or lexical art. It is inevitably intermixed with song, music, dance, ritual and craft. So, Bhasha was drawn to the craft of the adivasi communities, initially in western India, and subsequently to craft from all over India. This resulted in 'Bhasha's' craft collection and craft training initiatives, further leading to the formation of an adivasi craft-cooperative under the name 'Tribals First'. The objects one identifies as craft are not produced in adivasi communities for aesthetic pleasure alone. They are invariably an integral part of their daily life. Often, such objects carry with them an imprint of the supernatural as conceived in the myth and the imagination of the adivasis. The shapes, colours and forms of these objects reflect the transactions in the adivasi's collective unconscious. Often, one overlooks the fact that the metaphysical matrix of the adivasi thought process differs markedly from the philosophic assumptions of the dominant cultural traditions in India. Therefore, sometimes simple concepts and ideas, which look perfectly natural and secular, can provoke adivasis into reacting negatively, and even violently. Any intervention in an adivasi community is likely to have a better chance of making a lasting impact if it is preceded by a sympathetic understanding, if not a careful study, of the interior landscape of the adivasi mind. The rituals, arts and crafts of the adivasis reflect the complexities of their cultural norms and thought patterns as nothing else does.

I learnt the hard way that there is a common source for the dominance of the red colour in Adivasi arts, and their utter unwillingness to donate blood even when a kinsman is in dire need, namely, the supernatural belief that the domain of witchcraft is red in colour. This incidental insight came handy when we found ourselves involved in a hematological disaster called Sickle Cell Anemia. Reports from the Amarvati District of Maharashtra, inhabited by the Korku adivasis, about a large number of untimely deaths of children, and similar reports from Wynad in the south, had drawn our attention to the Sickle Cell phenomenon. Medical sciences maintain that a certain genetic mutation required to fight malarial fevers has made the Adivasis prone to the Sickle Cell disease. On learning about the Korku trauma, we decided to check the statistics of Sickle Cell anemia in our own area. Blood testing of the adivasis is a challenging task. So we decided to draw up mathematical models, and at the same time composed an extensive family-tree through a survey that took us over two years to complete, to isolate certain localities, villages and families who could provide clues to throw up the most reliable projections. We found that nearly thirty-four percent of Gujarat's adivasis have been carriers of the gene disorder, and about three and a half percent of the population is its direct victim. This means, about two hundred and ten thousand of Gujarat's seven million adivasis are likely to not attain the age of 30. What is even more saddening is that the existing health care system has not only been insensitive to the epidemic scale of the gene disorder, but that in most instances, it remains inaccessible. This revelation was shocking to say the least. As a result, Bhasha decided to launch its health care programme under the title 'Prakriti'. Obviously, we did not wish to create a large hospital but rather a small and functional clinic, and we planned to train local persons as community health workers, so that patients in a crisis situation could be identified and provided with immediate relief locally, and be referred to city clinics for long term treatment. Thus, beginning with aesthetics, we came down to anesthetics.

Specific diseases may have universal scientific definitions, but the general notion of 'illness' as distinct from 'well-being' does not have a universal grammar. In a given community illness and wellness are divided by an invisible line; and the introduction of new medicines keeps pushing the line, enlarging the domain of anesthetics, that is, the management of pain, and encroaches on the domain of aesthetics, which is, the management of pleasure. This, in turn increases the desire for instant curbing of pain, and at the same time the longing for an instant gratification of the senses. The distribution of pain and pleasure on the cultural spectrum is in direct correspondence with the distribution of craft and product on the economic spectrum of a given community. Often, shortages caused by larger economic forces push a social sector from its subsistence-farming character into becoming impoverished labour providers. The acute food shortages faced by the adivasis in Kalahandi and Koraput in Orissa, and the mass migration of the adivasis to the mining districts, are not exceptional stories. Though their main occupation is agriculture, adivasis have been under-nourished throughout India, and sadly enough a starvation death is no news for them.

Bhasha decided to address the issue of food security, and set up food-grain banks for adivasi women. Initially, we had decided to follow the government model of food grain banks; but we realized that they had come to be seen by adivasi villagers as charity distribution events, and so we chose to set up the grain-banks without any government contribution and entirely through local participation. We feel convinced that no effort towards reducing the sickle cell incidence was likely to succeed if it was seen in isolation from the question of forced migration and food-insecurity. Food-security and health care form for us a single concern.

Soon after the Bhasha Trust was established, it decided to institute an annual lecture series named after the legendary Dr.Verier Elwin, a long time friend of India's adivasis. For the 1998 Elwin Lecture, we chose the theme of Denotified and Nomadic Tribals. There are in India about 191 communities that were once wrongly notified as 'criminal tribes' owing to the colonial government's lack of understanding of nomadic ways of life. They were restricted by law to specific localities, prevented from movement, put to work as unpaid labour and stigmatized beyond redemption. After their 'denotification' in 1952, these communities, now known as the DNTs, continued to suffer the stigma, social isolation and acute economic disadvantage. Utterly dispossessed, these landless, illiterate and hounded people have been unsuccessfully trying to shake off their identities. Their estimated population is about sixty million. Moved by the Elwin Lecture delivered by the eminent activist Mahasveta Devi, we decided to establish the DNT-Rights Action Group. It was the first national campaign ever taken up for the cause of the DNT rights. In this campaign we moved the National Human Rights Commission and various ministries of the Central Government to abolish the Habitual Offenders Act, to provide a rights protection mechanism for the DNTs. Bhasha's energetic campaign for the DNT rights received an overwhelming response from the denotified communities. We had opened up a long festering wound. As a leader of that campaign I had to give very serious thought to turning the anger and frustration among the demonized, brutalized and politically vandalized DNTs into a constructive energy.

In order to contain the anger, I decided to use the most ancient method of getting people angry without making them destructive, which is 'theatre'. My experience of handling the violence within the minds of these communities has left me incurably convinced that theatre is probably the most powerful cultural means of sensitizing communities about the mutual entanglement and dependence of economic, social and cultural rights of several competing and clashing social sectors. 'Bhasha' has now its own theatre group under the name Budhan Theatre, named after a DNT killed in police custody. Apart from the 'Budhan Theatre', we have so far successfully established four annual cultural festivals in as many locations of Gujarat, one of which is Dandi – the place made sacred by Gandhi's salt-satyagraha. Adivasi and nomadic performers go to these four locations on their own and people from several states participate in thousands. These '*melas*' are now there to stay. A few years back, some children in the schools I run suggested to me that a children's magazine be launched. *Bol*, the magazine created by these children, has received subscriptions from more than ten thousand schools in Gujarat. My conclusion at the end of all these years of field experience in conservation of endangered languages is that unless survival of the community is not tackled as the first priority, the survival of the speech tradition of a given community cannot even be conceptualized

Maintenance and Revival Strategies for Indigenous Languages: Lessons from Australia

Dr. Nicholas Reid - Senior Lecturer, School of Behavioural, Cognitive and Social Sciences, University of New England, Australia

"When you lose a language, you lose a culture, intellectual wealth, a work of art. It's like dropping a bomb on a museum, the Louvre."
Kenneth Hale cited in The Economist (November 3, 2001)

The last decade has seen a resurgence of interest in the revival and maintenance of Aboriginal languages in Australia, where only about 12 of 250-odd languages are currently being acquired by children as a first language. This paper provides an overview of the language maintenance and revival initiatives that have been tried and tested in that time; places them against the political and social contexts that have shaped them; and attempts an assessment of the relative successes of the strategies attempted.

This paper has the explicit purpose of providing best practice advice to other countries, such as India, which have similarly large numbers of endangered languages, which they are planning to support, and wish to benefit from past experiences of other countries which have been engaged in language maintenance practices for some time.

The paper firstly provides an overview of the extent of language loss in Australia, and then examines a range of maintenance/revival initiatives, including:

- the role of Language Centres in undertaking linguistic research, collecting and analyzing archival materials, coordinating resource development, and developing curriculum materials, and undertaking language teaching/learning activities.

- the teaching of Indigenous languages within the school curriculum.
  - The bilingual school programmes in the Northern Territory, which operated during 1970-2009, but which have effectively been dismantled by the current territory government
  - NSW Board of Studies K-12 *Aboriginal Languages Curriculum*, a grassroots approach to introducing the teaching of Aboriginal languages into NSW schools, which after just 3 years now has 16 different languages being taught in 53 schools.
- issues in teaching training and professional development, looking at the courses available to train Indigenous educators in Indigenous languages teaching.
- the trialling of Masters-Apprentice programmes, which pair a native speaker with a 2nd language learner in an intensive language learning apprenticeship scenario. This concept, first mooted by Hinton (2006) has been started in the US and Canada, but in Australia is just in its infancy.

Finally this paper examines the political environments in which these various strategies have been tried, and demonstrates how if you don't get the wider picture right and combine higher-level support with grass-roots activity, then success in language revival is going to be very hard to achieve.

1. The Extent of Language Loss in Australia

The last two decades have witnessed a groundswell of rising concern about the loss of linguistic diversity around the world, and the Australian situation is particularly alarming. At the time of European settlement (1788) there were about 260 distinct languages spoken on the Australian continent. Today over two thirds of these have either ceased to be spoken entirely, or are critically endangered with small numbers of speakers in older age brackets only. Today only 16 languages are being actively acquired by children as their first language. Only about 10% of Indigenous people in Australia now speak an Indigenous language, and that figure is falling.

The 2005 National Indigenous Language Survey Report noted that ' … the situation of Australia's languages is very grave and requires urgent action … there is great community support in many parts of the country for reclamation and heritage learning programs'.

2. The Role of Schools in Maintaining Languages

Up until 2005 the history of language maintenance activities in Australia has been

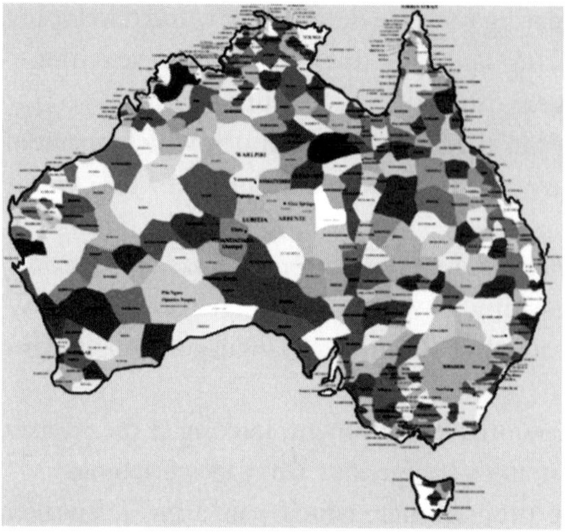

Map 1: the 260 Indigenous languages of Australia

quite haphazard, ranging from the work of official but under-resourced organizations such as FATSIL (Federation of Aboriginal and Torres Strait Islander Languages), through to local grass-roots community projects. There has also been some history of Indigenous language instruction in schools, but this too has been sporadic, subject to irregular funding, and widely varied in practice from state to state.

An important factor in this history has been an ongoing tension about the role of schools in language maintenance activities, with a lack of universal agreement about whether the mainstream education system is the appropriate vehicle for the transmission of indigenous culture and language. Indigenous Australians themselves have taken quite different stances over these issues, with the official FATSIL view "schools play a crucial role as a delivery point for language projects which are initiated in, and controlled by, the community. These language programmes are of central importance to the students' academic progress, personal development and cultural pride" (*FATSIL 2004*), standing in contrast to the view of, for example, Aboriginal academic and activist Noel Pearson who has argued that "Schools are not the places for cultural and linguistic transmission, and we must stop looking to schools to save our languages. This is because the primary purpose of schools is for our children to obtain a mainstream western education, including full fluency in English. Schools will never be adequately equipped to solve the transmission imperative, and all we will end up doing is compromising our children's mainstream education achievement" *(Pearson 2007*).

While these tensions remain as a feature of the Indigenous language maintenance landscape in Australia, since 2005 there has been an increasing focus on the education of Indigenous students, and a strong move to develop educational policy that supports Indigenous language maintenance and revival through the teaching of Indigenous languages in schools. A major step in this shift has been the adoption of a *National Statement and Plan for Languages Education in Australian Schools 2005-2008*, endorsed by the ministers of Education in every state. This statement affirms the educational value of all languages, but places a particular focus on the importance of teaching Australia's Indigenous languages.

Australian Indigenous languages have a unique place in Australia's heritage and in its cultural and educational life. For Indigenous learners, they are fundamental to strengthening identity and self-esteem. For non-Indigenous learners, they provide a focus for development of cultural understanding and reconciliation.

This National Plan lays out long-term directions for languages education, and facilitates collaboration in the development and use of state and national resources. The National Plan has facilitated the development of many language teaching projects, and below we shall touch on one of these – the NSW Board of Studies K-12 *Aboriginal Languages Curriculum.* First though, we turn to address some of the crucial profiling steps that must be undertaken before any serious language maintenance activity can be considered.

3. Profiling Language Situations

Effective planning requires the concepts and vocabulary to clarify types of language situations and types of language programmes most appropriate to them.

3a Language Profiling Models

There are many models of language profiling out there (*Bauman 1980, Burnaby 1997, and others*), and most of these are variants of Fishman's Graded Intergenerational Disruption Scale (GIDS) (*Fishman 1991*), summarised in **Table 1** below by Reyhner (1999) who fleshes the categories out with suggestions for activities relevant to each stage, drawn from Leanne Hinton's (1994) work on language revitalization.

Table I

Stage 8: Only a few elders speak the language.	Implement Hinton's (1994) "Language Apprentice" Model where fluent elders are teamed one-on-one with young adults who want to learn the language. Telephones can be use where dispersed isolated elders can be contacted by phone to teach others the language (Taff, 1997).
Stage 7: Only adults beyond childbearing years can speak the language.	Establish "Language Nests" after the Maori and Hawaiian models where fluent older adults provide pre-school childcare where they are immersed in their indigenous language (Anonby, In Reyhner 1999).
Stage 6: Some inter-generational use of language	Develop places in community where language is encouraged, protected, and used exclusively.

	Encourage more young parents to speak the indigenous language in home with and around their young children.
Stage 5: Language is still very much alive and used in community	Offer literacy in native language. Promote voluntary programmes in the schools and other community institutions to improve the prestige and use of the language. Use language in local government functions, especially social services. Give recognition to special local efforts through awards, etc.
Stage 4: Language is required in elementary schools.	Improve instructional methods utilizing Total Physical Response (TPR) (Asher, 1996) and other immersion teaching techniques. Teach reading and writing for higher-level language skills (Heredia & Francis, 1997). Develop two-way bilingual programmes where apporopriate where non-speaking elementary students learn the indigenous language and speakers learn a national or international language. Need to develop indigenous language textbooks to teach literacy and academic subject matter content.
Stage 3: Language is used in places of business and by employees in less specialised work areas.	Promote language by making it the language of work used throughout the community (Palmer, 1997). Develop vocabulary so that workers in an office could do their day-to-day work using their indigenous language (Anonby in Reyhner 1999).
Stage 2: Language is used by local governmental and in mass media in the minority community	Promote use of written form of language for government and business dealings/records. Promote indigenous language newsletters, newspapers, radio stations, and television stations.
Stage 1: Some language use by higher levels of government and in higher education.	Teach tribal college subject matter classes in the language. Develop an indigenous language oral and written literature using dramatic presentations and publications. Give tribal/national awards for indigenous language publications and other notable efforts to promote indigenous languages.

3b Tailoring Programmes to Language Profiles

In Australia the following *Australian Indigenous Languages Framework* categories have been widely employed to match language profiles to types of appropriate language programme.

Table 2: Australian Indigenous Languages Framework Categories

(1). First Language Maintenance

Students are first language speakers of the language. These programmes extend and develop students' language skills and may include the development of specialist skills such as interpreting and translating. They may be conducted as transition to English programmes for students in the early years of schooling.

(2). Second Language Learning

A strong language is taught to a wide range of learners (Indigenous and non-Indigenous) in the Languages area of learning — in much the same way as non- Indigenous languages are. Students have little or no assumed knowledge of the target language.

(3). Language Revival

A general term that covers three subtypes:*3.1 Revitalisation.*The language is still spoken by a small group of older speakers within the community. Language revitalisation aims to extend the use of the language into the younger generations of speakers. Indigenous students within these programmes will have considerable passive knowledge of the language. *3.2 Renewal.*The language is no longer actively spoken 'right through' or in its full form, but there are Indigenous people who actively identify with the language. Sufficient linguistic heritage remains within the community to develop a language programme. *3.3 Reclamation.*There has been a break in the transmission of the spoken language, but there is sufficient evidence from historical documentation and archival material for language reconstruction and learning.

(4). Language Awareness

The little bits that are known about a language can be incorporated into another area of learning (e.g., Studies of Society and Environment), but are not enough for sustained language learning. The focus is on teaching about Indigenous languages and on exploring socio-historical issues. Communicative fluency or competence is not a goal.

As discussed in section 5 below, the school language programmes that are currently underway in Australia range from some *first language maintenance* programmes in those few communties where children are still learning indigenous languages as their first language, through to many *revitalisation*, *renewal* and *reclamation* programmes in places where language transmission has been disrupted. A crucial factor underpinning the successes of school-based language programmes has been the careful analysis of each language situation, and intelligent decision-making about the types of language programme most appropriate to each situation.

4. Regional Language Centres

Throughout (mostly remote) Australia over the last 20 years there have been about 20 government funded 'Language Centres' which play a crucial role in supporting local Indigenous communities in their efforts to learn and teach their languages. Language Centres provide access to linguistic expertise, and training for Aboriginal people, undertake language recording, store and analyse archival materials, coordinate resource development, develop curriculum materials, provide translation services, and carry out a wide range of community and school-based language teaching and learning activities, and generally raise awareness in the wider community about the value of Aboriginal languages. Many are also active publishing houses and have produced dictionaries, learner grammars, and other language learning materials.

Most Language Centres cover a number of regional languages, and they are community oriented and independent of the education department. However they have proved to be an excellent resource on which later school-based programmes have been able to draw. Today many of the most successful school programmes in NSW are those which have been able to work cooperatively with a local Language Centre in developing curriculum materials. Most Language Centres now employ teachers in addition to linguists and language workers, to best foster close community-school relationships.

To get a sense of the role of Language Centres, try visiting the website of the *Many Rivers Aboriginal Language Centre*, which provides strategic support for Aboriginal communities of the northern and central coasts of NSW Awabakal - Wonnarua, Bundjalung, Darkinyung, Dhanggati, Gadhang and Yaygirr. See (http://www.muurrbay.org.au/mralc.html).

5. Indigenous Languages in the School Curriculum

By 2006 over 16,000 Indigenous and 13,000 non-Indigenous students are involved in learning one of 80 different Indigenous languages in over 260 Australian schools (*Purdie et. al. 2008*). These school programmes vary widely in type, depending on the degree of language endangerment and the kinds of resources available.

- About a third of these are first language maintenance programmes, mostly in the Northern Territory and South Australia in remote communities where languages are relatively strong.

- About half of the programmes fit the profile subcategories of 'revitalisation' where there are elder speakers, 'renewal' where there is sufficient linguistic heritage, and 'reclamation' where language reconstruction must proceed from archival materials.
- About 10% are 'Language awareness' programmes teaching about Indigenous languages without language learning as a goal.

The following two subsections briefly contrast first language maintenance programmes in the Northern Territory with language reclamation programmes in New South Wales.

5a Bilingual Education in the Northern Territory

The Northern Territory (NT) has Australia's greatest concentration of Indigenous communities where the levels of language endangerment are low enough that first language school programmes are possible, so it is in the NT that we find the greatest involvement in bilingual school programmes, in some cases extending back to the early 1970s. As of 2008 there are about 11 bilingual programmes in government schools and at least a further 4 in independent schools.

Most of these programmes are 'transfer' type models which teach solely in an Indigenous language at entry point, introduce the teaching of English as a second language, then in incremental steps each year reduce the Indigenous language component and increase the English language component, until the final years of schooling are taught mostly or solely in English.

The NT bilingual programmes are supported by the NT Department of Education, Employment and Training through a number of policy documents including *Indigenous Language and Culture in the Northern Territory Curiculum Framework*, and *Handbook for Aboriginal Bilingual Education in the Northern Territory*. The programme has been criticised by some Indigenous educators because of the top-down imposition of the transfer-to-English model. Some schools with greater control over their own bilingual programmes have rejected the inequality of this model, and instead opted for what is known as 'Two-way bilingual education', which places greater emphasis on the equal importance and status of both languages, and focusses on the educational benefits of balanced bilingualism.

The history of bilingual education in the Northern Territory is a sadly checkered one, and a salutary reminder of the need for consistency in government-level support. In 2005 the Minister for Education reaffirmed the role of bilingual education:

The government is also putting bilingual education back on the agenda. It is another important teaching methodology, with some initial evidence that results from bilingual schools appear generally better than other like schools... Furthermore we intend to have a stronger focus on valuing Indigenous language and culture through the curriculum. (Hansard, 24.08.05).

But in 2008 the Northern Territory Education Minister, Marion Scrymgour, responding to evidence of low literacy levels, effectively scrapped the bilingual programme in NT schools by demanding that the first four hours of school each day be taught in English in all Northern Territory classrooms. Supporters of bilingual education in Australia feel that the programmes have never been funded sufficiently for them to prove to their effectiveness. For example, despite the fact that English is taught as a second language, no Northern Territory bilingual programme has ever been funded to employ a trained ESL teacher. Opponents of the programmes focus on the failure of the funding levels to date to yield improvements in English literacy.

This cycle of unpredictable funding and political support that switches with successive state/territory governments, and federal government policy that is inconsistent with state/territory government policy, demonstrates a fact that is vital to the success of language maintenance activity - if you don't get the wider picture right and combine consistent higher-level support with community-supported grassroots activity, then success in language revival is going to be very hard to achieve.

5b The NSW Board of Studies K-12 *Aboriginal Languages Curriculum*

New South Wales (NSW) on the east coast state of Australia is the state with the longest history of European settlement. Aboriginal languages of this region have in many cases been unspoken for 3 or 4 generations, and many have been described as 'extinct' in past literature. Aboriginal people now prefer to refer to them as 'sleeping'. Across the past few decades it has widely been believed that these languages are effectively lost, although Aboriginal people have been quietly working on their languages, keeping careful records of archival materials, and engaging in community-based language revival activities, often with support from regional Language Centres. In the 2000s, particularly following the National Plan for teaching, there has been a growing pressure for school-based learning of aboriginal languages. In large part the rush of language-in-school activity in recent years has been fostered and driven by the 2003 launch of the NSW Board of Studies K-10 *Aboriginal Languages Curriculum.*

This curriculum for the years, 'Kindergarten' through to 'Year 10', has been developed as part of a policy aimed at preserving aboriginal languages of the region while also improving the educational outcomes of indigenous students. Developed by the statutory body that is responsible for all school curricula, it is binding on all schools that choose to run an aboriginal language programme, and is taught to both indigenous and non-indigenous children alike. However this is not a top-down imposition of a curriculum: Aboriginal language programmes only run in those schools where there is appropriate staff to develop local content and teach the programme, and where the local indigenous community is able and willing to support the initiative.

By 2006 there were 46 schools in NSW conducting an aboriginal language programme. 25 were run in primary schools, 9 in secondary schools, and 3 in central schools (see Table 3). Table 4 shows the number of programmes by language, and Table 5 by sector. At the time of writing, the number of schools has risen to 56 and is likely to continue to grow.

Table 3: NSW Aboriginal Language Programmes 2006 by year

School type	Years	Numbers
Primary (K-6)	K–6	15
	K–4	3
	2–5	1
	2–6	1
	K–2	2
	K–3	1
	3–6	1
	4	1
Secondary (7-12)	7	2
	7–8	1
	8	2
	9	2
	10–12	1
	12	1
Central (K-12)	K–10	1
	K–12	2
TOTAL		46

Table 4: NSW Aboriginal Language Programmes by Language in 2006.	No.
Bundjalung	8
Dharawal/Dhurga	5
Dharug	1
Gamilaraay/Yuwaalaraay/Yuwaalayaay	9
Gumbaynggirr	4
Ngiyampaa/Ngemba	2
Dunghutti/Thungutti	4
Wadi-wadi	1
Wangkumarra	1
Wiradjuri	10
Various	1
Total	**46**

Table 5: NSW Aboriginal Language Programmes by Education Sector in 2006	No.
Catholic	4
Department of Education and Training	41
Independent	1
Total	**46**

The NSW Board of Studies K-10 *Aboriginal Languages Curriculum* can be implemented in various ways:

- In Primary school there is no compulsory language study, but schools can either offer an aboriginal language within the 'Languages' key learning area (KLA), or they can deliver the aboriginal language/culture outcomes through the 'Human Society in its Environment' KLA, with a focus on learning about human society through language comparison.

- In NSW high schools (years 7-12) it is mandatory for all students to complete a minimum of 100 hours of language study, usually in year 7 or 8. The 'Languages' KLA usually gives high school students a choice between several languages (typically French, Japanese, Italian, Indonesian, etc), and the *Aboriginal Languages Curriculum* is usually delivered as part of this area, at least for those aboriginal languages with sufficient resources to support 100 hours of study. For those languages without such resources and offering general language awareness programmes, these can be implemented through the 'Human Society in its Environment' KLA.

Since 2003 an increasing number of schools have worked closely with the Aboriginal Curriculum Unit of the Board of Studies to develop local content for a range of programmes. Many started out as pilot language awareness type programmes offered within the 'Human Society in its Environment' KLA, and offering as little as one half hour per fortnight. However in the intervening years many of these have grown into better-resourced 'Language' KLA programmes offering up to four periods of study per week. A steadily increasing number of high schools are now moving towards running 100-hour mandatory programmes.

It is perhaps still too early to be talking about the successes of these programmes, and independent longitudinal research into the impacts of such programmes on the participation and performance of Aboriginal students is in planning but yet to be undertaken. Nevertheless there is anecdotal evidence from teachers and principals in many schools where such programmes have commenced, that the students and community have experienced a renewed valuing of their cultures through language learning, and that this has translated into a stronger sense that the school is a relevant force in their lives. The main factors that those involved have pointed to in accounting for the success of school-based programmes include:

1. Recognition that schools are important places for collaborative community ventures, and that school-based language learning can help language revitalisation.
2. School language programmes must be constructed around sound linguistic theories, based on strong second language acquisition practices, and embedded throughout with appropriate cultural values.
3. Language programmes must be supported by a central body like an Education Department or Board of Studies, who take primary responsibility for curriculum development, and teacher training.
4. That each school programme be based on a careful assessment of the language profile, with programmes tailored to meet the appropriate framework categories (see Table 2).
5. That each school programme be taught by a team, including;
   - a language specialist who has sufficient language skills and delivers the teaching programme in the classroom. Ideally they have some teacher training, but if not, this can happen in-class.

- a classroom teacher who helps the language specialist plan lessons, provides in-class support and training in good teaching practices.
- a linguist who compiles language materials, analyses them and adapts them for school use, and produces dictionaries and required background grammar notes, etc.

6. Recognition that revival programmes have broader goals than second language-learning programmes - they don't necessarily aim to produce fluent speakers. In addition to teaching about the structure of the language, they might also aim to provide their students with a better understanding of their linguistic heritage. They might take as a primary goal the provision of learning skills relevant to long-term linguistic and cultural revival/maintenance, rather than simply teaching reading and writing skills. And they might have such practically simple targets as improving Aboriginal student participation and rates of community involvement in the school.

5c The Major Issues Facing School-Based Teaching

Here I focus on three major issues that have been identified as crucial for the success of school-based Indigenous language programmes in Australia: teacher training, curriculum development, and resourcing.

- **Teacher Training**

Teachers in the NSW school programme vary from fully trained primary teachers, through to community members with no formal teaching qualifications, and who work casually in the classroom together with a trained teacher. These programmes largely began without proper teacher training options in place. Several Australian universities offer linguistics courses about Aboriginal languages, but these have no teacher training focus. Conversely, teacher training degrees within university Education faculties typically offer no specializations in aboriginal language teaching.

Over the first 6 years of the NSW *Aboriginal Languages Curriculum,* there has been a very limited set of opportunities for teachers and speakers of indigenous languages to learn the set of skills required for developing and delivering an indigenous language programme. The only real option for training educators has been the Master of Indigenous Languages Education at the University of Sydney. While highly successful, this has only produced a small number of graduates (10 in 2006, 5 in 2008, 10 new enrolments in 2009) because most indigenous people looking for training cannot meet the entry requirements for a Masters level degree. To address this anomaly, from 2010 the University of Sydney will add the earlier exit options of *Graduate Certificate* and *Graduate Diploma* to the Indigenous

Languages Education degree, but these still have some graduate entry barriers. The issue of how best to resolve the desirability of according potential teachers with some kind of recognition-of-prior-learning on the one hand, without on the other hand setting them up for studies they are not sufficiently prepared for, remains to be properly resolved.

At present most training of community language teachers occurs in informal Board of Studies workshops, and the Aboriginal Curriculum Unit has develped a two-day workshop called *Teaching Methodology for Aboriginal Languages.* The greatest current need within the NSW school programmes is for enhanced professional development for the community language teachers, who often have limited formal education backgrounds. Some NSW community language teachers have completed a Technical and Further Education (TAFE) course in Indigenous Language Study, but these are mostly offered in institutions in the Northern Territory far from NSW, and this remoteness has been a barrier to the uptake and completion of these courses.

Several other concerns over teacher training that have been identified by Purdie et al (2008) include;

- lack of secure ongoing funding for the various training options
- the general lack of career path options for Community Language teachers
- the training available tends to be ad-hoc and disconnected from further options, eg. TAFE courses do not articulate to university courses
- schools programmes are often totally dependent on a very small pool of people with the right language skills, and when they are unavailable, the whole programme can founder.

- **Curriculum Development**

Education departments are state-based in Australia, and some have done far more work in the area of Indigenous language curriculum development than others. The state of South Australia's *Department of Education and Children's Services* has led the way with well developed policies and syllabuses in several Indigenous languages over the last decade. Since 2006 the state of NSW's *Education Department* has also developed a single syllabus document which caters for the 70 languages of NSW. A central tenet of this syllabus is that there is a relationship in language revitalization projects between language learning, culture, identity and linguistics. The syllabus did not attempt to reinvent the wheel - it directly borrowed and adopted approaches already used in the teaching of non-aboriginal languages. It went through extensive consultation with aboriginal communities, teachers and linguists to ensure ownership protocols were handled appropriately, and to ensure that the content and linkages between language/culture and identity were appropriate. Pedagogically the syllabus draws on the approach known as 'communicative language teaching' in that it combines learning about the language itself with the development of real-life communication skills designed to generate spontaneous language right from the start.

This kind of model, where the Education Department promotes a generic syllabus, which in turn needs to be fleshed out at local level with specific content for particular languages, has proved to be very useful for NSW, and is likely to be valuable for other multi-language scenarios.

- **Funding Resources**

Endangered language teaching is typically characterised by fewer resources, the lack of access to a community of native speakers, and teachers who themselves aren't necessarily speakers. This makes it fundamentally different from normal foreign language learning, where the goals are simply to acquire some speaking/ reading skills. **Usually endangered language learning is part of a broader programme – to revive and maintain a culture.**

Second language learning can proceed without written resources, and there has been an ongoing debate in Australia about the extent to which languages with oral-only traditions should or should not have a culture of literacy imposed upon them, for the purposes of maintaining the language. However it has generally been the experience in Australia that where languages are taught under revival type programmes in formal school settings, that a lack of physical resources has been identified as a major inhibiting issue (*Purdie etal, 2008*). Those involved in teaching the NSW Aboriginal Languages curriculum have consistently identified the lack of written materials for use in the classroom, and the lack of good language-specific audiovisual resources, as their greatest in-class needs.

NSW schools running Aboriginal language programmes have had to try and allocate already stretched budgets to cover the development of new resources, and negotiate the funding of various kinds of outside support. Recent years have seen a wealth of highly creative, low-cost resources being developed, often with input provided by staff at Language Centres, but there is a genuine need to secure more reliable funding for resource development into the future.

The rapid escalation of digital technologies has also been widely seen as a boon to the development of low-cost language-specific resource materials, and has also allowed for the development of sophisticated media-rich resources for those who have adopted a lesser focus on literacy as their learning strategy.

6 Master-Apprentice Language Learning programmes

This concept, first mooted by Hinton (1997) has been operating for over a decade in the US and Canada, but in Australia is just in its infancy. The Master-Apprentice Language Learning Programme (MALLP) enables interested young adults to learn their language as quickly as possible, especially where that language is severely threatened and may only have a few speakers left. The strategy features a one-on-one learning relationship between a "master" (usually an older speaker) and an "apprentice" (usually a younger learner), who work together in an intensive language learning apprenticeship scenario for between twenty and forty hours per week, trying to only speak the target indigenous language. The goal is that after 3 years apprentices might in turn become masters.

6a Master-Apprentice programmes in California

The programme, first begun in California, is based on the concept that people learn a language best by being immersed in it for significant amounts of time, without translation to English. Rather than focus on formal lessons, the Master and Apprentice go about their daily lives, working or socializing at home or around the community, but making a conscious effort to speak only the target language. The programme funds each member of the pair $3,000 for 360 hours of teaching/learning.

The focus for each pair is on real communicative interaction involving listening and speaking rather than any focus on grammar or second language learning theory, in line with the approach to second language learning known as TPR 'Total Physical Response' (*Asher 1996*). However the programme does offer a range of supportive structures to the Master-Apprentice pairs, including workshop-based training and the development of generic resources. The concept has been quite successful in the North American context, with the programme described in Hinton (2001b) having seen over 65 Master-Apprentice pairs enrolled for more than a year. This programme type has since been tried in a variety of other contexts and countries. *[Further information can be found at the following website: http://www.fphlcc.ca/language/language-toolkit/fphlcc-language-programme-funding-calls/language-strategies/master-apprentice-programming]*

6b Master-Apprentice Programmes in Australia

The last few years have seen several attempts to initiate MALLP-type programmes in Australia.

The first Australian attempt at a more substantial multi-pair Master-Apprentice trial commenced in late 2009. The *Mirima Dawang Woorlab-gerring, Language and*

Culture Centre at Kununurra has begun training 6 Master-Apprentice pairs who will be spending 2 hours each day together in targeted language learning contexts.

It is too early to gauge the success of these programmes in the Australian context. They have real potential, but they are a strategy employed in worst-case endangerment scenarios, and the stakes are high. A successful outcome may produce just a single person with less-than-fully fluent speaking abilities. This is an important extension of language knowledge into a new generation – but still the language remains highly endangered and possibly with few or no options for the new 'master' to use the language in natural conversational contexts.

The success of such programmes is also highly dependant on the personalities and aptitude of the Master - Apprentice pairs. If they do not get on well together, or do not bring similar aptitude and enthusiasm to the venture, then such projects are at high risk of foundering quite quickly. It is also usually the case that 'masters' have no training in second language teaching methods. The best outcomes seem to be where; a) there is some initial training in second language teaching/learning methods, followed by ongoing scaffolded support rather than just the Master and Apprentice struggling as two individuals, and b) each member of the pair find the process itself rewarding.

Looking back to the birthplace of the MALLP-type model, there is now quite a good literature examining the factors that underlie the success of MALLPrograms in North America. Linn et al (2002) note that the commencement of MALLPrograms often triggers important attitudinal shifts in endangered language speech communities, raising awareness of the language's threatened status, and prompting wider community calls to action. Linn et al (2002) also provide a useful listing of attributes found across the most successful school- and community-based programmes, paraphrased below:

Table 6: Linn et al (2002) attributes of successful programmes	
Use teams	The best projects can draw on a range of support (speaker/elders, linguists, teachers, curriculum developers).
Using immersion, speak the language	It's not always possible, but aim as close to full immersion as you can.
Being family oriented	Successful programmes foster cross-generational language use.

Setting Goals	Learning a whole language is hard – make it more rewarding through achievable steps.
Building up, not out	It might be best to focus on thorough language for a few, rather than trying to teach everyone a little bit.
Balance in old and new	The tradition of a language is very important, but so is making it adaptable and appealing to the young.
Working through language variation issues	Issues about what kind of language is 'authentic' will arise – plan strategies for dealing with them.
Working through politics	Language revitalization will involve community and family politics – get the key people on board first.
Perseverance	Don't wait till all problems are solved to start, and don't stop just because some problem have arisen

7 Some Key Principles Emerging from Language Maintenance Experiences in Australia

There is no overarching comprehensive widely-accepted theory of language shift which explains why and how it happens and what can be done to reverse it. The situations of each country are a unique mix of socio-political and historical factors, so what works in one country cannot be assumed to be a recipe for success in another. The examples of Basque and Maori language revitalization are perhaps less relevant to countries like Australia and India with languages numbered in their hundreds. However the emergent lessons of Australia may be of value in planning approaches to language endangerment in India.

In their discussion of Indigenous language education in Australian schools, Purdie et al (2008) present six key principles:

Key Principle 1:

The Aboriginal and Torres Strait Islander peoples are the first people of this country and their languages are unique to it. The capacity to learn these languages and support their reclamation and long term maintenance as strong and viable languages is of great significance to both Aboriginal and non Aboriginal Australians.

Key Principle 2:

Ownership of each indigenous language belongs to a group of people who are its custodians: their language should only be taught in schools with their agreement.

Key Principle 3:

School language programmes should be developed and presented in partnership with the school and the owners of the language being taught.

Key Principle 4:

Learning an indigenous language and becoming proficient in the English language are complementary rather than mutually exclusive activities.

Key Principle 5:

The primary responsibility for maintaining, revitalizing or rebuilding indigenous languages does not rest with schools, although schools may have an important role to play.

Key Principle 6:

The most successful school programmes will flow from a collaborative approach involving indigenous communities, indigenous language centres, linguists, schools and teachers.

8 Why Should Language Maintenance and Revival Matter?

After many decades of escalating language loss in Australia many educators and policy makers are beginning to view language revitalization activities as an important way of both supporting the sense of self identity and cultural worth that aboriginal Australians have battled to maintain, whilst giving non-indigenous Australians the opportunity to achieve better cross-cultural understanding and a richer appreciation of their own country's heritage. The concept here, that there is 'social good' in supporting threatened languages, has been addressed directly by Nettle and Romaine (*2000: p36*):

Some, for instance, would say that other problems, such as eliminating poverty or protecting the environment, are more pressing concerns than the loss of languages. We will make the case that the need to preserve languages and the need for economic development in the world's peripheral societies are not opposing ones, as is widely supposed, but complementary aspects of the same problem. The idea that linguistic diversity should be preserved is not a sentimental tribute to some idealised past, but part of the promotion of sustainable, appropriate and empowering development. The problem of language death is thus a 'good problem', in that solving it would mean solving many other urgent and interrelated problems at the same time.

In addition to valuing languages because of their vital contribution to cultural identity, Australian educators and policy makers are also increasingly coming to view indigenous language education as having cognitive/academic benefits through the meta-linguistic awareness that knowledge of more than a single language brings, and intercultural benefits through the understanding of another culture and the comparative perspective on one's own culture which that provides.

For many decades Australia promoted English-only and did little to support its many indigenous languages. All the evidence suggests that this approach, through failing to value key elements of indigenous cultures, eroded aboriginal people's sense of identity and contributed to ongoing disadvantages for them. Slowly Australia has come around to value monolingualism less, and view the strong and varied cultural identities of all its citizens as positive contributing factors to the overall wellbeing of the country.

Like Australia, India has many languages that enjoy little recognition and have no official status. As linguistic diversity around the world decreases, now is the time to see this linguistic richness as a cultural treasure to be fostered and maintained by means appropriate to the Indian situation. In some ways India begins this process from a far better position than Australia, for while Australia pays lip-service to being a multicultural country, it still tends to promote a peculiarly assimilationist view of multiculturalism that values people's diverse backgrounds only if they stay in the background. Australia has never had the genuinely pluralistic multicultural outlook which India enjoys, and unlike India has never affirmed the status of multiple languages within its constitution. In this sense perhaps, India faces the task of acting to secure the future of its linguistic richness from a much stronger starting point, for it is a country that has, since its foundation, viewed its rich internal diversity as a strength.

Acronyms:

ESL: teaching *English as a Second Language*

FATSIL: the *Federation of Aboriginal and Torres Strait Islander Languages*

HSIE: *Human Society in its Environment* is one key learning area in NSW schools.

K-10: *Kindergarten* through to *Year 10* (approx ages 5 – 15)

KLA: a *key learning area* of the NSW school curriculum

MALLP: the *Master-Apprentice Language Learning Programme*
NSW: the state of Australia known as *New South Wales*
NT: the territory of Australia known as the *Northern Territory*
TPR: *Total Physical Response* is an approach to second language learning grounded in meaningful physical activity

References:

- Asher, J. 1996. Learning another language through actions: The complete teacher's guidebook. 5th edition. Los Gatos, CA: Sky Oaks Productions.
- Bauman, J. 1980. A Guide to Issues in Indian Language Retention. Washington DC: Center for Aplied Linguistics.
- Burnaby, B. 1997. Aboriginal language maintenance, development, and enhancement. In Cantoni, G ed. Stabilising Indigenous Languages. Flagstaff: Northern Arizona University.
- Chandler, P. and C. Haid, C. Jones, K. Lowe, J. Munro. Aboriginal Research: Impact of learning an Aboriginal language on Primary school students's Literacy in English.
- Hinton, L. 1994. Flutes of Fire. Essays on California Indian Languages. Berkeley: Heyday Books.
- Hinton, L. 1997. Survival of endangered languages: The California Master-Apprentice Programme. *International Journal of the Sociology of Language* 123. 177-191.
- Hinton, L. 2001(a). Language Revitalisation: an overview. In Hinton, L. and K. Years Hale eds. *The Green Book of Language Revitalisation in Practice*. London: Academic Press.
- Hinton, L. 2001(b). Sleeping Languages: can they be awakened?. In Hinton, L. and K. Hale eds. *The Green Book of Language Revitalisation in Practice*. London: Academic Press.
- Hinton, L. Ten Points for Successful Language Learning. Retrieved from http://www.aicls.org/pages/10steps.html#10steps6 10.10.09.
- Linn, M. and T. Naranjo, S. Nicholas, I. Slaughter, A. Yamamoto, O. Zepeda. 2002. Awakening the languages: Challenges of enduring language programmes; filed reports from fifteen programmes from Arizona, New Mexico and Oklahoma. In B. Burnaby and J. Rehner, eds. *Indigenous Languages Across the Community*. Flagstaff, AZ: Northern Arizona University.

- Lowe, K. and A. Ash. 2006. Talking each other's Lingo: The *Aboriginal languages K-10 Syllabus* and its role in Language Revitalisation in NSW. Paper presented to the 2003 conference of the Applied Linguistics Association of Australia.
- Purdie, N. and T. Frigo, C. Ozolins, G. Noblett, N. Thieberger, J. Sharp. 2008 *Indigenous Language Programmes in Australian Schools*. Report to the Australian Government Department of Education, Employment and Workplace Relations.
- Reid, N. 2009. English influence on the pronunciation of Aboriginal languages in the context of language revival and revitalisation. In Hobson, J. and S. Poetsch, M. Walsh, K. Lowe. eds. *Re-awakening languages: Theory & practice in the revitalisation of Australia's Indigenous languages*. NSW Education Department Board of Studies.
- Reyhner, J. and G. Cantoni, R. St Clair, E. Yazzie. eds. 1999. Revitalising Indigenous Languages. Flagstaff: Northern Arizona University.
- Rhydwen, M. and E. Parolin, J. Munro, S. Poetsch. 2007 Report on school-based Aboriginal language programme activity in NSW during 2006.
- Walsh, M. 2002. T*eaching NSW's Indigenous Languages: lessons from elsewhere.* Report commissioned by the NSW Government Department of Education, Office of the Board of Studies.

Endangered Languages: Observations and Proposals

Prof. Udaya Kumar Chakraborty - Department of Bengali, Jadavpur University, Kolkata, West Bengal

1) The Present Situation

At present there are about 6,800 languages worldwide. Scholars have observed that more or less half of these are endangered. Some languages have only 100 or 1000 speakers, and they are obviously bilingual.

The common perception regarding language and endangered language is that there is a broad classification of just two categories: living languages and dead languages. But in between these two extreme categories there is an intermediate category, which is termed 'endangered'. A further categorization divides these endangered languages into four [Source: UNESCO Red Book on Endangered Languages]:

1. Extinct languages
2. Nearly extinct languages
3. Seriously endangered languages
4. Endangered languages

It is a fact that minor and endangered languages are entering step by step into the death-area and heading towards extinction. Most of these are oral. Without written language-documents of their own for preservation, these oral languages are disappearing gradually.

Apart from this, there are exceptions, and other political and psychological causes behind language-death. Lepcha, an aboriginal language of the northern part of Bengal, is at present nearly extinct in Darjeeling district and endangered in Sikkim, although it is, in fact, not an oral language, but has a long written tradition with a script of its own. Manuscripts exist that were written in the 16th and 17th centuries AD. Nevertheless the language is edging towards extinction.

2) Language Death

Some steps have been taken world-wide for protecting endangered languages from certain death such as the following:

a) encouraging scholars to conduct research work on endangered languages;
b) engaging scholars, social workers, students and organizations in the documentation and preservation of these languages and cultures;
c) setting up innovative archives of endangered languages and culture;
d) introducing awards for innovative work on endangered languages;
e) encouraging conscious persons from endangered language communities to do innovative work such as organizing camps or encouraging schools to introduce their MT.

These are steps which are encouraging enough and can benefit endangered and minor language communities. But in my opinion, we have to do more. Let us observe the main problems of such endangered language communities in India, particularly in West Bengal.

3) Observations and Problems

During our field work some expected and common psychological findings were observed in West Bengal as follows:

1. Most male speakers use a mixed language. Even aged persons mix their MT with words from the dominant language or the language of prestige.
2. Teenagers are losing their MT.
3. Most primary and or secondary school children suffer from an inferiority complex.
4. They communicate with others in Bengali, Hindi or English. These languages are dominant languages as well as 'killer' languages in respect of endangered languages.
5. Most female speakers preserve their MT and are less hesitant in using it among themselves as well as in the presence of outsiders.
6. It is astonishing that male speakers hesitate to use their MT in the presence of outsiders; that they feel more comfortable in using the dominant language.

Apart from problems of poverty, endangered language communities often express the need for a proper education. The following observations can be made on this aspect:

a) Want of teaching material in the MT (often tribal languages) is a thrusting problem.
b) The affected communities want to learn through the MT.
c) They have no proper atmosphere of learning.
d) The schools are far from their residence etc.

We have started our work and are doing our best to revive endangered languages, using the following methods:

a) Documentation,
b) Digitalization,
c) Preservation of culture and language,
d) Highlighting linguistic and cultural activities,
e) Education through MT,

The last point is yet to see the light of day, and is not even at the preparatory stage in West Bengal. The Bhasacharya Suniti Kumar Chatterji Centre for Language Studies, Bengali Department of Jadavpur University, however, under the leadership of the writer of this paper, is preparing 15 teaching materials in Koda, Kurukh and Sherpa languages under the financial support of the Central Institute of Indian Languages. The authority of Jadavpur University is stepping forward in this regard and encouraging this project. We hope this project will serve to fulfill the need of teaching materials for these endangered language communities.

We should not forget that most endangered language communities live in great hardship. In West Bengal they are mostly below the poverty level. These people, at the grass-root level, are our target endangered language communities. They are the victims of reality and cannot be blamed for loss of MT. Therefore, the following additional suggestions are made:

f) Economic support as far as possible, and
g) MT based job opportunities for the younger generation.

4) Preservation of Language and Culture

The tribal people of India have a long history with an enriched tradition. But they are gradually loosing their paradise while coping with the modern world; they do not have the leisure to think about their culture, or prevent their language from extinction.

Some tribes, such as the Tamang, Sherpa, Bhotiya etc. who are basically more conservative by nature, manage to preserve their culture and language. Other tribes are not so conscious of their language and culture, such as Kora, Kurukh, Lepcha etc. They are trying to educate themselves in formal and English-medium schools. Some of them are economically stable and accept modern culture. In most cases, the dominant language acts as a 'killer' language. At the same time, western culture is being imitated, leading to changes in life-style, food habits, dress, ritual practices and so on, in what is actually a type of cultural transformation.

5) Language Shift: Need feeling, Language dominance, Prestige motive, etc

We know that there are many reasons behind this cultural transformation. We all float on the moving wave of the modern scientific world. The people of the third world are trying to survive, and next to this moving wave, the cultural activities of the endangered language communities seem to be standing still at the primitive stage.

It is hardly surprising, that the young generation, inspired by the modern trends accepted by the dominant language community, neglect their culture and language, knowing very well that as speakers of their MT they have no prospects, either inside or outside their community. As mentioned above, they are forced to communicate in the dominant language, are ashamed of their MT and are more comfortable in Bengali, the 'killer' language of West Bengal. Some of them are confused and feel they are Bengali as they live in Bengal and their MT has become Bengali, little realizing that a region and a language need not have a one to one relation.

In search of solutions

As already observed, poor family children are compelled to earn their livelihood and some attend school not for learning but to collect their mid-day meal, while most become drop-outs.

a) It is easier and better for thinkers and social workers from the affected language community itself to find solutions, rather than outsiders.

b) The task is to identify them and help them.

c) It is also necessary to raise awareness and consciousness among the affected communities about:

   i) their endangered MT and

   ii) The intrinsic aesthetic value of their cultural heritage.

Documentation or digitalization is not the only solution. Consciousness about MT and encouragement is a process that needs continuous hammering. The community should help itself, and that again, depends on economic stability.

Another reality is that there is a gap between educationists and policy makers from the Government and teachers in the classroom, field workers and the learners of the endangered language communities.

We have highlighted again and again that the thrusting reason is economic. The endangered language cannot give food to its speakers. And they are gradually getting distracted from their daily conversation at home or outside their home within the language community.

Need-feeling motive has already changed our mentality. Endangered MTs must be enabled to satisfy the demands. These languages should borrow words and syntactic structures from the dominant languages in order to be suitably enriched. Conscious speakers should prevent rejection of substitute words and phrases from their MTs. They should understand that because of the prestige motive, acceptance of such words and phrases will also prevent the death of these languages.

Each endangered language should be taken as a separate case. At the same time, a series of 'Wh' questions from the part of these minor and endangered language communities are haunting.

Q. Which language should I select?
Q. Which language is essential for my daily communication?
Q. Which language will give me my food?
Q. Which languages are normally introduced in my classroom?
Q. Who are my teachers in my classroom?

The replies to all these questions negate the endangered MT. Linguists know very well that the actual problem lies behind this type of language selection and rejection psychology.

6) Suggestion and Conclusion

The attempt has been to communicate that as poverty is the thrusting problem, the affected communites have no scope to think about their MT or their rich cultural heritage. To counter this problem a tremendous network is required. Documentation, Preservation or Archiving is not the only solution; they merely provide vehicles for research. Proper education is the means of bringing consciousness among them. That is, emotionally they will have the incentive to use their MT at home and among themselves. Field experience shows that even those who are more or less illiterate, have the same emotional feeling about their MT as us [*Ref. Chakraborty, U. K., Dr. Nilima Chakraborty & Mahuya Chakraborty, "Language Cognition, Language Preservation and Role of Mother Tongue (MT) in Education"*].

Thus it is seen that 'prestige motive' and 'need feeling' are factors for the rejection of MT.

The speakers of endangered languages have to learn at least three languages. Of these, two are learned in the classroom. They have to speak the dominant language outside of their community, so to get relief from being over burdened they reject the one language which has no material value to them in this realistic world, and that language is obviously the MT.

At present the children who are admitted in most formal schools face the problem that their study materials are not in the MT, nor do teachers speak in the MT. A solution is to introduce such endangered languages at schools at least from the primary level.

Books at this level should be 'shell-books' [*Ref. U. N. Singh; 2009; Theories of Danger and Breakdown of Communication*]. As the basic law of learning method is 'from known to unknown' so the teachers should start teaching from the MT to the dominant or eventual language. For this purpose at least one teacher should be selected from the endangered language community.

The revival of endangered languages depends upon such educational and economic planning. The educational authorities should accept these languages as tools for imparting education. The government and various media should encourage the MT through cultural activities. I have so far found just one or two little magazines in the 'Koda' language. But most have no means to provide for even such leaflet-type journals. Whatever the standard, such efforts should be encouraged.

Planning for economical gainfulness for these communities can give rise to their 'accepting mentality'.

Source and References

- This paper mainly depends on the field work of some endangered and minor languages such as 'Koda', 'Kurukh', 'Sherpa', 'Lepcha', 'Tamang' etc conducted during the last two years for the project on "Preparation of Teaching Materials in Minor and Smaller Languages" undertaken by the Bhasacharya Suniti Kumar Chatterji Centre for Language Studies, J.U. under CIIL financial assistance, project work under DRS (UGC sponsored) scheme, Bengali Department, Jadavpur University.
- Chakraborty, Udaya Kumar, Dr. Nilima Chakraborty & Mahua Chakraborty, 20 May 2009, paper on "Language Cognition, Language Preservation and Role of Mother Tongue (MT) in Education" presented in the panel discussion session in the two-day workshop on "Enabling Primary Education in a Multilingual Context: focus on West Bengal" held at Jadavpur University on 19 and 20 May, 2009, organized by The Paschim Banga Sarva Siksha Mission (PBSSM) and UNICEF, West Bengal and Jadavpur University.
- Chaudhury, Supriya, Samantak Das & Udaya Kumar Chakraborty, August 2009, Approach Paper on "Problems of Communication at the Primary Education Level in a Multilingual Situation with Special Emphasis on Minor (Endangered) Language Communities of West Bengal" prepared by School of Languages & Bhasacharya Suniti Kumar Chatterji Centre for Language Studies, Bengali Department, Jadavpur University.
- Singh, Udaya Narayana, 19 May, 2009, Paper on "Theories of Danger and Breakdown of Communication", presented in the two-day workshop on "Enabling Primary Education in a Multilingual Context: focus on West Bengal" held at Jadavpur University on 19 and 20 May, 2009, organized by The Paschim Banga Sarva Siksha Mission (PBSSM) and UNICEF, West Bengal and Jadavpur University.
- Census, 2001, Government of India.
- McCoy, Roger m., 2006, Field Methods in Remote Sensing, Rawat Publications, India
- Tamsang, K. P., A Grammar of the Lepcha Language, 1978, published by Mr. Lyangsong Tamsang, Kalimpong.
- Sprigg, R. K., 2005, Shedding Some Light on the History, Language and Literature of the Lepchas, Indigenous Lepcha Tribal Association, Kalimpong.
- Sitling, Ren G. T., 2006 (1929), Lepcha Primer-I, 2002, Lepcha Primer-II, Indigenous Lepcha Tribal Association, Kalimpong.

- Lepcha, Dup Shuzong, 2002, Lepcha Primer-III, IV, Indigenous Lepcha Tribal Association, Kalimpong.
- Lepcha, Dup Shuzong, 2007, Lepcha Reader, V, VI, VII, VIII & IX, Indigenous Lepcha Tribal Association, Kalimpong.
- Tamsang, K. P., 1998, The Unknown and Untold Reality About the Lepchas, Indigenous Lepcha Tribal Association, Kalimpong.
- Sing, Jawaharlal, 2008, Munda Bhasar Byakaran (A Grammar of Munda Language), published by Sadhan Mandi, Marang Buru Press, Mechada, Purba Medinipur.
- Misra, Bal Govind and Hans Raj Duo ed., 1980, Language Use in Himachal Pradesh, CIIL,Mysore.
- Itagi, N. H. and Shailendra Kumar Singh ed., 2002, Linguistic Landscaping in India, CIIL and Mahatma Gandhi Inetrnational Hindi University.
- Itagi, N. H., 1994, Spatial Aspects of Language, CIIL, Mysore.
- Dua, Hans R.1986, Language Use, Attitudes and Identity Among Linguistic Minorities, CIIL, Mysore.
- Annamalai, E., Bjron H. Jernudd & Joan Rubin ed., 1986, Language Planning, Proceeding of an Institute, CIIL, Mysore.
- Bishnu, Sudhir Kumar, 2009, Pranta Uttarbanger Bhasa-Upabhasa (Languages and Dialects of Border Area of North Bengal), Boioyala, Kolkata.
- Nath, Mrinal, 1999, Bhasa O Samaj (Language and Society), Naya Udyoge, Kolkata.

Prevention is Better than Cure: The Case of "Small", But Still Thriving Languages

Dr. Gail Coelho - Department of Linguistics, University of Delhi

1. Introduction

The circumstances in which languages are endangered in India vary greatly, although certain recurring factors can be identified. Some languages are spoken by very small communities (less than 10,000) with low social status, living in the midst of larger and more powerful communities that speak a different language. Many of these are already moribund; i.e. they are no longer the first language learned by children – e.g. languages such as Gorum and Gutob (Munda branch, Austroasiatic family) in Southern Orissa and Northern Andhra Pradesh. However, some of them, such as the Dravidian languages in the hill areas of Tamil Nadu, Kerala, and Karnataka are currently viable; i.e. they are still learned as the first language by children in the community. Some are spoken by extremely small communities (estimated at less than 300) that live in almost complete isolation from other communities; e.g. the Jarawas, Sentinelese, and Shompen in the Andaman and Nicobar islands. These are endangered not so much because of the danger of shift to the dominant language in the region, but because the population of speakers may themselves die out. Others are spoken by large communities (more than 1,000,000), but are endangered despite their size because they do not enjoy state support. Examples of such endangered large languages are Sindhi, which is an official language, but not a state language, and Tulu (spoken in Mangalore, Karnataka), which is neither an official language nor a state language.[1]

Thus, programmes for language revitalization or maintenance should be designed to suit specific cases, each of which will require their own approach. This paper presents a case study of one language, Betta Kurumba, which is spoken by an adivasi community living in a hilly region across the states of Karnataka, Kerala, and Tamil Nadu. The community is small and is culturally subordinate to more "powerful" language communities. The language is not yet moribund, but is potentially endangered. Such languages might appear at first glance to be in no immediate need of state support for revitalization. However, prevention is better than cure – once a language becomes moribund, it is much harder to revive it. Therefore, the threat of endangerment should be addressed while the language is still thriving, and programmes implemented now with the aim of preventing language shift and of partially reversing the areas in which shift has occurred.

To design a language maintenance programme, it is necessary to first study the existing situation with a view to identify:

- What factors have a positive effect on language maintenance,
- What poses a potential threat to maintenance,
- What facilities or practices already exist that can be utilised for the promotion of maintenance,
- What new facilities or practices need to be introduced for this purpose,
- And finally, what potential problems can be expected in implementing the programme.

A consideration of all the varied factors involved in maintenance is beyond the scope of this paper. I shall focus on three main issues that stand out in my mind as important: (a) Maintenance of domains of use for the adivasi language, alongside the dominant language(s) – such multilingualism is inescapable given present realities; (b) attitudes to the use of adivasi languages, and (c) maintenance of the community as a unit, with its cultural traditions. For each of these I argue that there are positive factors already existing that promote language maintenance, otherwise the languages would have been lost to us by now. However, there are strong threats to their continued maintenance, and measures must be taken to guard against these threats.

[1] *See the extensive literature on endangerment (see e.g. Mahapatra 1991, Crawford 1996, Grenoble and Whaley 1998, 2006, Mehrotra 1999, Verma 2001) for generalizations about the factors responsible for endangerment*

2 The Language and its Background.

Betta Kurumba is not listed as a separate language in the Indian census surveys, which instead mention Kuruba (aka Kurumba within Tamil Nadu) as a dialect of Kannada. The Kurubas or Kurumbas actually consist of several different ethnic groups, each of which probably speak a separate language (*see Zvelebil 1981, Hockings 1989, 1997 for a discussion of the languages and ethnic groups of the region)*. Groups that call themselves Kurumba consist of the Betta Kurumbas, Mullu Kurumbas, Urali Kurumbas, and Jenu Kurumbas (alias Kattunayakans within Tamil Nadu). Two Ph. D. dissertations by Jayapal (1979) and Coelho (2003) provide clear evidence that Betta Kurumba is a separate language and not a dialect of another language. Further, the Betta Kurumbas identify themselves as a distinct community and have certain cultural practices that enforce their distinctiveness, such as ex-communication of those who marry outside the community.

The Nilgiris itself can be divided into two geographic and cultural zones – the Upper Nilgiri area and the Nilgiri-Wynaad area (*Bird-David 1997*). The adivasi groups of the Upper Nilgiri area occupy territories within Tamil Nadu – Todas, Badagas, Kotas, Irulas, and some of the Kurumba groups. The adivasi groups of the Nilgiri-Wynaad area, on the other hand, occupy territory that goes beyond the Nilgiris into the Western Ghat sections of Kerala and Karnataka. Based on the information given to me by the Betta Kurumbas, their land lies primarily in Wyanaad district, Kerala; however, the discussion in this paper will centre on the Betta Kurumba situation within the Nilgiris, because this is the section I am familiar with through fieldwork.

Before the 19th century, the adivasis of the Nilgiri mountains were relatively isolated from the languages and "mainstream" cultures of the lowlands (i.e., the Deccan Plateau and the coastal plains). The hill groups, therefore, developed fairly independently of the lowland areas, although the languages of both regions belong to the Southern branch of the Dravidian family. Each of the adivasi groups that inhabit the Nilgiri mountains and the adjoining Western Ghats apparently speak a separate language, although further research has to be done to determine the extent to which each group differs in speech. There is no record of the adivasi groups having developed any *lingua franca* for communication with one another; therefore, at least some people in each adivasi group must have been knowledgeable of some of the other adivasi languages or dialects. However, it is unlikely that they had knowledge of languages spoken outside of the hill areas.

The near isolation of the Nilgiris ended in the 19th century when the British set up towns and tea and timber plantations in the region. This attracted large numbers of settlers from the lowlands, who were mainly speakers of related South Dravidian languages – Malayalam, Kannada, and Tamil. With Indian Independence and the formation of states, the Upper Nilgiri zone (referred to above) became part of Tamil Nadu with Tamil as the official state language. The Nilgiri-Wynaad zone, on the other hand was transected by state boundaries, with portions incorporated into Karnataka, Kerala, and Tamil Nadu. These changes have, of course, had political, social, and economic effects on the adivasis. They have become marginalized in their own homeland and their traditional lands have come under the control of persons from other communities – either through private ownership, or through the establishment of protected forest lands under the control of the government. In terms of lifestyle, the adivasis have largely moved from being self-reliant to employees of persons from other communities. In education, they must now participate in an alien system of education consisting of formal schooling with the state language as the medium of instruction, plus English as a possible additional language.

The linguistic effect of these changes has been partial language shift from an earlier pre-19th century stage when they presumably spoke almost exclusively in their own mother tongue to a bilingual situation in which they use their mother tongue in the restricted domain of intra-community interaction and the state language for inter-community interaction. The experience of other communities whose languages have died has shown us that bilingualism is often the precursor of full shift to the dominant language, particularly when an imbalance of power exists between the two or more communities involved in the language contact situation. These experiences have also shown us that once a language becomes moribund, it is much harder to bring into play the resources and willpower necessary to revive the language. It is better to ensure that the partial shift that the Betta Kurumbas and similar communities have undergone towards their current state of multilingualism does not deteriorate into complete shift to the dominant regional language, leading to the death of their mother tongue.

3 Prospects for Language Maintenance Among the Betta Kurumbas

3.1. Domain Differentiation

As stated above, the Betta Kurumbas use their mother tongue for intra-community communication and the state language for inter-community communication. The mother tongue is likely to survive as long as this domain differentiation remains intact. However, the mother tongue has low prestige and social, economic and political factors exert pressure on the Betta Kurumba community to assimilate towards the dominant culture and its language. Therefore, there are strong chances that the dominant language will gradually encroach on the domains in which the mother tongue is used, eventually leading to death of the mother tongue.

Assistance in language maintenance should therefore be aimed at preventing the dominant language from such encroachment. In fact efforts should be made to encourage the reverse process: encroachment of the mother tongue into domains in which the dominant language is used. This reverse process can be encouraged in three primary areas where the dominant language now is exclusively used:

- School education,
- The cultural practice of writing, and
- Media resources, such as radio and TV.

The most important area in which the mother tongue should be introduced is in education. School occupies a large part of a child's day, therefore, the language learned in school and the cultural exposure received in school has a strong influence on children. It influences a child's sense of identity; it is the language in which children gain a major part of their knowledge about the world and learn to think about the world; it is the language in which children learn to communicate with their peer group in school. If the language of the school is exclusively the dominant language, children could get into the habit of using this language for communication with peers, even with peer-groups from their own community while at home. In this case, a generational difference could develop in children's pattern of language use at home – the dominant language with their peer group and the mother tongue only with their elders. Over time as these children grow up and have children of their own, their children would be exposed to conversation conducted by their parents primarily in the dominant language, with the result that the mother tongue is not passed on to the next generation.

Bilingual education must, therefore, be a vital part of a language maintenance programme, particularly since it is already well-established that bilingual education furthers the development of academic skills and is an important factor in affirming the linguistic and cultural identity of the students (*see e.g. Cummins 2009 for a summary of the benefits of bilingual education*). The most effective bilingual programme, it seems to me, is one that uses a phased system in which all the classes in the first one or two years are in the mother tongue, and later classes gradually introduce more and more of the dominant language. The mother tongue should, however, continue throughout schooling, for at least one class. Adivasis themselves should be trained as teachers and should take an active part in planning the syllabus. The syllabus should be based to a large extent on the cultural practices of the adivasi group; for example, since the Betta Kurumbas were originally forest gatherers, classes for their children could include demonstrations of traditional house-building, honey-gathering (in a safe setting), observation of animals and plants, etc. The actual teaching practices should be adapted to the needs of different adivasi groups; for example, some adivasi groups may learn better in a non-formal outdoor setting, rather than in a classroom. [2]

The most important requirement for such bilingual programmes is the development of textbooks in the mother tongue. This, of course, involves the development of an orthography, which is best handled by modifying the script of the dominant language to make it suitable to the phonemic system of the relevant adivasi language. It should be noted, however, that while the development of an orthography by itself is a relatively easy task for a linguist, the resultant introduction of literacy in a community is not an easy matter, since writing involves the introduction of a whole new cultural practice. For literacy to become truly embedded as a practice, the need for writing would have to be created among the people. School education is an obvious arena for creating such need. Another possibility is to initiate magazines in which Betta Kurumbas can be encouraged to publish stories, articles about themselves and their views on the world, etc.[3] A third possibility could be recognition within the community of the need for creating written records of their traditions in the eventuality of language death.

Literacy development will also involve dealing with sociolinguistic issues, one of which is how to handle dialect differences, since writing frequently involves the codification of one variety, legitimising it over other varieties present

---

[2] *This list is based partially on information provided by Ramdas, who helps run a school for advasis set up by Accord, an NGO based in Gudalur, Nilgiris.*

[3] *Bhasha, founded by Ganesh Devi in Tejgarh, Gujarat, has already shown the way by publishing a magazine to which the adivasis in that region contribute articles.*

in the community. In addition, communities like the Betta Kurumbas, whose lands have been bifurcated by state borders, face the issue of deciding upon which script to use for the new orthography. If the script of the local state language is used, the community would be split into those who use the Kannada script within Karnataka, the Malayalam script within Kerala, and the Tamil script within Tamil Nadu, all to write the same language. This would further heighten the division that has already been created in the community by the bifurcation of its traditional homeland across three states. On the other hand, if one script is chosen for the entire community, the children of one state would have the privilege of learning only one script for the mother tongue and state language, while the children of the other two states would have to learn two different scripts. The community will have to work together to resolve the dilemmas arising from these issues. Linguists themselves should be actively engaged over time in assisting the community with these sociolinguistic issues and in the work of creating suitable educational material. Too often linguists limit themselves to designing an orthography and publishing a book with a list of words to demonstrate use of the orthography, and then make no attempt to follow up by working with the community in the much more painstaking task of actually developing the practice of writing.

3.2. Attitudes to the Use of Adivasi Languages

An important factor that favours the maintenance of minority languages in India is our tolerance of cultural diversity. India is a country that accepts the use of many languages and it is expected that each community has its own speech form. In the Nilgiri-Wynaad area, this acceptance is aided by the fact that the dominant state languages all belong to the same language family as the adivasi languages. The adivasi languages are seen as dialects or corrupt forms of the dominant language rather than a different language, and several words in the adivasi languages can be recognized by the dominant community reducing the sense that their speech is "different" or "alien". However, although these languages are accepted, they are not respected. The languages get ridiculed, which can lead speakers to feel inhibited to use their language among others. Further, there is virtually no awareness among non-adivasis in the region of the value and richness of adivasi languages and cultures. As in other parts of India, the non-adivasi people of the Nilgiris consider the adivasis "primitive" and believe that they need to be educated into the ways of more "advanced" civilizations.

In terms of government policies (which I would include under the topic of attitudes), a positive factor is that Indian governmental policies are not ones that involve the active suppression of adivasi languages, unlike regions of the world in which aggressive programmes have been carried out to prevent use of minority languages. However, state governments practice passive neglect to varying degrees. In Tamil Nadu, while plenty of programmes are in place to promote pride in Tamil, no such programmes exist to promote pride in the adivasi languages. There is an Adivasi Research Centre in M.Palada, near Ooty, with a museum containing displays about select adivasi groups in India. However, the display is limited and functions are no more than a tourist attraction, visited by casual tourists, but not by the people of the Nilgiris themselves.

Fortunately, this is an area in which NGOs are already active and have been fairly successful. One NGO deserves special mention in this respect: '**Accord**' and its sister organization the '**Adivasi Munnetra Sangam**', based in Gudalur, Nilgiris. Accord has set up an adivasi school called Vidyodaya and a hospital and has acquired land for collective ownership by the adivasis in the Gudalur area. The school has made a concerted effort to promote self-pride; its teachers are drawn as far as possible from the adivasis, and the teachers are, therefore, able to speak to the children in their own language. Adivasi traditions are given a place in its curriculum through classes on the history of the adivasis, and sessions during which elders are called in to tell stories and songs in adivasi languages.[4] Since the school caters to different adivasi groups, this enhances the childrens' knowledge of ethnic groups other than their own. The school also takes care to deal with problems that students may face in attending school; thus, according to Ramdas, who helps run Vidyodaya, the school has virtually no drop-out rate, unlike other schools in the area, such as government-run tribal residential schools.

However, a lacuna in the efforts of even NGOs is that awareness-building among the non-adivasi communities in the Nilgiris has not received sufficient attention. It is essential to foster positive attitudes among the adivasis by making people aware of the richness of these traditions. I would, therefore, recommend setting up a regional centre in the Nilgiris that makes information about the languages and cultures of the adivasis available and disseminates this information widely through interactive work with non-adivasi communities. This could

---

[4] *However, mother tongue instruction has not yet been implemented because of a lack of suitable textbooks.*

involve a museum-style display that provides information about the rich adivasi knowledge of medicine, house-building, food-gathering, among other things, as well as information about their music, dance, story-telling traditions, and religious rituals. The museum could also present the Nilgiris from the perspective of the adivasis themselves. For example, maps of the Nilgiris could show the territories that belong to different adivasi groups, marking sub-divisions claimed by different clans. Such maps could also show landmarks (such as streams or sections where particular plant species grow) that are important to the adivasis, but remain unmarked on conventional topographical maps of the area. It is particularly important that the centre have interactive sessions with non-adivasi people in the Nilgiris through public lectures, educational classes in schools, cultural festivals, etc. Publications should be brought out to disseminate this information further through video and audio CDs, as well as attractive books designed for children and adults containing adivasi folktales, information about medicinal knowledge, etc. These can be made available in local bookstores for tourists and permanent residents of the Nilgiris. Needless to say, the adivasis themselves should participate at all levels in the activities of this centre. Further, the centre will require trained linguists and anthropologists to contribute their skills towards ensuring that the information is of high quality and as free as possible of inaccuracies.

3.3. Maintenance of the Community as a Unit:

For a community to continue to use its language, it must continue to maintain itself as a community and maintain its cultural traditions because it is in the context of these cultural traditions that the language is most likely to be used. This is evident from that fact that when all other domains of language use have been lost, several moribund languages are still used in the domain of religious rituals.

A factor that strongly favours maintenance of cultural traditions is continuing habitation within the traditional homeland. This is particularly true of hunter-gatherer or farming communities, whose traditions are closely tied to the environment their cultures have developed in. A positive factor for the Betta Kurumba prospects of language maintenance is that the community has not been entirely displaced from their native lands. Sections of the Betta Kurumba community in the Nilgiris still live in the Mudumalai forest sanctuary and have limited access to forest produce. Moreover, the Betta Kurumbas are disinclined to migrate to other areas in search of work. This is partly due to the pleasant

Nilgiri environment and the availability of plenty of work in reserved forests and plantations, but an important reason is also that they cannot practice their religious traditions away from the homeland. Their death ritual consists of an invocation ceremony to the ancestral spirits who are called from the dead person's clan territory and asked to escort the spirit of the person to this territory. The Betta Kurumbas reported to me that this ritual must be performed within Betta Kurumba lands. Further, their religious worship must be done only in their own temples – they may visit the temples of other deities as tourists, but it would anger their own deities if they worshipped there.[5]

However, the question arises of how long these ties to the land will last. Will the Betta Kurumbas' own religious beliefs persist under the influence of a dominant community with other beliefs? Will work become unavailable within the Nilgiris and economic pressures overcome their religious beliefs, resulting in migration elsewhere to earn a living. In addition, the threat of being moved from their traditional land by force is an ever present one. This threat comes either from private landowners who want tribal-land, or forest authorities in the region's protected forests who see tribal practices as inimical to plant and animal conservation. Even while living in the forest, their rights to use forest produce is severely curtailed making them dependent on materials that must be purchased, rather than gathered from the forest. The resultant need for cash puts them under pressure to assimilate to mainstream cultural practices. For example, when I first began field work among the Betta Kurmbas in the mid-1990s, the Betta Kurumbas living within Mudumalai sanctuary used to build houses of bamboo and grass from the forest. By now, almost all their houses are built of concrete with metal or asbestos sheeting for the roofs. This change has come about partly because the forest authorities make it very difficult for the Betta Kurumbas to cut bamboo and grass. The result is that the Betta Kurumbas now need cash for their new housing needs, reducing their self-reliance and independence from the dominant culture's ways.

It is important therefore that the community's right to pursue their traditional ways and remain in their homeland be protected. The recent passage of the The Scheduled Tribes and Other Traditional Forest Dwellers (Recognition of Forest Rights) Act, 2006 is a welcome step in this direction; however, it remains to be seen how well the law will be implemented. Conservationists should be

---

[5] *Despite this assertion by my consultants, I have noticed that a few Betta Kurumbas do join the annual pilgrimage that many Hindus in southern India make to the Ayyappa temple at Sabrimalai in Kerala.*

persuaded to recognise the important role that tribals can perform in assisting conservation because of their own intimate knowledge of the forest. Further, the adivasis should be assisted into utilising their knowledge of forest resources in economically viable ways. This assistance is currently being provided by an NGO in the Nilgiris called '**Keystone Foundation**' (based in Kotagiri), which helps the adivasis in marketing their forest produce for a fair price, and has also introduced certain new income-generation practices (such as bee-keeping) which do not depart too heavily from the previous practices of local adivasi groups.

4 Conclusion

It is both desirable and possible that measures be taken to prevent the rapid death of minority languages in India. As stated above, the measures must include steps to maintain those languages that are not yet moribund. Three important factors that must be addressed in such language maintenance efforts are: (a) The maintenance of domain differentiation, and possible reversal of this differentiation such that the mother tongue comes to be used in areas where the dominant language is currently used; (b) promotion of positive attitudes to tribal languages and cultures, both within the community and among non-adivasi communities; (c) protection of adivasi rights to pursue their traditional cultural practices and their right to continue living in their traditional homeland.

References

- Bird-David, Nurit. 1997. The Nilgiri tribal systems: A view from below. In Hockings (ed.), pp. 5-22.
- Coelho, Gail. 2003. A grammar of Bet?t?a Kurumba. University of Texas at Austin doctoral dissertation, Austin.
- Crawford, James. 1996. Seven hypotheses on language loss: Causes and cures. In Gian Cantoni (ed.), *Stabilizing Indigenous Languages*. Arizona: A Center for Excellence in Education Monograph.
- Cummins, Jim. 2009. Fundamental psycholinguistic and sociological principles underlying educational success for linguistic minority students. In Ajit K. Mohanty,
- Minati Panda, Robert Phillipson, and Tove Skutnabb-Kangas (eds.), *Multilingual education for social justice: Globalising the Local.* Hyderabad: Orient BlackSwan.
- Grenoble and Whaley. 1998. Toward a typology of language endangerment. In Lenore A. Grenoble and Lindsay J. Whaley (eds.) *Endangered languages:*

Current Issues and future prospects. Cambridge: Cambridge University Press.

- *Saving Languages: An introduction to language revitalization.* Cambridge: Cambridge University Press.
- Hockings, Paul, (ed.) 1989. *Blue Mountains: The ethnography and biogeography of a South Indian region.* Delhi: Oxford University Press.
- *Blue Mountains revisited: Cultural studies on the Nilgiri Hills.* Delhi: Oxford University Press.
- Jayapal, S. 1979. Kurumba grammar. Annamalai University doctoral dissertation, Annamalainagar.
- Mahapatra, B. P. 1991. An appraisal of Indian languages. In R. H. Robins and E.M. Uhlenbeck (eds.), *Endangered Languages.* Oxford: Berg Publishers Mehrotra, Raja Ram. 1999. Endangered languages in India. *International Journal of the Sociology of Language* 140:105-114.
- Verma, Mahendra K. 2001. Language endangerment and Indian languages: An exploration and a critique. In Anvita Abbi, R. S. Gupta, and Ayesha Kidwai (eds.), *Linguistic structure and language dynamics in South Asia: Papers from the proceedings of SALA XVIII roundtable.* Delhi: Motilal Banarsidass Publishers.
- Zvelebil, Kamil. 1981. Problems of identification and classification of some Nilagiri tribes. *Anthropos 76*: 467-528.

Session 3

Impact of Hindi and other Scheduled Languages on Unwritten Languages

Language Endangerment in the Himalayan Chain: The Impact of Nepali on the Tibeto-Burman Languages of Nepal, India and Bhutan

Dr. Jean Robert Opgenort - University of Leiden, Netherlands

1. Introduction

The topic of this paper is the current language endangerment in the Himalayan Chain, in particular with respect to the impact of Nepali on the unwritten Tibeto-Burman languages in India, Nepal and Bhutan.

We will look at the various factors in the past and present that make people favour Nepali — a major regional language — at the expense of their own mother tongue. We will also look at what can be done in practice to reverse the trend of language loss in the Himalayan region.

This presentation is organized into four sections. Section 1 examines the present situation of the endangered languages spoken in the Indian Subcontinent and the Himalayan Chain. In Section 2, we will focus on the Tibeto-Burman languages of the Himalayan region. Subsequently, the success of modern Nepali mainstream culture is discussed in Section 3. Finally, in Section 4, I will discuss what can be done to reverse the trend of language loss.

2. An Irrecoverable Loss of Unique World Views

There are approximately 6,500 languages in the world, half of which are not surveyed or have not been adequately studied according to the online *Ethnologue* catalogue, and many of which are dying at an exceptional scale. According to the third UNESCO Atlas of the World's Languages in Danger (2009), there are currently 2,500 endangered languages around the world. This puts more about 40 per cent of the World's linguistic richness at peril. This is a worrying situation. As UNESCO so rightly declares on its own web site (http://www.unesco.org/culture/ich/index.php?pg=00148):

"Every language reflects a unique world-view with its own value systems, philosophy and particular cultural features. The extinction of a language results in the irrecoverable loss of unique cultural knowledge embodied in it for centuries, including historical, spiritual and ecological knowledge that may be essential for the survival of not only its speakers, but also countless others.

The global situation is reflected in India and the Himalayan Chain, where more than 280 languages out of the 500+ languages spoken today are in danger of vanishing for good from the face of this earth. India, Nepal and Bhutan, which together constitute less than 2.5 per cent of the world's land area and are home to 11.5% of the endangered languages in the world, form one of the most endangered linguistic patchworks in the world."

The third UNESCO Atlas of the World's Languages in Danger distinguishes five different levels of endangerment:

1. Unsafe (vulnerable)- The language is used by some children in all domains, and used by all children in limited domains.
2. Definitely endangered-The language is used mostly by the parental generation and up.
3. Severely endangered-The language is used mostly by the grandparental generation and up.
4. Critically endangered-The language is used mostly by very few speakers, of the great-grandparental generation.
5. Extinct-No speakers exist.

The data from the Atlas (http://www.unesco.org/culture/ich/index.php?pg=00206) also show that 60 out of the 280 languages spoken in India and the Himalayan Chain are severely or critically endangered, whereas ten languages are considered to be extinct. Even though the situation in India, Nepal and Bhutan seems slightly better than average in the world, where more than half of the languages are decidedly endangered or extinct, the classifications should be treated as provisional, given that reliable data for many of the smaller languages, with regard to both health and number of speakers, is not always available for the various parts of the world.

3. The Tibeto-Burman Languages of the Himalayan Region

The Himalayan region forms one of the most intricate ethnological and linguistic mosaics in the world. This vast area is home to Indo-Aryan languages — a branch of the Indo-European language family — the most widespread and best-documented language family with nine languages in the world's top 15 languages in number of speakers. After the Indo-European language family, Sino-Tibetan — or rather 'Tibeto-Burman' — is the most populous family in the world, containing close to a billion speakers. Except for Chinese, most of the Tibeto-Burman languages have rather small numbers of speakers, are unwritten and poorly documented. The greater Himalayan region is also home to several Dravidian and a few Daic languages.

The Himalayan region constitutes the region where the majority of endangered languages in the subcontinent can be found, and Tibeto-Burman languages form the majority of languages under threat. Even though much on the conditions of language loss in Himalayas has yet to be learnt, it must be kept in mind that the endangered languages are not in any sense inferior or backward, but that they are merely losing the uneven confrontation with more dominant cultures and their languages.

More than half of the languages under threat in India are Tibeto-Burman languages in North East India, mostly in Arunachal Pradesh and Nagaland, and about one dozen Tibeto-Burman languages in the western Himalayan states of Himachal Pradesh and Uttarakhand.

In Nepal, the bulk of Tibeto-Burman languages are spoken by small populations and considered endangered. We list more than 40 unsafe or definitely endangered languages, more than a dozen severely or critically endangered languages and one extinct language. The smallest and most endangered Tibeto-Burman languages have very few speakers and are on the verge of extinction.

In Bhutan, none of the native Tibeto-Burman languages is considered to be safe. Even Dzongkha, which is the official national language of Bhutan, is marginalised by the extensive use of English throughout Bhutan and by Nepali, which is spoken in much of southern Bhutan.

4. The Success of Nepali

Even though there are several reasons for endangerment of the language communities[1], the current language endangerment situation in the Himalayan region is largely the result of cultural assimilation, which is a process by which the culture of a minority

[1] *For instance, Raji and Raute, in the Bheri and Seti districts of western Nepal and the submontane region of the central Himalayas in Uttarakhand, are examples of fully undocumented languages that are severely endangered because the hunter-gatherer lifestyle of the speakers is under threat with the destruction of the original forest habitat; while landslides have almost completely wiped out the two villages where the Kohi or 'Koyu' Rai of Eastern Nepal are located (Toba, Toba & Rai 2001).*

group is gradually influenced by a more dominant culture. One of the dominant cultures undermining linguistic diversity in the central Himalayas is modern Nepali culture.

Nepali, an Eastern Pahârî language, is the official language of the country of Nepal, where it is the mother tongue for more than 11 million people for the most part living in the western part of the country and in the Terai belt in the south. Nepali is also the dominant language for media, trade, public domain and education in the country and the *lingua franca* for communication among different language groups throughout Nepal. In India, Nepali is one of 22 scheduled languages and the mother tongue for more than 2.8 million speakers (Census 2001). Nepali is an official language and *lingua franca* of the state of Sikkim, an officially recognised language in the state of West-Bengal and spoken in the state of Assam. In Bhutan, about one third of the population speaks Nepali.

Nepal

Many decades of state neglect, the simultaneous cultivation of a national identity based on Nepali and marginalization and oppression of indigenous groups are the basis of the present decline of minority languages in Nepal.

The Spread of Nepali

The spread and success of Nepali started with the unification of Nepal by P[tvî NârâyaG Úâh in the latter half of the 18th century, when Nepali — or 'Khas Kurâ', Gorkhâlî or 'Parbate' — became the national language of the newly formed kingdom.

Retired soldiers were given land in subjugated indigenous areas and came as colonists to settle in the newly acquired areas. With the expansion of the kingdom, the area where Nepali was spoken expanded from west to east.

After the Gorkhâ conquest, some of the larger Tibeto-Burman language groups such as the Gurung and Magar settled outside their traditional homeland, from eastern Nepal to southern Bhutan and northeastern India. Outside their traditional area, these groups adopted Nepali as their native tongue.

From the unification in 1768, through the Rana (since 1857) and Panchayat (since 1962) periods and up to as recent as 1990, the government of Nepal promoted monolingualism by pursuing a 'one nation, one language' policy and suppressed the rights of linguistic minorities. Only Nepali was permitted in education and broadcasts.

In 1990, Nepal won its democracy after the People's Movement brought an end to absolute monarchy. The new constitution acknowledged the multilingual character of the state. Article 18 of the Constitution allowed communities the fundamental right to promote their own language and to use it as the medium of instruction at the primary level. Twelve minority languages could be used on a regular basis on the national broadcast media. The right to primary education in the mother tongue was granted, but remained largely unimplemented.

A period of economic and political turmoil followed the advent of democracy. The Nepalese Civil War, which was a conflict between government forces and Maoist rebels that lasted from 1996 until 2006, further deteriorated the language situation, as the wealthy elites from the villages fled to Kathmandu and other cities, causing further local impoverishment.

After the 2006 Democracy Movement (or People's Movement 2) against the monarchy and the adoption of an Interim Constitution in 2007, linguistic minority groups have been given additional rights to use their mother tongue in local organizations and government offices. The seventh amendment of the interim constitution currently proposes that a President, Prime Minister or any government official can take oath in their mother tongues.

An Uneven Situation

Speakers of indigenous languages nowadays find themselves in an uneven situation of *diglossia*. In contrast to Nepali, which is very widespread as it is the dominant language for media, trade, public domain and education and the *lingua franca* throughout the

The author with a friend

entire country of Nepal, the indigenous languages are mostly used in the home domain, between members of the same linguistic community and confined to the area where they live. The speakers of minority languages belong to one particular group and, in general, outsiders do not speak these languages. Because the members of language groups acquire knowledge of Nepali in school or through work, they usually speak their own minority language and Nepali. Unlike Nepali, which is taught at school, the indigenous languages are mostly unwritten. They only exist in the memory.

Since most speakers of minority languages are bilingual, even those languages that are not definitely endangered are victims to a gradual process of linguistic convergence towards Nepali. These languages survive, but they are losing their distinctiveness as they borrow vocabulary and morphological and syntactic features.

In recent years, improvements in transport and communication and economic forces have even further eroded local language and culture. Massive waves of migration have accelerated the loss of indigenous languages. Individuals moving to the urban areas (where people of different ethnicity live together) in search for work or for the purpose of education, or families migrating to the Terai in search of land, often find their mother tongues less relevant to their needs and they rapidly shift to Nepali. As Toba, Toba and Rai (2001: 14) note, '... those who come from the hill areas gradually lose their mother tongue and are bilingual only during a transitional period. In many, if not most cases, parents do not teach their mother tongue to their children with the consequence that these children grow up as monolingual Nepali speakers.' Spouses from different linguistic communities who settle outside the indigenous area also usually end up speaking Nepali. Sometimes, these indigenous people have a strong negative attitude towards their mother tongue, which they consider useless as a serious life skill and also less prestigious than Nepali, and so they do not teach their MT to children.

The Wambule Language

Wambule is an example of a small minority language, which I have classified as 'unsafe' (as the language is used by all children in all domains), but which is victim to gradual process of linguistic convergence toward Nepali.

The Wambule language belongs to the Kiranti family of Tibeto-Burman, which includes some thirty-odd languages spoken in eastern Nepal. Some 5,000 people living near the confluence of the Sunkosi and Dudhkosi rivers speak Wambule. The Wambule have a distinct culture with a rich oral tradition and their own *Mundhum* religion.

Wambule has no script of its own. The language is written in Devanagari script. Individuals who are organized in the Wambule Society of Nepal have made some necessary adaptations to accommodate distinctive Wambule sounds that are not represented in Nepali, such as the implosive sound. The society was founded some 16 years ago and has published several books, including a Wambule dictionary, a book on the Wambule tribe, a book with Wambule poems, Libju-Bhumju magazine and a Ramdale Salang music album. The society regularly organizes poetry contests in the indigenous area as well as cultural gatherings in the Kathmandu Valley, where many active members of the society live and work, such as the well known lyricist Byakul Maila (Pradip Kumar Rai) who received the honour of becoming the composer of the new national anthem of Nepal *Sayai lhuEgâ Phûlkâ Hâmî Eumâ Mâlâ Nepâlî*. The society is also involved in making primary education materials.

Like many other indigenous tribes living in the mid-hills, the Wambule live in small villages that are mostly inhabited by their own people. The majority of Wambule people work as peasant farmers. In a few larger villages, we find a primary school where the teachers are Nepali mother tongue speakers. All children learn to speak Wambule at home and to read and write Nepali at school. At a certain distance from the Wambule villages, there are other villages or a few individual houses where Nepali speaking castes or other Tibeto-Burman tribes speaking different languages live, with which the Wambule speak Nepali.

India

According to the 2001 Census, Nepali is the 16th of the 22 scheduled languages[2] of India in terms of number of speakers' strength, with more than 2.8 million mother tongue speakers. Nepali is an official language and *lingua franca* of the state of Sikkim (with more than three hundred thousand speakers), an officially recognized language in the state of West-Bengal (with more than a million speakers) and also widely spoken in the state of Assam (with more than half a million speakers). In India too, Nepali is spreading at the expense of Tibeto-Burman languages, both native and imported.

According to van Driem (2001: 906), Nepalese colonists driven by overpopulation in eastern Nepal, the demographic upheavals in the wake of the Gorkhâ conquest and the pull of employment opportunities in the tea gardens, began to settle in Darjeeling[3] at the end of the XIXth and beginning of the XXth century. And it was only a few decades later that Nepalese settlers started flooding the valleys of Sikkim proper.

Sikkim, which lost its sovereignty in 1975 when it was incorporated into India, is the only state with an ethnic Nepalese majority. According to the 2001 Census, Nepali is spoken by 60 percent of the Sikkimese population. The indigenous Tibeto-Burman population groups of the former kingdom of Sikkim, the native Lepcha (or 'Róng tribe) and the Dränjop (or Bhomiyâ of Dränjo 'Sikkim'), constitute a minority of less than 10 per cent.

In contrast to many Tibeto-Burman languages, which have no script of their own, the Lepcha have their own indigenous script and a literary tradition that dates back some three hundred years. Lepcha is one of the eleven official languages of Sikkim that is taught in schools (at the lower level) and used in the media. Nevertheless, Lepcha has already effectively been lost everywhere in favour of Nepali. The total number of Lepcha mother tongue speakers across India is somewhere between 4,000 individuals (*van Driem 2001*), 29,854 (*Plaisier 2006*) and 50,629 (Census 2001). Lepcha is a definitely endangered language. In contrast to the Wambule, for whom speaking Wambule constitutes an important part of Wambule identity, the Lepcha frequently have to converse with other ethnic Lepcha who have already lost the ancestral mother tongue in a language other than Lepcha.

Besides more than 2.8 million mother tongue speakers, the Indian 2001 Census also gives data on some 100,000 people mainly living in Sikkim and West-Bengal who returned a Nepalese language as their mother tongue: 37,265 speakers of Limbu, 18,342 speakers of Sherpa, 17,494 speakers of Tamang and 14,378 speakers of Rai languages. Even though the Census defines mother tongue as the language in which the mother was talking to the person in his/her childhood, it remains unclear how many people still speak this mother

---

[2] *The Eighth Schedule to the Indian Constitution is an important language policy statement. Scheduled languages have preferential treatment regarding language development activity. These 22 languages are bestowed with certain facilities, including those to absorb language technology initiatives of the Indian government (Technology Development in Indian Languages).*

[3] *The British managed to acquire Darjeeling from the Sikkimese king in 1835. Prior to that, Darjeeling formed a part of Sikkim and for a brief period of Nepal. The British converted the area into tea gardens.*

tongue. The so-called 'mother tongue' may actually refer to the ancestral language of the ethnic group to which the people belong, rather than the language they speak at home. In other words, the given census data should be double-checked, since some of the large Tibeto-Burman language groups from Nepal who have settled outside their traditional homeland, from eastern Nepal to southern Bhutan and northeastern India, are most likely to have adopted Nepali or some other major regional language as their native tongue.

Bhutan

The national language of Bhutan, Dzongkha, is one of the two Tibeto-Burman languages that now have official national status, the other one being Burmese in Burma. In comparison with Sikkim and Nepal, the linguistic situation in Bhutan is relatively stable. Yet Nepali is also spreading at the expense of Tibeto-Burman. Even Dzongkha is marginalized by the extensive use of English throughout Bhutan and by Nepali. The most endangered language in Bhutan is Lhokpu, which is threatened by linguistic assimilation to the surrounding communities of Nepali colonists in southwestern Bhutan.

5. Healthy Multilingualism to Reverse the Trend

We have looked at the past and present pull and push factors that make people favour Nepali at the expense of their own mother tongue. People moving to the urban areas in search for work or education rapidly shift to national languages, and do not teach their mother tongue to their children. What can we do now to reverse the trend of language loss?

To begin with, we must also acknowledge that even though major languages such as Nepali, Hindi, Bengali and English constitute a threat to the minority languages in the Indian subcontinent and the Himalayan Chain, these important languages also enable speakers of smaller languages to communicate beyond local levels. Knowing a major language is therefore of vital importance to many small, poor and rural communities, just as knowing English is essential to communicate internationally.

Monolingualism therefore is not an option. Instead we should promote a healthy bilingualism, which values both the mother tongue and a *lingua franca*, and as such does not necessarily lead to language loss. A healthy bilingualism should not only be promoted though education (at the primary level), but also at home given that people mistakenly think that children can learn to speak only one language well, whereas the opposite is actually true. Schools can develop a child's usage of both languages (listen, speak, engage in folklore and literature) and raise its self-esteem. Classes for adults who never learned about their language can foster positive language attitudes, which are needed for passing on the language to one's children. However, language-teaching programmes require good learning materials (respecting the world view of the indigenous people) and good mother tongue teachers. The state and the dominant cultures must also acknowledge and support the cultural and linguistic rights of minority groups, and introduce the minority languages in the public sphere and media. Article 30 of the Convention on the Rights of the Child, which was ratified by the Government of India, Nepal and Bhutan, states that no indigenous child should be denied the right to use his or her language and practise his or her culture. This article applies to any child and any language.

The case of Lepcha of Sikkim clearly shows that official state support and education alone is not enough, and that only the community can save its own language by passing it on to their children. Linguists can play an important role in sparking renewed interest in a language and encourage people to preserve their language, as the members of the Himalayan Languages Project have regularly noticed. As such, linguistic research can not only provide documentation of endangered languages for the scholarly community, but also benefit the language communities. I would like to call upon the entire linguistic community to start doing fieldwork immediately and assist in this much needed effort to preserve our world's linguistic heritage.

References

- Borchers, Dörte. 2007. 'Reasons for language death: myths and counter-evidence', pp. 1-21 in Roland Bielmeier and Felix Haller, eds., *Linguistics of the Himalayas and Beyond* (Trends in Linguistics Studies and Monographs 196). Berlin–New York: Mouton de Gruyter.
- Bradley, David. 2007. 'East and Southeast Asia', pp. 349-424 in Christopher Mosely, ed., *Encyclopaedia of the World's Endangered Languages*. London: Routledge.
- Brenzinger, Matthias. 2007. *Language Diversity Endangered* (Trends in Linguistics: Studies & Monographs 181). Berlin–New York: Mouton de Gruyter.
- Crystal, David. 2000. *Language death*. Cambridge: Cambridge University Press. Driem, George van. 2001. *Languages of the Himalayas*. Volumes 1 and 2. Handbook of Oriental Studies. Section Two: India. Leiden/Boston/Köln: Brill.
- Driem, George van. 2007. 'South Asia and the Middle East', pp. 283-347 in Christopher Mosely, ed. *Encyclopaedia of the World's Endangered Languages*. London: Routledge.
- Government of India. Census of India 2001. http://www.censusindia.gov.in/. Krauss, Michael. 1992. *The world's languages in crisis*. Language 68 4–10.
- Michael Krauss. 2007. 'Classification and terminology for degrees of language endangerment'. pp. 1–8 in Christopher Moseley, ed., *Encyclopedia of the World's*

Endangered Languages, London: Routledge.

- Mettle, Daniel & Suzanne Romaine. 2000. *Vanishing Voices. The extinction of the world's languages*. Oxford: Oxford University Press.
- Noonan, Michael. 2005. *Language Documentation and Language Endangerment. Dialogue of Cultures*. Talk held at the University of Iceland, April 14th, 2005.
- Opgenort, Jean Robert 2002. *The Wâmbule Language. Grammar, Lexicon, Texts and Cultural Survey of a Kiranti Tribe of Eastern Nepal*. Amsterdam: Jean Robert Opgenort.
- Opgenort, Jean Robert. 2004. *A Grammar of Wambule. Grammar, Lexicon, Texts and Cultural Survey of a Kiranti Tribe of Eastern Nepal*. Brill's Tibetan Studies Library.
- Languages of the Greater Himalayan Region, 2. Leiden: Koninklijke Brill.
- Plaisier, Heleen. 2006. *A Grammar of Lepcha*. Universiteit Leiden: doctoral dissertation.
- Plaisier, Heleen. 2007. *A Grammar of Lepcha*. Brill's Tibetan Studies Library. Languages of the Greater Himalayan Region, 7. Leiden: Koninklijke Brill.
- Rastogi, Kavita. 2002. "Raji': Language of a Vanishing Himalayan Tribe'. *Linguistics of the Tibeto-Burman Area* 25.2: 155–167.
- Regmi, Bhim Narayan. 2008. *Developing a Devanagari-based multi-language orthography for Nepalese languages*. Paper presented at the Second International Conference on Language Development, Language Revitalization and Multilingual Education in Ethnolinguistic Communities, 1-3 July 2008, Twin Towers Hotel, Bangkok, Thailand.
- Toba, Sueyoshi and Ingrid & Novel Kishor Rai. 2001. *Diversity and Endangerment of Languages in Nepal*. UNESCO Kathmandu Series of Monographs and Working Papers: No 7.
- Turin, Mark. *Linguistic Diversity and the Preservation of Endangered Languages*. A Case Study from Nepal. Kathmandu: International Centre for Integrated Mountain Development (ICIMOD), 2007.
- Yadav, Yogendra Prasad. 2009. *Linguistic Diversity in Nepal: Situation and Policy*. Lalitpur: Social Inclusion Research Fund (SIRF)

Growth of *Arunachalee Hindi* and its Impact on Tribal Languages of Arunachal Pradesh

Lisa Lomdak, Arunachal Institute of Tribal Studies, Rajiv Gandhi University, Arunachal Pradesh

1. Introduction

Ever since its introduction as a second language in the schools of erstwhile North Eastern Frontier Agency (NEFA), the Hindi language has experienced a phenomenal growth in its usage amongst the different tribes of (now) Arunachal Pradesh. In the failure of promoting one tribal language as a state language the introduction of Hindi has served an important function of a link language amongst the Non Arunachalee population residing in Arunachal and also within the linguistically different tribal groups. Over the decades, despite the presence of languages like Assamese and English, no language other than Hindi has made such a significant impact on the tribal languages in terms of expansion of lexicon, innovative grammatical structures and popular usage. As a result, the domain of use of Hindi extended from the classroom to all other spheres of life such as offices, the market place, cultural institutes etc. and gradually and steadily it is in the process of establishing itself as the *lingua franca* of the state. It continues to systematically grow as a distinct variety of Hindi popularly known as *Arunachalee Hindi*.

The advantages of using Hindi are many but this process is now leading us to a critical state of language loss. Firstly, it is significantly replacing the mother tongue of tribal communities in the domain of homes. We have come to a critical situation where generations of youngsters are acquiring *Arunachalee Hindi* rather then their own mother tongue for purposes of conversation and communication. Secondly, it is alarming that they find no motivation to learn their native languages as it is confined "to just adhering to and asserting your cultural roots." The other side of the situation is that as Arunachal Pradesh is still indecisive about the selection of a common script, it prefers using the Roman script and IPA symbols rather than the Devanagari script. We see that the status of the Hindi language, especially in the context of tribal languages of the state, presents a unique dichotomous position. From a study on this unique situation we can infer some important insights into the issue of language endangerment in the state. In addition, one may wonder as to why, when multilingualism is considered an asset and never a burden, the situation has so changed today in the multi lingual societies of Arunachal Pradesh? This study attempts to address these issues by drawing instances from the present linguistic scenario of the state.

Let us first look at the criteria of endangerment listed by UNESCO.

The Criteria of Endangerment

- Absolute number of speakers
- Proportion of speakers within the total population
- Intergenerational language transmission
- Shifts in domain of language use
- Community members attitude towards their own language
- Availability of materials for language education and literacy
- Response to new domains and media
- Type and quality of documentation
- Governmental and Institutional language attitudes and policies, including official status and use

In view of the above criteria of endangerment, the future of languages in Arunachal Pradesh definitely shows serious signs of being endangered by the end of this century.

Before we begin the main discussion on the impact of Hindi in the state, it is imperative that we understand the reality of linguistic diversity in the state. Situated in the North- Eastern part of India, according to the 2001 Census, the population of the state is 1,097,968. Of these 705,158 persons are Scheduled Tribes (ST), constituting 64.2 per cent of the total population.

2.1 Languages

Arunachal Pradesh today is divided into various heterogeneous linguistic groups. Their languages are to a large extent mutually unintelligible. The majority belong to the Tibeto-Burman language family. The other major languages belong to the Tai-Kadai and Tibetan group of language families.

Tani

Languages like Adi, Nyishi, Galo, Tagin, Apatani and Mishing constitute a comparatively larger group of speakers who share close linguistic and cultural affinities with each other. This group covers the central and the largest part of the state. (Fig. i.)

Mishmi

The Idu, Taraon and Kaman Mishmis are often classified under Tani, but in reality there are no linguistic affinities with the Tani group. However it may be noted that there are many commonalities across these tribes evident in various cultural practices.

Jingpho-Konyak-Bodo

The Singpho language variety apart from Arunachal Pradesh is also spoken in Assam which is influenced by Tai languages. The Tangsas are also classified under the Jingpho-Konyak-Bodo. However, there exists a considerable amount of linguistic diversity amongst these two groups.

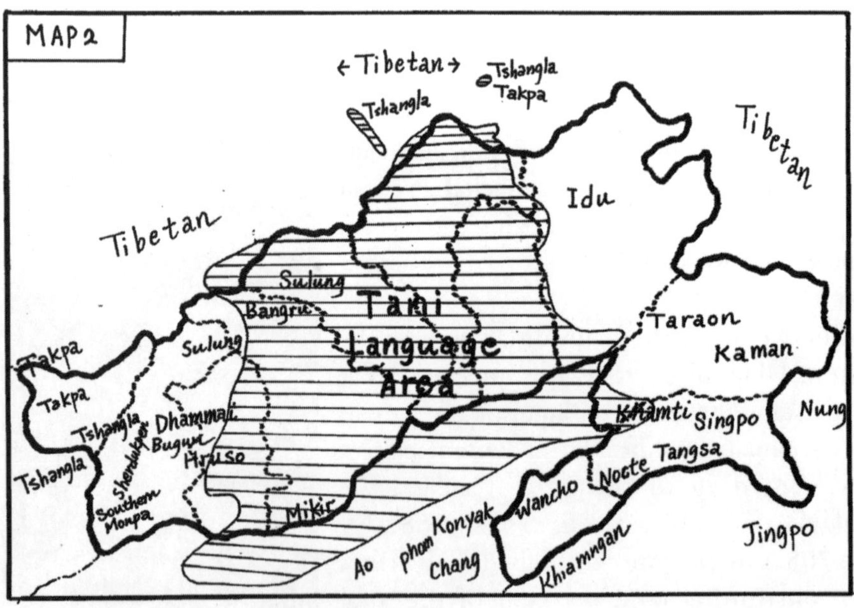

Figure 1. Map showing language distribution in districts of Arunachal Pradesh (Sun, 1993)

Naga-konyak

Nocte-Wancho languages are often classified with the Naga-konyak group and share close cultural afifinities with neighbouring state Nagaland.

Boddhic languages

The Boddhic languages and presence of Tibetan dialects can be seen in areas where languages like Monpa, Sherdukpen etc are spoken. Hruish languages like Aka, Miji are also concentrated in the West kameng district of Arunachal Pradesh.

Tai-Khampti

The khamti language belongs to the Tai Kadai family. The Khamti language shares close linguistic and cultural affinities with the Tai-Ahoms of Assam.

All these languages are Non-Scheduled Languages (not recognized or listed in the VIIIthe Schedule of the Indian Constitution). This is also indicative of the number of speakers of these languages. (To be included in the Schedule, speakers must number at least 10,000) The official language of the state is English. Hindi is the second language of the state. There is talk of the Monpa language being promoted as the third language of the state. We notice that here too the Mother Tongue of a local community is posed as the third language in the state.

2.2 Scripts

The major portion of the tribal communities of Arunachal Pradesh represents a culture based entirely on oral traditions, or the absence of a script. The memories of a script are often reflected in the folktales that the community shares. One version common amongst the Tani community about the absence of script is that, "*...the script was written in the hyde of a deer...later when there was no food to eat the men ate up the hyde....hence the script was lost forever...*" The history of any spoken language explains that these languages continued to survive because there was a constant flow of inter-generational transmission of mother tongue language among the speakers.

All of Arunachal is not devoid of a script. The Monpa and Khamti communities have well developed scripts. The Monpa follow the Tibetan script. And the Khamti have a script known as Lik-tai. What is important is that the texts written in these scripts are preserved in the form of religious texts and are usually regarded as sacred and confined to religious and ritualistic spheres. It is still promoted in the community; for example, in the Khamti area, the script is taught in Pali language schools by monks. However the motivation to learn one's own script is diminishing among the masses nowadays.

Apart from the above two, most of the tribal languages of Arunachal are unwritten. An immensely rich oral tradition of our age old wisdom, folklore and indigenous knowledge systems still exists. But in the present circumstances the transmission of this knowledge system is threatened due to the diminishing number of speakers of the respective languages.

3.1 Bi-Lingual and Multi-Lingual Society

It is common in Arunachal to find one language in various regional varieties. This variation is largely due to geographical distances between the communities, and also to clan groupings in some tribes. For instance the Monpa language of the West Kameng district is divided into three dialects according to geographical location: the Dirang variety (Northern), Tawang variety (Central) and Kalaktang variety (Southern). The speakers of these dialects often say that their variety is mutually unintelligible with the other groups within the Monpa. However one ends up learning the other varieties for communication purpose. Bilingualism was a natural process and a convenient strategy the community developed in order to survive.

3.2 Domain of Language Use

This presents us with a situation where we see that a tribal child in Arunachal Pradesh grows up in a bi-lingual or in some cases a multi-lingual society.

Firstly, the child is exposed to his native mother tongue at home by the mother or family members. Later, as the domain of language use is extended to other areas the child naturally grasps several other varieties within the language.

Secondly, a child who grows up in a town away from his village learns to speak in *Arunachalee Hindi* to his friends if they belong to other tribes. The obligatory choice of language use is often reflected in the lamentations of young children, "I can't make friends because I can't speak Hindi". The other major source of the Hindi language is through the cable network television. Television channels with cartoons, popular music, movies etc contribute significantly in creating a multi-lingual space for the growing child. Apart from *Arunachalee Hindi,* in most cases one also gets exposed to languages like highly colloquial forms of Assamese and Nepali from domestic help.

Thirdly, in schools the child is exposed to English and Hindi in the form of textbooks. The teachers' medium of instruction is either of the two. This is also the space where the child develops the *Arunachalee* variety of Hindi as part of his verbal repertoire.

The teaching of the mother tongue at the primary level of education has been scrapped from a large number of schools in the state. However one cannot also equate knowing local prayers, songs and dances taught in the schools with knowing the language. Apart from this the youth today are not aware of any form of regional language being taught as part of the school education.

3.3 Hierarchy of Language Use

On a closer study there seems to exist a hierarchy in language use within tribal groups. This may be the result of the changing importance of various languages at different points of time. We see that firstly, the older generation, both educated and uneducated, who belong to different tribes, usually speak to each other in Assamese, an Indo-Aryan language of the neighbouring state, Assam. Assamese was tested in examinations (a language paper) and was the medium of instruction before the introduction of English in school education during 1970-71. Assamese was also a link language during those days. It is also observed that in those areas where Khamti, Singpho and Tangsa are spoken, the children tend to speak in Assamese. The reason for this is that apart from the geographical proximity of the tribes with Assam, they share a common history and matrimonial alliances with the Ahom Kings of Assam.

Secondly, even to an outsider it will appear that *Arunachalee Hindi* is spoken by the younger generation and especially by children. This phenomenon is evident across all the tribes. *Arunachalee Hindi* is a language that is used to bond with friends. Even when these children meet outside the state this is the language that links them. In case they wish to share some secret message the most common strategy is to switch to a broken form of Assamese.

Thirdly, English is regarded as the language of the educated class. It is spoken mostly in formal contexts like classrooms, offices and formal functions. But it is also highly popular among students brought up in boarding schools.

From the above discussion we can see the multi-layered acceptance and usage of several languages in Arunachal Pradesh.

4. Growth of *Arunachalee Hindi*

Arunachalee Hindi is simply understood as Arunachal Pradesh's Hindi, a variety of Hindi now gradually being accepted amongst Hindi speaking belts of India. It is spoken everywhere in Arunachal Pradesh. The speakers of this variety are aware of it being a deviant of the Hindi prescribed in the textbooks and also the Hindi spoken by the native speakers of the language. Some of the linguistic features are absent from this variety of Hindi. For example there is an absence of retroflex sounds, there are no gender markings on the verbs or on Nouns [including humans], and use of first person plural '*hum*' to signify both Singular 'I' and 'we'. The speakers of this language are growing day by day and the language is being acquired as the first language and replacing the mother tongue.

Despite the presence of Assamese and English, no language other than Hindi has made a significant impact on the younger generation. As stated earlier it serves as a link language between all the heterogeneous linguistic groups of the tribals themselves. It also serves as a medium of communication in a contact situation with the people who belong to the non-tribal population. To some sections, the introduction of Hindi as a Second Language in Schools of NEFA has promoted a sense of national integration in the region. Educationists state that its promotion in the region perhaps became intense after the Chinese incursions in 1962. It was a common sight to see a Hindi teacher even in remote villages which could only be reached over suspension bridges. In 1964 when the first college, Jawaharlal Nehru College, opened up in Pasighat, one of the first departments was the Hindi department. Many have benefitted today and make a career out of the Hindi language especially in the area of teaching and mass media. Therefore we see that there was enough institutional support to promote the Hindi language in the state.

To a linguist like me I can sense the process of growth of distinct forms of *Adi Hindi, Monpa Hindi, Nyishi Hindi, Idu Hindi*. Every community seems to have owned it by giving it a distinct form which is characteristic of the speakers of the particular community.

4.1 Factors that Facilitated the Popularizing of *Arunachalee Hindi*

If we study the situation three decades ago, we get an insight into the present scenario. Firstly, the older generations have memories of learning Hindi from the jawans of the Army posted in various parts of Arunachal. "*hum luk/log army log , Assam Rifles se seekha hei." (we have learnt it from the Army of Assam Rifles)*. Secondly, the migrant population mostly consisting of Central Government employees, bussinessmen (Marwaris), labourers from Bihar, Assam, and Bengal played a significant role in giving *Arunachalee Hindi* definite expression in its formative years. Thirdly, according to my observation, the cultural assimilation that took place between various Hindu Missionaries like the Ramakrishna Mission, Vivekananda Kendra Vidhyalayas and Sharda Mission instilled the Hindu way of life to tribal students. It played a significant role in instilling a sense of national integration amongst them and made them conscious of an identity greater than their community identity. This assimilation is also evident in the Donyi-Polo religion of the indigenous people which shows many elements of the Hindu religion. Likewise members of the community perceive many practices similar between their indigenous culture and Hindu culture. My point is that the knowledge of Hindi language facilitated this assimilation to a great extent.

Most importantly, the people of Arunachal Pradesh were aesthetically drawn to the melodious music of both Assamese and Hindi songs. The All India Radio service played an important role in the promotion of Hindi film music and language through news programmes and continues to do so till today. These cultural factors therefore played a crucial role in popularizing Hindi to a great extent in the region.

However with the advent of cable TV networks in the 1980s, the use of Hindi increased to a great extent. It is a fact that, "an Arunachalee feels more comfortable watching news on the Hindi Channel than on an English channel." Also after the introduction of FM radio service *Arunachalee Hindi* has just broadened its scope and acceptability in the wider popular culture of the state.

Today, one can see that Hindi, *Arunachalee Hindi* to be precise, is the most effective language used by the politicians of the state to address a general gathering in the market or any other social function. And it serves as a great medium to especially reach out to the youth.

From the above study we can observe that apart from the institutional support to promote the Hindi language, the cultural and political factors have also contributed in popularizing the use of Hindi to such an extent as to give it a distinct identity, *Arunachalee hindi.*

5. Are the Tribal Languages of Arunachal Pradesh Endangered Today?

The answer to the question above is definitely yes. As stated earlier the future of languages in the context of Arunachal Pradesh definitely shows serious signs of being endangered by the end of this century.

It is important to note that the usability of *Arunachalee Hindi* became effective once the non-tribal population started conversing with tribals in *Arunachalee Hindi.* Ever since that moment in the past the variety got accepted as a form of speech in contact situations.

Now the children are acquiring *Arunachalee Hindi* and not their mother tongue as their first language. It is seen particularly so in the case of urban settings where both the working parents well versed in their native tongue are absent from home for long hours. As a result the child is left in the care of domestic help who speak either in Hindi or Nepali or Assamese to the child. And the child naturally picks up the language of convenience. These children and youth now constitute a category that are educated in English, influenced by western popular culture and speak in *Arunachalee Hindi*. They have a passive knowledge of their mother tongue but cannot speak it.

The situation in the villages however, presents quite a different picture, where everyone around the child is a fluent and competent speaker of the mother tongue. But after the introduction of Dish TV, Tata Sky and other cable networks into the villages, Hindi has reached the rural areas too. There have been instances of children speaking only *Arunachalee Hindi* now. However these are isolated cases but one cannot ignore these trends.

The other areas where *Arunachalee Hindi* affected the culture a great deal is in the use of kinship terms. Greatly criticized by the elders of the community, kinship terms in tribal languages have been replaced by Hindi and English terms significantly. It is especially seen at homes where there is cable TV. For instance, the terms for brother-in-law or sister-in law have been replaced by the Hindi *jijaji, bhabi,* etc. Also the use of *Chacha* (paternal uncle), *mama* (maternal uncle), *bhaiya* (elder brother), *didi* (Sister) etc. is quite common.

It has also replaced and resulted in less use of the grammatical features of the mother tongue. For instance, knowledge of language games, numerals, classifiers, names of months, names of flaura and fauna etc. are all reducing to a large extent amongst the younger generation.

The attitude of non-speakers of the mother tongue to a large extent is negative and indifferent. They feel no motivation for learning their language as '…it is of no use in the wider context…' They assert that "...apart from home and community space there is no scope of using the language. If one doesn't speak one's language it doesn't limit one's opportunities in any way. So not speaking your language is okay. You can learn it later…" This mind set is reflected in almost all of the non-speakers of the mother tongue. To some it is just a means to assert your identity which is often viewed as constricting and narrow in outlook. This generation gap is widening in great proportion.

Then what is the alternative? This brings us to an important issue of which regional language is to be promoted? The present paper cannot discuss this issue here for limitations of scope and space. However, the issue addresses a relevant and old debate on which script should be adopted in order to unify the linguistically divided groups of Arunachal Pradesh.

6. The Debate on Selection of Common Code of Script

Which script should be chosen for the unwritten languages? This pertinent question is not new amongst many tribal elites and literary societies. The issue is as old as the formation of the state. It raised many social and political issues for the people. As mentioned earlier, given a situation of great diversity each community naturally wanted their own community to be promoted, misinterpretation of which resulted in great conflict situations.

The Devanagari script of Hindi was rejected due to its grammatical complexities and orthography. As most of the official dealings and education were conducted in English, naturally the tribals opted for a script that had prestige, power and easy accessibility in terms of technical advancement. An elderly person states "English alphabet is easier to write than Hindi." However in classroom situations Devanagiri serves as a convenient medium of instruction for pedagogical purposes to teach any language especially in terms of representation of sound and sentence translation.

As a solution to the matter at an individual level every tribe through their joint Welfare societies and literary societies decided to promote their script firstly at community level. Roman alphabets with modifications or diacritics were conventionalized for accommodating unique phonetic elements and tones. This has been successfully used by *Adi Agom Kebang* i.e. Adi Literary Society, to document the proceedings and various literary activities. For the community members it is indeed a great achievement for the pursuit of documentation of knowledge and language.

Similarly, the Galo welfare society in consultation with linguists, have come up with a script written in IPA symbols and Roman script which has been used in a Galo-English dictionary. The compilers claim that the learning of the new symbols can be used both in computers and cell phones. Therefore the advantages of the script is that it is 'techno friendly' and easy to learn. However, its applicability, implementation and popularity are yet to be studied.

Another script that was received with mixed reactions was Dr. Toni Koyu's *Tani Lipi* (Tani script). Some sections applauded his attempts in inventing a unifying code of script for the larger Tani group. It was promoted through the State Government by dedicating a section of the newspaper of the state. Several documentaries on

Doordarshan were telecast showing steps to learn and use it. But another section consisting of community members mostly academicians and younger generation vehemently opposed the idea of learning a whole new set of symbols as a script. "...why the need to learn a whole new set of symbols when we have Roman and Devanagari script at hand. Why not utilize these..."

Every effort of promoting one regional language as a common language met with failure. It is in these circumstances that *Arunachalee Hindi* emerged as a common code of language i.e. *lingua franca.*

7. Institutional Support and Documentation

We can mention many initiatives taken by the people and Government to document the languages of Arunachal Pradesh. For instance, documentation of tribal languages has been carried out by the Directorate of Research, Arunachal Pradesh. Since its inception one of the objectives was to prepare pedagogical material in the form of language guides for learning and teaching of tribal languages to the central government employees coming to the state. Various academicians within the community are continuing in documenting their rich oral tradition and other indigenous knowledge systems in the form of books and research papers. In the districts of East Siang and West Siang languages like Adi and Galo have introduced their mother tongues in the school education at primary level respectively. The Arunachal Institute of Tribal Studies, Rajiv Gandhi University offers language package courses which are taught by the native speakers staying in the university campus. In recent years one can also see a lot of linguists taking keen interest on documenting the less explored languages of Arunachal Pradesh.

In the domain of mass media too efforts are on to promote and preserve the local languages. Doordarshan Itanagar, Radio FM, All India Radio etc dedicate slots for news or programmes conducted in regional languages. It is observed that there are programmes and films made with local languages with English subtitles, but movies with Hindi dialogues reach a wider audience especially amongst the illiterate.

So, the awareness of language endangerment is not a new concept to the people of Arunachal Pradesh. As we can see from the above study that community members have done significant work to preserve their culture and language. The problem is why aren't they effective? Why are the numbers of speakers of mother tongue continuing to shift to other dominant languages? Why are the non-learners of mother tongue still not motivated enough to learn their language?

What we severely lack is an excellent and effective Audio-Visual Documentation for pedagogical use of the languages. We lack the technical knowledge to enhance our endeavours to preserve our language and reach out to the larger younger generation. This is the area where we should and can focus. The reason is that this is the popular medium to which the younger generation connects the most. Learning from the story of revitalization efforts of Aboriginal languages in Australia, I sincerely feel that the target group i.e. children and youth, who are educated in English, influenced by western popular culture and speaking in *Arunachalee Hindi*, and those that have a passive knowledge of their language, but cannot speak the language, should be able to access language materials in the form of CDs, videos, bi-lingual dictionaries and language websites even on the internet. We should work on making the easy accessibility of language learning and language teaching materials. Only then can we enhance our efforts to reach out and make available mother tongues to the real learners of the language.

8. Conclusion

To conclude from the study I would like to state that the tribal languages of Arunachal Pradesh are potentially endangered. The problems leading to language endangerment have been addressed before and within the state people have made efforts to teach the language amongst those who do not or have stopped speaking the mother tongue. But the efficacy of language development programmes seems to get neglected as low priority is given to them. The recent factors for the endangerment of languages in Arunachal Pradesh are mainly due to a process of urbanization and homogenization. Raising materialistic pursuits and also aspirations to come up to the mainstream directly or indirectly, plays a decisive role in one's linguistic choice. The youths should understand that the motivation to learn one's mother tongue is not only to maintain our identity but to preserve and know the age old wisdom and knowledge systems of our communities.

References

- Blair, Heather, & Freedmen, Shirley (1995), "Do Not Go Gentle into That Good Night. Rage, against the Dying of the Light" *Anthropology & Education Quarterly*,26, No. 1, pp 27-49. Blackwell Publishing on behalf of the American Anthropological Association http://www.jstor.org/stable/3195906 (Accessed: 08/10/2009 04:31)
- Dorian, Nancy C. (1994) Purism vs. Compromise in Language Revitalization and Language Revival, *Language in Society*, Vol. 23, No. 4, pp. 479-494 Published by: Cambridge University Press ,http://www.jstor.org/stable/4168553 (Accessed: 07/ 10/2009 14:36)

- Fakuade, Gbenga, Matudi Gambo & Abdullahi Bashir (2003) Language Shift from Mother Tongues towards Fulfulde in Adamawa State, Nigeria: Causes and Consequences,*Anthropological Linguistics*, Vol. 45, No. 3, pp. 296-315 Published by: The Trustees of Indiana University on behalf of Anthropological Linguistics, http:// www.jstor.org/stable/30028897 (Accessed: 07/10/2009 09:01)
- Galo Language Development Committee (2009) *Galo- English Dictionery,* First Edition, Galo Welfare Society, Itanagar, Arunachal Pradesh
- Hale, Ken, Michael Krauss, Lucille J. Watahomigie, Akira Y. Yamamoto, Colette Craig, LaVerne Masayesva Jeanne, Nora C. England (1992) Endangered Languages, *Language,* Vol. 68, No. 1 (Mar., 1992), pp. 1-42 Published by: Linguistic Society of America http://www.jstor.org/stable/416368 (Accessed: 07/10/2009 08:45)
- Ladefoged, Peter (1992) Another View of Endangered Languages, *Language,* Vol. 68, No. 4 , pp. 809-811 Published by: Linguistic Society of America , http:// www.jstor. org/ stable/416854 (Accessed: 07/10/2009 08:56)
- Mallikarjun,B., An Expolration into Linguistic Majority -Minority realations In India, Central Institute of Indian Languages, Mysore 570006, India
- McCarty, Teresa L (2003) Revitalising Indigenous Languages in Homogenising Tiimes, *Comparative Education,* Vol. 39, No. 2, Special Number (27): Indigenous Education: New Possibilities, Ongoing Constraints (May, 2003), pp. 147-163 Published by: Taylor & Francis, Ltd. http://www.jstor.org/stable/3099(Accessed: 07/10/2009 09:24)
- Mibang, Tamo (1997) An Attempt For Language Development , *Studies In The History, Economy And Culture Of Arunachal Pradesh,* pp 428-434, Himalayan Publishers
- Ostler, Nicholas (2003) A Loss for Words, *Foreign Policy,* No. 139, pp. 30-31 Published by: Washingtonpost.Newsweek Interactive, http://www.jstor.org/stable/ 3183728 Published by: Washingtonpost.Newsweek Interactive, (Accessed: 07/10/ 2009 09:31)
- Silverstein, M. (1998) "Contemporary Transformations of Local Linguistic Communities" *Annual Review of Anthropology,* Published by: Annual Reviews http:/ /www.jstor.org/stable/223377(Accessed: 07/10/2009 08:46)
- Sun, Tianshin Jackson (1993) *A historical –comparative study the Tani (Mirish) branch in Tibeto Burman,* PhD Thesis, University of California, Berkeley
- Turin, Mark (2005) Language Endangerment and Linguistic Rights in the Himalayas: A Case Study from Nepal, *Mountain Research and Development,* Vol.

25, No. 1, pp. 4-9 Published by: International Mountain Society Stable http://www.jstor.org/stable/3674361 (Accessed: 07/10/2009 08:51)

- Tyagi, Yogesh (2003) Some Legal Aspects of Minority Languages in India, *Social Scientist*, Vol. 31, No. 5/6, pp. 5-28 Published by: Social Scientist , http://www.jstor.org/stable/3518031 (Accessed: 07/10/2009 09:28)
- UNESCO ,*First Language First: Community-based Literacy Programmes for Minority Language Contexts in Asia* , Bangkok, 2005. ISBN 92-9223- 052-2.
- Wuethrich, Bernice (2000) Learning the World's Languages: Before They Vanish, *Science, New Series,* Vol. 288, No. 5469 , pp. 1156-1159 Published by: American Association for the Advancement of Science , http://www.jstor.org/stable/307522 (Accessed: 07/10/2009 09:04)

Conservation and Development of Pahari Languages/Dialects

P.S. Negi Loktus, IAS - INTACH Convenor
Kinnaur, Lahaul and Spiti, Himachal Pradesh

1. Introduction

The Linguistic Survey of India, the first and perhaps the only one, was undertaken by the Government of India around 1894 AD. The need of a 'throroughgoing' linguistic survey of India was spelt out in a resolution adopted by the Congress of Orientalists at its Vienna Session, held in 1886, recognizing the innumerable languages and their dialects spoken by the people of India.

Sir G. A. Grierson was assigned the task of carrying out the survey. This monumental work accomplished by Grierson was produced in eleven volumes (10,000 pages) between the years 1903- 1928, containing what is believed to be only one-eighth of the material collected during the survey. It was further summarized by Dr. Siddheshwar Verma of Vishveshvaranand Vedic Research Institute (VVRI) between 1955-1960 and rewritten by Dr. S. K. Swami of the VVRI in 1967-68.

The Linguistic Survey covers the Himalayan languages; Bhoti; the languages of the Eastern Sub Group, the Western Sub Group, the North Assam Group, the Tibeto-Burman family of Languages, Munda, the Dravidian-Gaudian Languages, Mon-Khmer and the Siamese-Chinese family, the Iranian family and the Gipsy languages. In the Western sub-group of the survey are included the dialects of the Trans Himalayan areas – Kanawari i.e Kanaures sKad of Kinnaur; Manchati/Patni of Lahaul; Chamba Lahuli; Bunan (Gari); Bhoti of Spiti and Kanashi of Malana.

2. Pahari Languages

Pahari languages/dialects spoken in the sub Himalayan region have three main divisions: Nepali, Central Pahari in Kumaon and Garhwal and the Western Pahari Language group spoken in Jaunsar Bawar, Himachal Pradesh and the Western parts of Kashmir etc. These Pahari languages/dialects, according to Grierson, belong to the Indo–Aryan family; but researches done in modern times have revealed that the languages – Kanawari of Kinnaur and Manchati of Lahaul and some other dialects of the Himalayas are indigenous to India.

As described above, the Western Pahari language sub group covers Kanawari i.e. Kanaures sKad of Kinnaur; Patni or Manchati, Chamba Lahuli, Bunan and Tinnan in Lahaul, Kanashi of Malana and Bhoti in Spiti. Manchati and Kanashi are in some way related to Kanaures sKad. In turn, Kanaures sKad is related to the Munda dialects of Central India.

During the last 35 years or so the Department of Language and Culture of Himachal Pradesh has done some identification/listing of the dialects spoken in the state, but not substantially. A survey of the dialects was done eight years ago by the Central Institute of Indian Languages (CIIL) based in Mysore in association with the Department of Language and Culture. So far no report of the analytical survey has been submitted. In any case, the survey does not cover the Trans Himalayan dialects. The Academy of the Department, has in the meantime, developed a *Shabdavali* (Vocabulary) of about 55,000 words in respect of some major dialects spoken in the lower areas of Himachal Pradesh. But, no survey for listing/identification of the dialects of Kinnaur, Lahaul and Spiti (Trans Himalayan region) has been carried out by the Academy.

3. Languages/Dialects of Trans Himalayan Kinnaur, Lahaul & Spiti

In the first decade of the 20th Century when Grierson's team was busy compiling the linguistic survey of India, Pt. Tikka Ram Joshi of the erstwhile State of Bushahr compiled a 'Dictionary and Grammar of Kanawari' (1901 – 1911) single-handed. Further efforts were made in later years to compile a vocabulary of the dialects of Kinnaur. These are:

- 'A Primer of the Kanawari Dialects' by W.C. Negi
- 'A List of Words in Kinner Desh' by Rahul Sankrityayan
- Kanauri Vocabulary in two parts – English-Kanauri & Kanauri-English, by Rev. T. Grahame Bailey (1909), primarily of Hams sKad of Kinnaur.
- A Descriptive Grammar and Vocabulary of Chanali Dialect of Lahaul by Dr. D.D. Sharma.

The above studies are not exhaustive, nor are they the works of linguists. There is a need to conduct investigative research on the languages and dialects of the Trans Himalayan areas of Himachal Pradesh.

3.1 Dialects of Kinnaur

There are seven dialects/languages spoken in Kinnaur and each of them is area specific. The population of the natives of Kinnaur is around 66000 in an area of 6520 sq km and it amazing that there are as many as seven dialects for this small population. These dialects have a mix mainly of 'Shu' (Kiraat dialect/language), Sanskrit, Hindi, Bhoti, Bon, Munda & Dravidian-Gaudian languages. Major dialects spoken are:

- Hams sKad in the lower areas of Kinnaur, from ancient times the *lingua franca* of the people of Kinnaur, and known as Kanaures sKad.
- Jangrami, in the Lippa Valley,
- Shum-cho-sKad in Kanam, Lhabrang, sPilo and Karla.
- Sunnampa sKad in the Gongyul Valley, although in some villages of this valley people speak Hams sKad and Shum-cho-sKad.
- Chhitkuli in Chhitkul and Rakcham villages,
- A mix more of Chhitkuli and less of Bhoti in Nesang, Kuno and Charang villages.
- Bhoti is spoken in Hang Rang Valley – Puh, Namgya, Tashigang, Nako, Chango, Shealkhar, Maling, Leo, Chuling and Hango villages.

Many words are common in all the above mentioned dialects, but some of them differ in respect of the nouns and tenses of verbs. These are said to be Indo-Aryan Languages indigenous to the areas specified in the list above, but they have more indigenous content than Indo-Aryan.

Lamaistic-Buddhist monasteries were established in the upper areas of Kinnaur district after the 12th Century AD or so. In the absence of Hindu Brahmans, or priests, in the District, the natives used 'Chos' i.e. Buddha-vachana, *mantras* particularly for birth and death ceremonies, which are in the Tibetan language, interspersed with vocabulary from the local dialects of Kinnaur. Another reason for the Tibetan influence in some of these dialects is the trade between Kinnaur and Tibet which has existed since 1683 AD. Now that the area has opened up again after Independence, officials and traders from outside have come into the District and modern education has been introduced through schools; Hindi vocabulary is therefore extensively used. The local dialects do not have their own scripts and use the Devnagari script of Hindi these days, while the Urdu (nastaliq) script was earlier used.

Earlier, Hams sKad was the *lingua-franca,* and it continues to be so in the lower and middle areas. In the upper areas, Shum-Cho sKad, an easy language with a touch of Sanskrit and Hindi, is the *lingua-franca*. An interesting though alarming development has taken place in the usage of the region's dialects in modern times i.e. the children studying outside Kinnaur and the children of spouses speaking different dialects from the local mother tongue, speak and converse exclusively in Hindi. Even in conversation with the deities, the Shu-dialect[1] now includes Hindi , English and Urdu vocabulary (because the revenue records are in Hindi and Urdu). The natives realize that the local dialects will face extinction in the near future.

3.2 Dialects of Lahaul and Spiti

Dialects spoken in Lahaul are:

- Tinan in Chandra Valley
- Bunan (Gari) in Bhaga Valley
- Manchati in Pattan or Chandra-Bhaga Valley.
- Chanali in Pattan Valley
- Chamba-Lahuli in Udaipur sub division of Lahaul

These dialects of Lahaul are said to be Indo-Aryan. However, Bunan has over 50% Bhoti words because of the earlier Ladakhi influence.

Manchati is the dialect spoken by the majority in Lahaul. However, Lahulis can converse in most other dialects when they meet people from other valleys.

Spiti

Bhoti is the standard language of Spiti. The religious *Chos* are in the Tibetan language.

As in the case of the dialects of Kinnaur the dialects of Lahaul and Spiti are also run over by Hindi on account of the introduction of education through schools and the use of the Hindi medium. Hindi words are extensively used, particularly by the younger generation and by those natives who have settled outside Lahaul, particularly in Kullu.

The local INTACH Chapter has done a preliminary survey on the status of the dialects of Kinnaur, Lahaul and Spiti. Although these dialects might face extinction, perhaps by the end of the next generation, none of them is as yet in a state of attrition. However, conservation efforts are needed to avoid an otherwise certain future loss.

4. Recommendations

It is recommended that investigative research on the languages/dialects - 10 of them listed in Kinnaur and 6 of them in Lahaul & Spiti - in the Trans Himalaya should be conducted at the earliest. These languages/dialects do not have scripts of their own. And, the fact that each dialect is area specific should help us analyse the movement of communities into the interior Trans Himalayan area which is also criss-crossed by the fabled silk/trade routes.

[1] *Shu dialect is used by the Shu Mathes for conversation with the Shu (deities) on Rathang in public proceedings. An investigative research is needed to establish linguistic affinity the Shu dialect has with the Kiraat dialect, if any.*

At least seven tribes moved into parts of Kinnaur and some four tribes moved into Lahaul and Spiti at different times before the 10th century AD. This is borne out by the fact that Ring-Chen-Bzan Po (958-1055 AD) had listed, during his lifetime, many villages of Kinnaur, Lahaul and Spiti for establishing Lhakhangs (*religious*). Legends date some of these human settlements as far back as the 4th century BC. Dravidians, perhaps Gaudians of the Dravidian-Gaudian group, and some other tribes had moved into the interior during the period of the great deluge, i.e. around 3500 BC, when the human habitats in the northern plains at the foot of the Western Himalayas were inundated. This is said to be a reason for the affinity between the dialects of Kinnaur and Lahaul with Munda, a dialect of Central India. Researches based on Grierson's Linguistic Survey have revealed that the Kanawari language has more traces of the non-Tibeto-Burman sub-stream than any other Himalayan dialect, and that the old language must have belonged to the Munda family, (as in '*Uneyk*' for Sun and '*Tee*' for water).

5. Conservation Work

Some urgent conservation work should be undertaken for the preservation and development of certain dialects spoken by the majority in Kinnaur and Lahaul & Spiti, as listed below:

- Kanawri-Hams sKad, the *lingua franca* of Kinnaur
- Kanawri-Sum-cho-sKad, the *lingua franca* of upper Kinnaur
- Shu dialect – though esoteric[2] needs to be conserved to help preserve oral traditions which must always remain oral. The reason for this is that the *Chiranings* i.e. the revelation made by the Oracles on behalf of the Deities, and the *Shu – Geethang* (divine song) sung are totally oral. Because the *Chiranings* are not read out or recited as these are revealed orally, nor are the *Shu – Geethang* sung by reading the text of the song. These need to be documented and kept in the archives of the deities to save them from distortion and mis-interpretation.
- Manchati dialect of Lahaul spoken by the majority people of Lahaul.
- Bhoti spoken in Hang Rang valley of Kinnaur and in the Spiti sub division of Lahaul and Spiti district.

INTACH Central Office may take up with the State government of Himachal Pradesh the recommendations made in this paper. The Chapter is already at its own level actively engaged in efforts to persuade the State government to undertake conservation projects in this regard.

---

2 *Understood only by the Chief Kardar (Mohtmeem); Shu-Mathes who holds conversation with the Deities; Oracle who makes revelation while in trance on behalf of the Deities, Pujaris and other functionaries of the Deity.*

Preliminary Research on Tibeto-Burman Language of *Zhang Zhung* and Related Western Himalayan Languages of *Kinnara Kirata*

Tshering Dorje - Buddhologist, Knowledge Holder, Lahaul and Spiti, Himachal Pradesh

Introduction

Till the recent past, people outside Tibet, hardly had any knowledge about the Zhang Zhung (Zz. here after) language and ancient Bon religion of Tibet. Recent researches of scholars have indicated that Zz is from the Tibeto-Burman (TB) linguistic family, and was spoken by the people of Western Tibet and adjacent Himalayan regions.

The kingdom of Zhang Zhung was located in Western Tibet and played an important role in Central Asia before the 7th century AD. This kingdom was annexed into the Tibetan Empire by Srong Tsan Gampo, the King of Tibet, in the 7th century AD and Zz was gradually replaced by Tibetan; the latter became the dominant language with the introduction of Buddhism and the Tibetan writing system. Finally Zz died out around the 12th century, but survived in the Himalayan region among the Kinnar populace where it is still in use.

After the unsuccessful Lhasa uprising against China's occupation of Tibet, thousands of Tibetans fled from their homeland and took asylum in India. They were settled in various refugee camps by the Indian Government. I had the chance to visit one such camp near Solan in the Shimla Hills, where the Tibetan Bonpo community had taken shelter. I was curious to learn about the Bonpo spiritual way of life and was able to discover the very root of my mother tongue and other branches of the Tibetan linguistic family spoken in the Western Himalayan Region.

While discussing the Bon way of spiritualism, I met Ven. Sangye Tanzin Jongdong, a monk, and learned that the teachings were propagated in Zz in the country of Zhang zhung, and had come initially from Tag.Zik (may be the Tajikistan of today). The Abbot handed me a Tibetan-Zz dictionary, written in Tibetan characters. I was amazed when I found many words of my dialect and several other dialects, spoken by different ethnic groups in the Western Himalayan region of Himachal Pradesh and further east in Uttarakhand.

I have tried to classify the TB languages, generally known as Kinnara Kirat (Kk), spoken by several different ethnic groups in the Himalayas.

Classification of TB Languages of Western Himalayas.

(Link between Zhang Zhung and Kinnar a Kirat languages of TB)

My research reveals that Zz has a very close linguistic affinity with the Kinnara-Kirata (Kk) languages. It seems that both may have originated from the same root of TB and that both the speaker groups may have had a common ancestor. About the ancient Kinnara tribe, vivid mention has been made in the Epic and Purana literature of India. The King of Kinnara attended discourses of the Buddha at Griddha Kuta mountain, near Rajagriha, the capital Magadha.

Kalhan's Rajatarangini gives us information about the occupation of the Trigata country by the Kirata. Chamba a tiny hill country in the Western Himalayas was also annexed by the forces of the Kirata community during the reign of Raja Shaila Verman in the 10th century C.E. The chronicle of Nepal refers to the country being ruled by aboriginal ruling families of Kirata or Kiranta prior to the conquest by the Licchavis, a group of Northern Indian origin, whose history goes back to the Buddha's time. Following the Licchavi conquest, Kiratas migrated to the east of the valley. Ancient Nepal has been referred to as Kiranta, probably the central and eastern part of today's Nepal, and the language spoken by the different tribes was known as Kiranti, before the establishment of the Gorkha dynasty. Among the Kiranti speaking tribes are included Tamong, Gurung, Sunwar, Magar, Rai, Limbu, Thakali and a host of others.

Nothing has been particularly mentioned about the trans-Himalayan country of Zhang Zhung in early Indian records, though several names from the north of India have been mentioned. Among these, I would like to emphasize two, "Kimpursha Varsha" and "Hun Desha". Kinnara has also been mentioned as Kimpurusha in the early records of India. Being Zz language speakers, the nomadic people of the Zhang zhung country might have been referred to as Kimpurusha in early India. As with Huna, Zhunga may be a corrupt version of Zhang Zhung. Hence it is Huna or Zhunga desh. The Chinese refer to it as Yangtung.

It may not be out of place to mention the Bon religion, the pre-buddhist faith of the Tibetans. Before the propagation of Indian Buddhism in Tibet in the 8th century AD, the Tibetans practised a religion known as Bon or Bonpo, which involved the worship of natural forces, heavily blended with folk beliefs and rituals. It is said that this was propagated by the great preceptor gShen-rab Mio for the first time in the country of Zhang Zhung in the Zz language. He had come here from Ta.zig or Tag.zig region (Tajikistan?); though some European scholars trace him to Sogdiana and Bactria. Owing to the introduction of Buddhism in Tibet and conversion of the royalty to the new faith, Bonpo gradually fell into oblivion. However, a handful of believers remained faithful to gShen-rab's doctrine. To them survival of the Bon doctrine was supreme, though they assimilated some spiritual practices, including logic, from Buddhism. This came to be known as later propagated Bon or Swatika Bon. Bon has variously been translated by scholars and Bon priests as 'implore', 'beseech', 'murmur', 'recite', 'chant', 'invoke', 'summon' etc. My view is that the word comes from 'boun', that is, 'Brahmin' or 'priest' in the languages of the Indian Himalayas including Nepali. This may have become 'Bon' in Tibetan languages, or 'priest absolute'. The reason Zz did not vanish without trace is that it is purported to be the tongue of the Bon religion.

Session 4

Language of Education and Empowerment (Language & Power)

The Language Loss Pandemic and Language Wellness Issues

Prof. Panchanan Mohanty - Centre of Applied Linguistics and Translation Studies, University of Hyderabad

1. A Prelude

On 19 September 2009, *The Hindu* published a news item as follows:

Hogs to be reintroduced in forest

West Bengal's Forest Department has decided to reintroduce the critically endangered pigmy hog in North Bengal's Gorumara forest.

The department has sought a feasibility report for the project from the Zoological Survey of India (ZSI).

After a successful release of the hunched, barely two-feet long, [sic] furry hogs into the wild at Sonai Rupai Wildlife Sanctuary and Nameri National Park in Assam in 2008, the Forest Department wants to replicate the experiment in the forests of north Bengal, since it falls in the region that is the original home of the wild suids (pigs), said A.K. Sanyal, additional director of ZSI.

"The pigmy hogs were seen at the Gorumara forest till a few years back, which is why it was decided to reintroduce them there as a measure to restore the biodiversity of the area," said P.K. Ray, the State's Additional Principal Chief Conservator of Forests (Wildlife).

"Earlier, they were easily located in Nepal, Bhutan and India, but they are not found anywhere other than Assam today – a situation that must be changed," said Dr. Sanyal.[1]

---

[1] The Hindu (Hyderabad, India), 19 September 2009, p. 20.

The significant expressions used in this news item are: "…it was decided to reintroduce them there as a measure to restore the biodiversity of the area" and "… a situation that must be changed". Before commenting on these expressions, it would be in the fitness of things to quote some statistics about the level of endangerment of various species of animals and birds vis-à-vis languages all over the world. The following data taken from Harrison (2007:7) is self-explanatory:

Fish: 5%, Plants: 8%, Birds: 11%, Mammals: 18 %, Languages: 40+%

The precarious condition of languages is conspicuous, but it was not noticed till the 1990s. That is why, when a large number of projects have been supported with very liberal funding everywhere for the preservation of biodiversity, nothing like that has happened to conserve the linguistic and cultural diversity among the peoples of the world. The above news item evidences the seriousness of the Government of India to conserve and preserve biodiversity whereas the same kind of concern for endangered languages is unheard of. Restoration and change of the situation by introducing hogs in the forests of West Bengal is certainly important from the environmental and ecological point of view. It must be emphasised here that survival of a language that holds a speech-community, its culture, and its knowledge systems together is also equally important. But news items regarding the efforts to preserve languages are extremely rare in the Indian news media. What is shocking is that about one third of the total population of the world's languages has not been documented yet. This means there is no record of more than 2000 languages. If by chance, these languages die before they are documented, we will lose an enormous amount of indigenous knowledge without even knowing what we have lost. This is certainly not commensurate with the interests of the world's intellectuals.

The Summer Institute of Linguistics *Survey* published in 1999, presents the following figures about the status of a number of languages under the threat of extinction: There were 51 languages with one speaker each and 28 of them were in Australia. About 500 languages had less than 100 speakers, 1500 languages less than 1000 speakers, 3000 languages less than 10,000 speakers, and 5,000 languages less than 100,000 speakers. If we tabulate this data, we will see that a staggering 96% of languages are spoken by a meagre 4% of the population and a meagre 4% of the languages are spoken by a staggering 96% of the population. Even though this situation is visibly catastrophic, it has not been able to draw the attention of the people who matter in this world. On the basis of two judgements from the Foundation of Endangered Languages that about 50% of the world's languages will face extinction in the next 100 years, Crystal (2000: 19) has calculated that "To meet that time frame, at least one language must die, on average, every two weeks or so. This cannot be very far from the truth." There is a still more alarming prediction that "...upto 90% of the world's languages may well be replaced by dominant languages by the end of the 21st century, which would reduce the present number of almost 7,000 languages to less than 700." (*Brenzinger & de Graaf n.d.:1*). But the irony is that, unlike the issue of preservation of biodiversity, hardly any serious steps are being taken at the national or international levels for protection of these fast vanishing voices. A few volunteer groups have been trying to make their voice heard by the world's citizens, but it is not loud enough and hence, the outcome is far from adequate.

There is a near complete silence with reference to the situation in India where plurality is practised and variation is expressed in day-to-day life. This has naturally led to discrimination among the languages of India in spite of the constitutional safeguards. Due to economic and political reasons some languages are perceived to be more than equal by other speech communities, and that is why the domains and spaces of the latter languages are slowly shrinking giving way to occupation by the former. In this paper, I will discuss some of these issues along with suggestions for empowerment and revitalization of endangered languages with reference to the Indian context.

2. Language Situation in the Developed World

The inhabitants of the present United States of America spoke some 250 to 350 indigenous languages before the arrival of European immigrants more than two centuries ago (Crawford 1999). Linguistic and cultural diversity was tolerated in that country for about a century and after that an English-only attitude spread and occupied both public and private spaces. For instance, an English-only instruction was mandated in California in 1855. Then, the Bureau of Indian Affairs started implementing its language suppression policies ruthlessly around the 1880s (Ibid.). As a result, English bossed over the innocent minor languages and, over a period of time, English monolingual education became the mainstream. The Americanization Department of the United States Bureau of Education passed a resolution in 1919 recommending that education in all schools, i.e. both public and private, be imparted in English including the elementary classes (*Garcia 1992*).

In spite of the 1964 Civil Rights Act that regulated against discrimination on the basis of colour, race and origin, intervention of the judiciary as well as efforts of various activist groups, English remains the dominant medium of instruction in the U.S. educational system. Regarding intervention of the judiciary, the 1970 lawsuit by some non-English speaking Chinese students against the San Francisco School District is considered a landmark and known as the 'Lau vs. Nichols case'. Though it was rejected by the federal district court and another court of appeals, the Supreme Court admitted it in 1974 and ruled: "There is no equality of treatment merely by providing students with the same facilities, textbooks, teachers and curriculum; for students who do not understand English are effectively foreclosed from any meaningful education." (*Baker 2001: 186*). As a result, a compensatory 'poverty programme' was introduced which encouraged a few teachers to use the 'home languages' in classroom while imparting education in English. The name 'poverty programme' indicates the government's attitude towards the people who are supposed to go through it. Even President Ronald Regan was quoted to have said the following in *The New York Times* of 3 March 1981 with reference to educating the linguistic minorities in their languages: "It is absolutely wrong and against the American concept to have a bilingual education programme that is now openly, admittedly, dedicated to preserving their native language and never getting them adequate English so they can go out into the job market." (Ibid. 187-8) Hence, the famous joke I have heard from my American friends: "If you speak many languages, you are multilingual. If you speak two languages, you are bilingual. If you speak one language, you are American." Therefore, it is no wonder that 155 out of the 175 native American languages are in the endangered category (*Krauss 1992*).

Let us now have a bird's eye-view on the situation in Europe. The European Union declared the year 2001 as the European Year of Languages and the desired goal was to lay the foundation for a multilingual Europe: "All those leaving compulsory education should be able to communicate in at least two European languages in addition to their mother tongue and then be able to build on that knowledge for the rest of their lives."[2] But the ground realities seem contradictory. Many European countries believe that "... knowledge of the heritage language is something that is unnecessary at best and detrimental to integration into the dominant society at worst." (*Schmid 2002: 355*) This is clearly reflected in withdrawal of funding for various heritage language teaching programmes in European public schools.

The situation in Australia is no better. After a detailed analysis of the Australian situation, Fishman (1991) has come to a grim conclusion that these Aboriginal languages do not have any long-term survival prospects. Whatever

---

[2] *http://www.europe.eu.int/comm/education/policies/lang/languages/actions/year2001_en.html*

may be the propaganda regarding protection and preservation of the 'small' languages, all these facts uncover the stark realities prevailing in the developed world.

3. Is India a Safe Haven?

Of late, scholars have started presenting case studies on language loss and language shift in different linguistics seminars and conferences in India. It is undoubtedly a good sign, because it is indicative of an increase in the level of awareness in the phenomenon. But there are two questions that demand attention:

i. Is the Indian situation comparable to those prevalent in the U.S., Europe and Australia?
ii. Is it enough to discuss the problems only? If not, what are the remedies?

Let us discuss these questions in some detail.

A close look at the Indian situation makes it evident that it is different from the situation in the developed countries. As we have seen above, monolingualism is the fundament on which linguistic structures have been built in the western world, whereas multilingualism is the very basis of Indian society. Most of the *adivasi* or primitive languages have diminished in the U.S. and Australia within hardly two centuries, whereas hundreds of languages have survived on Indian soil through millennia. Indian languages have learned to co-exist though they have converged with each other and at the same time maintained their individual identities. This has been demonstrated in a fascinating study by Gumperz and Wilson (1971) on the linguistic situation in an Indian village named Kupwar. The three languages spoken in this village are Kannada, a Dravidian language, and Urdu and Marathi that belong to the Indo-Aryan family. Bilingualism and multilingualism in this village are wide-spread, and it is common to see people switching back and forth between at least two languages. This has made the grammatical structures of these three languages so similar that a word-for-word rendering among them is possible. Finegan and Besnier (1989:386) have called this phenomenon "Having your cake and eating it too." Though Myers-Scotton (1992:33) has argued that "...code-switching is involved in language death." and "...at least some instances of language death may involve the pervasive addition or substitution of the grammar of another language in the code-switching situation.", the Kupwar example cited above does not substantiate this argument. Since she has elaborated her views on the basis of African languages, it can be claimed that the linguistic situation of India is different not only from that of the Western world, but also from the African one.

It is, of course, true that many languages known to us have died over a period of time, and such natural deaths are inevitable. Some major and powerful languages like Sanskrit and various Prakrits that received support from rulers, religious leaders and the masses are included in this type of death. But as far as the minor languages are concerned, Lo Bianco and Rhydwen (2001: 394) have proposed two types of loss: "...an abrupt dislocative and extreme form and a slower, generational, attrition. The former often results in the total disruption of all transmission (and of any later re-learning prospects) of the language, while the second can, at best, retain within the living memory of speakers sufficient language resources on which to base a revival or renewal activity. The former may be called language loss by *rupture* and the latter language loss by *attrition*." Though this distinction is made with reference to the indigenous languages of Australia, it is applicable to the loss of minor languages in general. Interestingly, 'language loss by rupture' is typically a western phenomenon and has hardly taken place in India. But the second type of loss, i.e. 'language loss by attrition' is a common feature across the Indian subcontinent.

4. Get Scared or Look Ahead?

There have been a number of scary forecasts regarding the fast decline of languages. Way back in the 15th century certain English academics had predicted that after the people received a better education in languages like Latin and French, English would not remain a 'language of learning' (*Mackey 2003:64*). Again, in a symposium on the fate of minority languages in America, the participating linguists predicted, in the 1940s, that most of these languages, including French, would die by the end of the 20th century (Ibid.). Then, in his 1894 article entitled "Bengali Literature", R. N. Tagore stated: "... the Bengali language had no status and enjoyed no respect; knowledge of Bengali brought no one either glory or money; expression of thought in Bengali was difficult and it was almost impossible to bring ideas to the people. It was neither patronised by the Rajas nor inspired by scholars." (*Kluyev 1981:115*). But contrary to these predictions and statements, today English is the most dominant international language, French has a more elevated status in Quebec than earlier, and Bengali is a developed and strong language in the Indian subcontinent. The lesson we learn from these predictions is that all of them need not always be true. Therefore, we must worry about means of change and improvement and not get so scared that we allow the situation to deteriorate. Now the question is: How do we improve the situation?

Though the linguistic situation in India is inextricably complex, language planning activities certainly do not match that complexity and have, in fact, been superficial to a great extent. Schiffman (1996) has proposed a concept of 'linguistic culture' that can greatly influence the prospects of a country's language policy. He has argued that unless we understand the covert linguistic culture of a country that consists of the belief systems, ideas and attitudes about its languages, we cannot achieve success in implementing the overt language policies. I am not aware of any study conducted to discover the covert linguistic culture of India. So, it is natural for the overt language policies to lie hidden in the files of government offices.

We know that Indian society is in an unprecedented state of flux and transition, and that a large number of Indians belonging to different strata have been making efforts to join the national/international mainstream which has resulted in radical changes in the global economy. As a result, the good old joint family structure has broken down and nuclear families are the trend now. All these people live in 'houses' and the concept of 'home' has become a thing of the past. They are uprooted from the 'home-land' and have left the 'home-language' behind.

Ostler (2005: 526-8) has interpreted the statistics of the world's top twenty languages in an innovative and interesting way. The positions of these languages are as follows:

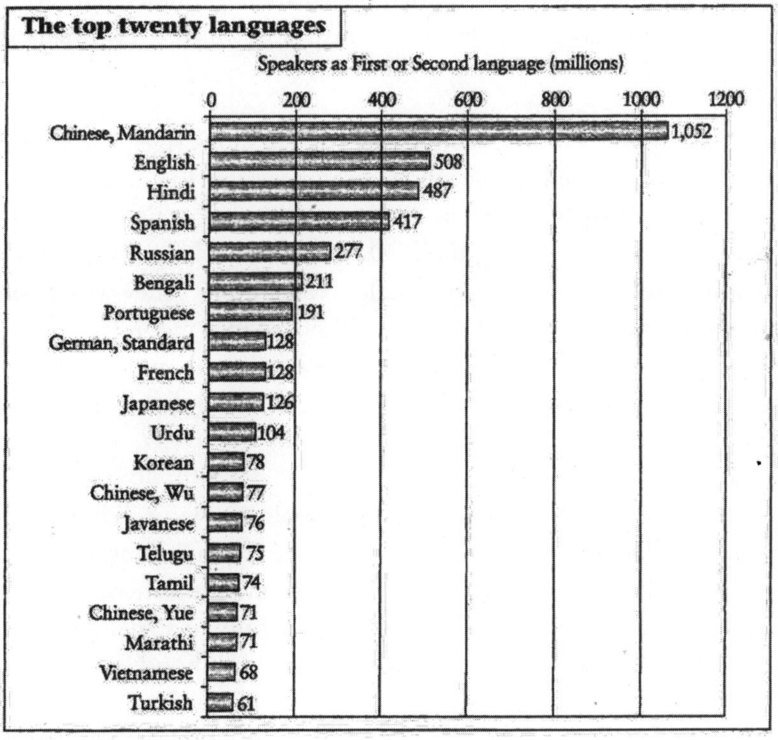

(from Ostler 2005: 526)

Ostler (Ibid.: 527-8) has observed: "In the world's top twenty, all the languages have their origin in the south or east of Asia, or in Europe. ... What accounts for their growth, then? It is noticeable that a great many of the languages (nine out of twenty) are spoken in the civilisations sustained by rice as a staple crop (Bengali, Japanese, Korean, Wu and Yue Chinese, Javanese, Tamil, Marathi, Vietnamese). Evidently, rice is capable of supporting dense and extensive populations, and its cultivation, through controlled flooding, requires a high level of organization. Other languages which are not predominantly in the rice area are spoken in the neighbouring areas that have assumed political control of the rice areas (Mandarin Chinese, and Hindi and Urdu, which are linguistically in direct continuum if they are distinct at all)". If we add Telugu, which belongs to the rice-eating area and has been left out by Ostler, to the above list, 50% of the world's top twenty languages are spoken in the area where rice is a staple food. These interesting observations strengthen the above hypothesis that the relationship of 'rootedness' to a land is a key factor in preservation of languages. The implication is that a change in the physical environment will obviously alter the linguistic and cultural environment of the concerned society. Due to large scale migrations from villages to towns and cities as well as rapid spread of the urban pop culture, the second generation everywhere has neither a 'home-land' nor a 'home-language'. They are a part of the 'motley mainstream' which is essentially similar all over the world.

These civilised persons do not know that the ferocious tiger, the shrewd jackal, the copycat monkey as well as the silvery moon are our /ma:mi/ 'maternal uncle' (*Mohanty 2008*); and the dark patch on the moon's surface is caused by a brown rabbit's dead body, which is lying there. Or that while taking a vaccine if children look in the direction of their maternal uncle's 'sweet home', they will experience no pain. They also do not hear a pied-crested cuckoo calling /mita/ 'friend' in summer. The folk belief is that this bird does not drink water stored on the earth; so when it is thirsty, it calls to its friend cloud to release rain-water so that it can slake its thirst while flying.

Most of these persons have not sung a prayer in Oriya or Telugu or Maithili, nor have they laughed delightedly at hilarious jokes in their mother tongue. They have not heard lullabies from their mothers and grandmothers before going to sleep and have never jumped with joy or clung fearfully to a friend while listening to the animated narration of a story during their childhood. At the most, they have heard and sung some English and Hindi nursery rhymes without understanding their meaning and read English translations of the *Panchatantra, Ramayana, Mahabharata*, and fables from other parts of the world. All these have handicapped them to such an extent that they do not know the names of the Indian months and what the months, such as Vaishakha (April-May), Jyestha (May-June), Ashadha (June-July), and Shravana (July-August), etc. signify. Let us consider the following Oriya saying:

jyeSThe kadaLi a:sa:Dhe kia:
pota na pota hoiba Thia:

It means: 'Banana saplings in the month of Jyestha and screwpine saplings in the month of Ashadha will grow very well whether you plant them properly or not.' There is no need to emphasize the importance of such sayings to farmers. But most educated farmers are not even aware of their existence. It needs to be mentioned here that the older generation living in quiet Indian villages are not at all familiar with the English calendar. Their life moves according to the traditional Indian calendar which most modern citizens do not understand. Many of the latter people also find it difficult to name more than five flowers, five fruits, five birds and five animals in their own languages. They may know more words for these in English or Hindi even if they have never seen them. Here I must cite what Whorf (1956:135) observed regarding the cause of fire-accidents in the U.S. at the time: "My analysis was directed toward purely physical conditions, such as defective wiring, presence or lack of air spaces between metal flues and woodwork, etc., and the results were presented in these terms. Indeed it was undertaken with no thought that any other significances would or could be revealed. But in due course it became evident that not only a physical situation *qua* physics, but the meaning of that situation to people, in the start of the fire. And this factor of meaning was clearest when it was a LINGUISTIC MEANING, residing in the name or the linguistic description commonly applied to the situation. Thus, around a storage of what are called 'gasoline drums', behavior will tend to a certain type, that is, great care will be exercised; while around a storage of what are called 'empty gasoline drums,' it will tend to be different-careless, with little repression of smoking or of tossing cigarette stubs about. Yet the 'empty' drums are perhaps the more dangerous, since they contain explosive vapor. Physically the situation is hazardous, but the linguistic analysis according to regular analogy must employ the word 'empty', which inevitably suggests lack of hazard. Following this logic we can argue that the persons for whom it is hard to name more than five flowers, five fruits, five birds and five animals in their own languages would perceive the natural environment around them as an undifferentiated and not-so-useful continuum. If this argument is accepted, then how can we expect them to be sensitive to and concerned about the conservation of bio-diversity? For these reasons, a sound knowledge of the mother tongue is crucial for appreciating bio-diversity and the protection of the environment. Not only that, the native words for lower order numerals, kinship, and body parts have been replaced to a regrettable extent by those of English and Hindi in these people's language.

I have been utterly surprised and disappointed to see one of my colleague's daughters run to her mother to find out the meaning of /a:lua/, an extremely common Oriya word denoting 'light', because her grandmother told her in Oriya / a:lua libheide/ 'Switch off the light'. The little girl knew the English word 'light', but not the Oriya /a:lua/, though her home-language was Oriya. Many such examples can be cited to show how Indian home-languages are shrinking and giving way to English and/or Hindi.

Needless to say, *diglossia* is a part of life for most indigenous linguistic communities in this country. They speak the L(ow)-language for effective social functions and the H(igh)-language for prestige-oriented and informative functions. When a community starts using the H-language in effective and social domains, it is a clear sign of endangerment. Thus, the above example is simply a case of language loss. If this can happen to Oriya, the official language of the state of Orissa and one of the languages recognised by the Constitution of India way back in 1950, the condition of the minor tribal and indigenous languages can easily be imagined.

5. Language Revitalization and Empowerment

This brings us to the question of language revitalization and empowerment. Giles (1977) has proposed the concept called 'ethnolinguistic vitality' to predict the maintenance of a language by its speakers. He has emphasized three components:

a) the speech community's attitude towards its language,
b) the size of the community and its distribution, and
c) institutional support for the language concerned.

I am not aware of any large scale study to determine different Indian language speakers' attitudes towards their own languages. But all studies on endangerment of Indian languages, whether major or minor, adduce evidence in support of a weak and/or negative attitude towards these languages. Needless to say, proper documentation and rank-ordering of various Indian languages with reference to their speakers' attitudes are absolutely necessary so that the languages at the bottom of the list can be immediately attended to.

The size of a community is undoubtedly a determining factor in preserving a language. It would be preferable to rephrase this criterion as 'concentration of speakers or speech-community in one place'. Though the governments of Maharashtra, Orissa, and Tamil Nadu have to provide the required facilities for teaching Telugu to Telugu speaking children in the respective states, this need not be our primary concern. We must first concentrate on the status of Telugu in Andhra Pradesh itself where Telugu is the dominant language. At another level, maintenance of the Dravidian tribal language Kui by the migrant Kandha *adivasis* or aboriginals at Bhubaneswar, the capital of Orissa, is a secondary problem. The main concern is whether Kui is maintained in its home-land within the interior districts of Orissa. But as we know, a large section of Kandha *adivasis* are monolingual Oriya speakers today (*Mohanty 1994*). Therefore, revitalization in such cases is a priority.

The third component of institutional support for language education in India is at best a parody of what it should have been. Two of my non-Oriya speaking students, who had completed their school and college education in Orissa, including studying Oriya as a subject in school, are not able to speak Oriya. It is well known that tribal language education has never been a serious business in this country. I have met hundreds of teachers from every nook and corner of India at the Centre for Cultural Resources and Training, Hyderabad, who have not even heard of the National Curriculum Framework 2005 (NCF 2005) after four years of its existence. Many learned people as well as teachers think that tribal languages are 'dialects' because they are not written; and for that reason, they need not be taught or used as media in education. All these warrant a complete revamp of mother tongue/ first language teaching at every level, and a thorough planning for tribal language education in this country.

Under the impact of globalization, a number of changes are taking place in this country over which we have no control. Therefore, the breaking down of joint families cannot be reversed. The movement of linguistic groups from their home-land to other language speaking areas for greener pastures cannot be checked. Interlingual marriages cannot be prevented. But we can do a number of things that will ultimately lead the endangered language speaking communities to empowerment.

- The first and the easiest step is to record data on each and every language spoken in this country in the decennial Census reports.

- The next significant step would be to provide these languages with scripts of their own in consultation with the concerned communities, because it will give them a separate identity along with a proud feeling that their language is comparable to the so-called developed languages. We know that tribal communities possess a very rich oral literature and a vast wealth of alternative knowledge systems. Once a writing system is in place for each of these languages, the speakers may be encouraged to document these treasures, and in the process this will bring recognition and visibility.

- Newspapers, books and magazines can also be published for the people speaking these languages which will involve them in working with them.

- Radio and television are not only an integral part of every household today; they are the most powerful media. With the kind of advanced technology available in India, it is quite feasible to start community radio and television channels for most of these indigenous linguistic groups. This will not only revitalise the domain of creative literature but also open up new entertainment avenues which, in turn, will act as a filter and prevent the speakers softening towards other dominant languages.

- The goal of the Indian Bilingual Education Programmes meant for the linguistic minorities is not conducive to promote stable and additive bilingualism, because a switch from the first language to the dominant second language within a few years gives the speakers a clear impression that their languages are not-so-important from the political, economic and cultural points of view. Pattanayak (1981:90) has rightly remarked: "Unless a strategy for transition from the home language to school language is built into the elementary education of tribal children it is almost impossible to meet their learning needs." This integration is an immediate necessity. On the other hand, speakers of the major and dominant languages may be encouraged to learn these minor languages, possibly by making the knowledge of such a language obligatory for various jobs in the government sector.

- One of the major tasks of the National Knowledge Commission of India is 'creation and preservation of knowledge systems'. I have mentioned earlier that the indigenous languages are unexplored store-houses of alternative knowledge systems. Ethnic medicine is a very good example. Therefore, the NKC should make an all out effort for documentation and preservation of indigenous languages and cultures before it is too late. Then, 'transforming India into a knowledge society' is one of the main objectives of the NKC; therefore, the alternative and indigenous knowledge base has to be an indispensable part of it. This will also fully conform to the spirit and ethos of pluralistic India. All these support what a wise man had stated: "... nothing benefits a country more than to treasure the languages and cultures of its various peoples because in doing so, it fosters intergroup understanding and realises greater dividends in the form of originality, creativity and versatility." (*Herder, quoted in Fishman1978: 49-50*).

- Another significant step would be to establish a national body that would not only redress the problems faced by the minor and indigenous speech-communities, but also be entirely devoted to teaching, research, documentation and preservation of the minor and indigenous languages of this country.

6. Concluding Remarks

To conclude, I would like to emphasise that linguistics is a highly democratic discipline in the sense that it strongly believes in equality among languages. Every language, whether it is Toda in the Nilgiri Hills or Savara in the dense forests of southern Orissa, has a right to live its full life and is equal to any 'international' language in this world. That is why Sapir (1979: 219), one of the founders of modern linguistics, had long ago remarked: "When it comes to linguistic forms, Plato walks with the Macedonian swineherd, Confucius with the head-hunting savage of Assam." I should close this discourse with what Holmes (2000:183) has said in another context: "Let the meta-discussion begin."

References:

- Baker, C. 2001. *Foundations of Bilingual Education and Bilingualism*. Clevedon: Multilingual Matters.
- Brenzinger, M. (ed.) 1992. *Language Death: Factual and Theoretical Explorations with Special Reference to East Africa*. Berlin, New York: Mouton de Gruyter.
- Brenzinger, M. and T. de Graaf n.d. Documenting endangered languages and language maintenance. Contribution to the UNESCO Encyclopedia of Life Supporting Systems (EOLSS) 6.20B.10.3. (downloaded from internet on 15-10-2009) Crawford, J. 1999. *Bilingual Education: History, Politics, Theory and Practice*. Los Angeles: Bilingual Educational Series. (4th ed.)Crystal, D. 2000. *Language Death*. Cambridge: Cambridge University Press.

- Finegan, E. and N. Besnier 1989. *Language: Its Structure and Use.* San Diego: Harcourt Brace Jovanovich Fishman, J. A. 1978. Positive bilingualism: some overlooked rationales and forefathers. in *International Dimensions of Bilingual Education*, ed. by J Alatis. Washington, DC: Georgetown University Press, pp. 42-52.
- Fishman, J. A. 1991. *Reversing Language Shift.* Clevedon: Multilingual Matters.

  Garcia, O. 1992. For it is in giving that we receive: A history of language policy in the United States. Paper presented in the conference on 'American Pluralism: Toward a History of Discussion' held at SUNY, Stonybrook on 7 June 1992.
- Giles, H. (ed.) 1977. *Language, Ethnicity and Intergroup Relations.* London, New York: Academic Press.
- Grenoble, L. A. and J. Whaley 2006. *Saving Languages: An Introduction to Language Revitalization.* Cambridge: Cambridge University Press.
- Gumperz, John J. and Robert Wilson 1971. Convergence and creolisation: a case from the Indo-Aryan/Dravidian border in India. In: *Pidginization and Creolization of Languages*, ed. by Dell Hymes. Cambridge: Cambridge University Press, pp. 151-167.
- Harrison, K. David 2007. *When Languages Die : The Extension of the World's Languages and Erosion of Human Knowledge*. Oxford: Oxford University Press Holmes, James S. 2000. The name and nature of Translation Studies. In: *The Translation Studies Reader*, ed. by L. Venuti. London and New York: Routledge, pp. 172-185.
- Kluyev, Boris I. 1981. *INDIA National and Language Problem*. New Delhi: Sterling Publishers.
- Krauss, M. 1992. The world's languages in crisis. *Language* 68, pp 6-10.
- Lo Bianco, J. and M. Rhydwen 2001. Is the extinction of Australia's indigenous languages inevitable? In: *Can Threatened Languages Be Saved?*, ed. by J. A. Fishman. Clevedon: Multilingual Matters, pp. 391-422.
- Mackey, William F. 2003. Forecasting the fate of languages. In: *Languages in a Globalized World*, edited by G. Maurais and M. A. Morris. Cambridge: Cambridge University Press, pp. 64-81.
- Mohanty, A. K. 1994. *Bilingualism in a Multilingual Society: Psycho-social and Pedagogical Implications.* Mysore: Central Institute of Indian Languages.
- Mohanty, Panchanan 2008. The other maternal uncles in Indian languages. In: *Ethnographic Discourse of the Other: Conceptual and Methodological Issues*, ed. by

Panchanan Mohanty, Ramesh C. Malik and Eswarappa Kasi. New Castle: Cambridge Scholars Publishing, pp. 69-90.

- Myers-Scotton, Carol 1992. Codeswitching as a mechanism of deep borrowing, language shift, and language death. In: Brenzinger (ed.) 1992, pp. 31-58.
- Ostler, N. 2006. *Empires of the Word: A Language History of the World.* New York: Harper Perennial. (first published in 2005).
- Pattanayak, D.P. 1981. *Multilingualism and Mother Tongue Education.* Delhi: Oxford University Press.
- Sapir, E. 1979. *Language: An Introduction to the Study of Speech.* London: Granada. (first published in 1921).
- Schiffman, H. F. 1996. *Linguistic Culture and Language Planning.* London and New York: Routledge.
- Schmid, M. S. 2002. A new blueprint for language attrition research. In: *First Language Attrition: Interdisciplinary Perspectives on Methodological Issues,* ed. by M. S. Schmid, B. Köpke, M. Kaijzer and L. Weilmer. Amsterdam, Philadelphia: John Benjamins Publishing Co., pp. 349-363.
- Whorf, B. L. 1956. *Language, Thought, and Reality: Selected Writings of Benjamin Lee Whorf* (ed. by J. B. Carroll). Cambridge, Mass.: The MIT Press.

European Instruments for Protecting Endangered Languages: Communiqué

Dr. Tomasz Wicherkiewicz - Department for Language Policy, Adam Mickiewicz University, Poland

With not so many encouraging exceptions, linguistic diversity is regressing everywhere throughout the world, and some languages have been disappearing from areas where they have been historically present, earlier representing a distinctive feature of those areas/regions' identity. Although most of such losses are expected to occur in Asia, South America, Australia & Oceania, there are numerous weakened languages in Europe too.

The situation of regional & minority language[1] in Europe is diverse and heterogeneous: the numbers of speakers of those traditionally spoken elements of the European linguistic heritage range from a few people (like the last three speakers of Karaim in Poland or 9 speakers of Livonian in Latvia) to several million (e.g. speakers of Catalan, i.e. more than some of the European states' official languages – e.g. Swedish, Finnish or Danish…), some are co-official, others are spoken exclusively in private situations. All these languages, nevertheless, have one factor in common: they are all, to some extent, in a vulnerable position, with some even threatened by extinction – a trend that can only be reversed if states or supranational institutions take resolute action. As Europe decided to create and implement actively not only national but also (or even predominantly) supranational structures, in the process of the unification, new (common), effective and comparable' instruments were needed.

---

[1] *in the European legal and administrative terminology, the endangered/indigenous languages are commonly referred to as "lesser-used languages" (as in the name of the European Bureau for Lesser-Used Languages) or "regional or minority languages" (as in the title of the European Charter for Regional or Minority Languages).*

In the past, linguistic rights were mainly protected by the *European Convention of Human Rights*. In terms of linguistic rights, it set mainly negative rights, in the sense that it obliged states to abstain from acting in certain ways as opposed to positive rights, which include, of course, freedom of expression and prohibition of discrimination on grounds of language. The limitations of that 'negative rights' approach became apparent from a relatively early stage.

It was therefore felt necessary to have more specialized international/European treaties, as follows:

- *Framework Convention on the Protection of National Minorities*
- *European Charter for Regional or Minority Languages*

They show a different attitude to the question of linguistic rights: the latter being a completely new instrument devoted to languages on a cultural base, without focusing on the status of the speakers themselves. These two complementary instruments, which both entered into force in 1998, provide indeed for clear positive rights for linguistic minorities.

The *European Charter for Regional or Minority Languages* is a convention designed on the one hand to protect and promote regional and minority languages as a threatened aspect of Europe's cultural heritage and on the other hand to enable speakers of a regional or minority language to use it in private and public life.

The principal dimension of the *Charter* is cultural. It is designed first to protect and promote regional and minority languages "as a threatened aspect of Europe's cultural heritage", and second to enable speakers of a regional or minority language to use it in private and public life. Languages are presented and treated from an "ecolinguistic" perspective - separately from their speakers: they are like species which can face extinction, they pertain to the cultural heritage of the Continent. Indeed, according to the *Preamble* of the *Charter*, languages to be protected remain the cultural capital of Europe: they do not belong solely to their speakers. The main objectives for protection and promotion of regional or minority languages are threefold:

- *democracy*: as already mentioned one of the crucial goals of the *Charter* is promotion of such values as democracy, diversity, multilingualism and multiculturalism; for the first time in its history, since a quarter-century, the concern of European and international policy makers includes also preservation of weaker, thus endangered artefacts and intangible values, such as languages;

- *culture*: safeguarding Europe's cultural diversity, particularly in the form of multiplicity of European languages, which is generally considered a common heritage and as such worth preserving despite growing unification of the continent;
- *ecology*: languages should be, and more and more often are, perceived as an element of the natural human ecosystem, thus a loss in the linguistic mosaic is a harmful loss to the cultural environment.

Therefore, for the first time in history, not only are official languages subject to legal instruments of protection, but the *Charter*, forms an invaluable instrument for preserving, protecting and promoting languages which are less present in public spheres in their countries, or which are actually moribund and as such doomed to erosion and finally extinction.

The *Charter* covers regional and minority languages, non-territorial languages and less widely used official languages. It is intended to ensure that regional or minority languages are used:

- in education,
- in the media,
- to permit and encourage their use in legal & administrative contexts,

- in economic & social life,
- for cultural activities, and
- in transfrontier exchanges.

The *Charter* is based on an approach that fully respects national sovereignty and territorial integrity. It does not conceive the relationship between official languages and regional or minority languages in terms of competition or antagonism. Development of the latter must not obstruct knowledge and promotion of the former. A deliberate decision was taken to adopt an intercultural and multilingual approach in the *Charter*, with each category of language taking its rightful place. In each state the cultural and social reality must be taken into account.

The *Preamble* to the *Charter* stresses the value of interculturalism and multilingualism, democracy and cultural diversity. However, the preamble also recognizes that the protection and promotion of regional or minority languages should not be to the detriment of official languages and the need to learn them, and that such protection and promotion must be within the framework of national sovereignty and territorial integrity. The aim is the creation of societies in which cultural and linguistic difference is a source of stability, rather than the opposite.

The *Charter* sets out the main principles and objectives upon which States must base their policies, legislation and practices, and which are regarded as providing the necessary framework for the preservation of the languages concerned.

The eight fundamental principles and objectives:

- recognition of regional or minority languages as an expression of cultural wealth;
- respect for the geographical area of each regional or minority language;
- the need for resolute action to promote such languages;
- the facilitation and/or encouragement of the use of such languages, in speech and writing, in public and private life;
- the provision of appropriate forms and means for the teaching and study of such languages at all appropriate stages;
- the promotion of relevant transnational exchanges;
- the prohibition of all forms of unjustified distinction, exclusion, restriction or preference relating to the use of a regional or minority language and intended to

discourage or endanger its maintenance or development;
- the promotion by states of mutual understanding between all the country's linguistic groups.

The *Charter*, as with all international conventions, should undergo a process of ratification; first being signed by the state government, and later ratified by the respective state parliament. By Autumn 2009, it had been ratified by 24 States[2], and another 9 have signed it[3], out of the 47 States of the Council of Europe, Poland is the most recent state-party to ratify it...

References:

- Dunbar, Robert & Gwynedd Parry (eds.) 2008. The European Charter for Regional or Minority Languages: Legal Challenges and Opportunities. Strasbourg: Council of Europe.
- Moring, Tom & Robert Dunbar 2008. The European Charter for Regional or Minority Languages and the media. Strasbourg: Council of Europe.
- Trifunowvska, Sne•ana & Fernand de Varennes (eds.) 2001. *Minority Rights in Europe – European Minorities and Languages.* The Hague: T.M.C. Asser Press.
- Woehrling, Jean-Marie 2005. *The European Charter for Regional or Minority Languages. A critical commentary.* Strasbourg: Council of Europe.

[2] *Armenia, Austria, Croatia, Cyprus, Czech Republic, Denmark, Finland, Germany, Hungary, Liechtenstein, Luxembourg, Montenegro, Netherlands, Norway, Romania, Serbia, Slovakia, Slovenia, Spain, Sweden, Switzerland, Ukraine, United Kingdom, and Poland.*

[3] *Azerbaijan, Bosnia and Herzegovina, France, Iceland, Italy, Macedonia, Malta, Moldova, Russia.*

Valedictory Session

H. E. Professor Piotr Koldkowski-Polish Ambassador to India

It is a great honour for me to be here with so many distinguished scholars and to participate in a seminar like this one. I suppose that the issue of endangered languages is one of the most important in the modern world. It is not well understood and valued by our public opinion. This is not to say that there is no group of committed scholars or NGOs who are doing an excellent job to make us aware of all the linguistic and social processes taking place in the globalizing world. But to emphasize a cultural phenomenon which is not always clearly perceived by the general public, I have learnt, that half of the 6700 languages spoken today are in danger of disappearing before the century ends. That so called rare languages are being increasingly replaced by various economically politically or socio-culturally dominant ones. Every two weeks the last fluent speaker of a languages passes away and with him or her goes literally hundreds of generations of traditional knowledge encoded in those tongues. This process can only be slowed if urgent action is taken by governments and international institutions and local authorities. I do understand that not many people with power have a full understanding of the situation in spite of making verbal declarations.

There are scholars who feel that we should not interfere in natural linguistic and social processes. It comes as no surprise that currently there are several options for involvement with endangered languages. It has been observed that the choice depends on national and institutional philosophy, and resources available. The first option, as I understand it, is to do nothing, to accept changes in language use as normal. The philosophy asserts that it is natural for languages to undergo several changes, transformations, and finally to vanish. A second option assumes that we should document the languages, or enable other linguists to do so, recording as much data as possible. Arguments for being involved in such documentation, include the safeguarding of linguistic diversity, contributing to a knowledge bank for language universals, and the western idea that the knowledge is of itself valuable. The third option is to attempt some sort of a language salvage revitalization, or maintenance programme including language development strategies such as in education, literature, translation etc. Well there are certain problems in prioritizing needs for such interventions. Should we even try to save languages from extinction? Should we include even the smallest groups? And you have mentioned about only a dozen of speakers for certain languages… should we consider cost efficiency and the number of people who might be benefited? By raising these issues we have to bear in mind that basically what keeps a language alive is its social function so only the people who can stop the language from shrinking or dying, are the ones who are the speakers of the particular language. So from my personal subjective point of view, the last option is really worth considering. As I strongly believe that by losing a language once spoken by a big or a small community, we lose a part of our human identity, and reduce our human heritage. In fact we may become culturally poorer, though more globalized in a negative sense. And incapable of understanding the wisdom once passed down from generation to generation. By losing hundreds of languages in the near future, we are likely to become more superficial in dealing with our history, culture and beliefs.

I come from a country which did not exist on the map of Europe for more than a hundred and twenty years. In fact our language was the most admired treasure, our most precious sign of cultural and national identity. The Polish language, more than birth or religion was the most essential ingredient of our identity. Its usage was banned or discouraged in many institutions at that time. Much effort was made to preserve it at all costs. We have made a memorable place with our language; the language is our homeland. So I hope I am not wrong in saying, that particular communities and its members who lose their language, lose their homeland, become displaced people who are likely to have problems with their own cultural identity.

Helping people preserve their endangered language is to help them to preserve their multi cultural and multi ethnic identity which not only guarantees creative and successful development, but gives them the sense of inclusiveness. In my opinion, the state itself through various institutions is seriously committed to keeping its linguistic traditions alive and that allows its citizens to believe its shared values and cherish their own sense of belonging to a dominant community which is not blind to cultural and linguistic aspirations of its various members. Languages are humankind's principal tools not only for expressing ideas and emotions, they are vehicles of cultural expression So safeguarding endangered languages is a crucial task, in maintaining cultural diversity worldwide. Without these rare languages we shall become socially and culturally very poor, maybe it is some sort of a sanskritic *gharibi*, that we may face one day in the future. I should also remember about the social and psychological consequences of losing rare languages. *Hamari bhasha, hamari sanskriti*. Thank you very much.

Recommendations

Prof. Udaya Narayana Singh

Professor Udaya Narayana Singh, in his valedictory address which followed, summarized the presentations of the scholars and made the following recommendations:

- The Government of India may consider initiating a Scheme for Revitalization of Endangered and Potentially Endangered languages – some outside the 8th Schedule of the Constitution but recorded by the Census of India, and those that may not have been recorded in published documents so far.
- The data with respect to smaller language groups – i.e. Mother-Tongues not spoken by 10,000 or more persons, may now be released with an archival detail for mother-tongue labels over differenrt decadal censuses. For instance, we do not have the names and locations of more than 3000 mother-tongues or languages noted in the Census 2001 document.
- An effort may be made to draw international expertise in our revitalization efforts.
- It should be the endeavour of the Scientific Community of linguists and language specialists in India to modify the UNESCO Atlas of the World's Languages in Danger (2009) database so that a more correct assessment of endangerment is possible.
- Introduction of mother tongue language education experiments in selective zones may be undertaken.
- In view of the fact that a large number of Indian languages are threatened for various reasons, and in order to know their role in education, knowledge-production, informatics, science and technology, commerce, media, literary productions, law & justice and governance, an independent National

Commission for Languages may be set up by the Government of India which could give annual report to the Governments at the centre as well as to the state governments about the status of Indian languages, and suggest steps to be undertaken where sustenance and support are to be provided.

Additional Recommendations by ICH Division INTACH

Interaction should be started with the Human Resources Development Ministry involving:

1) Central Institute of Indian Languages for partnership where required
2) NCERT and State CERTs in a selectively progressive programme
3) This interaction should be kept alive with periodic and regular meetings and exchanges

INTACH convenors should be alerted on the issues involving endangered languages and sent a template to list the languages in the regions represented by them with their endangered status if any. This should be done in conjunction with relevant regional linguistic experts, and tapping on contacts made during the Seminar.

Subsequent to this, selected programmes can be put on course in experimental or other modes.

The programmes should keep in mind the following:

1) Urge linguists and researchers to document and work on endangered languages where possible, including oral literature and other oral material including translation.
2) Involve local commuities through heritage school clubs and convenors and to get involved in producing newsletters and other material.
3) Encourage media exposure, television and radio programmes.
4) Encourage development of textbooks and readers in local schools for affected communities.

5) Adopt various measures to instill pride and provide empowerment by studying best practices shown up in presentations at the Seminar by, for example, Ganesh Devy, Gail Coelho and Dr Sreenathan (the case of Andhra Pradesh) and Professor Peter Austin. The areas, methods, institutions and NGOs mentioned by them can be studied individually for replication.
6) Study script issues which vary significantly from area to area.
7) Awareness building through non-affected schools, i.e. schools without students from endangered language speaking communities.
8) Promotion of minority/adivasi rights.
9) Study the European Charter for Regional or Minority Languages explained by Dr Tomasz from Poland and its validity for Indian situations.
10) Closely follow the progress of Linguistic Survey of India.
11) Multidisciplinary approach as practiced by Prof. Ganesh Devy and recommended by Prof Rmakrishna Reddy and Prof Anvita Abbi.
12) Introduction of Reverse Education as recommended by Prof Anvita Abbi.

Profiles of Speakers

Prof. Anvita Abbi - Chairperson, Centre for Linguistics JNU New Delhi

Born in family of celebrated Hindi writers, grew up to be linguist dividing time between teaching in university and working on lesser known languages and tribal languages of India.

Zealous field linguist, who has scanned through northern most tip of India, such as areas represented by Himalayan languages to southern most tip, areas represented by languages of Andaman Islands. In last 35 years worked on every language family of India, and wishes to unravel linguistic typology of these varied languages. Author of ten books and approximately 50 articles in various research journals, Principal Investigator/ Director of mega project Vanishing Voices of the Great Andamanese, located at Jawaharlal Nehru University, New Delhi. Researched on large number of marginalized and endangered languages of India.

Visiting Scientist in 2000 and 2003 at Max Planck Institute, Leipzig, Germany, nominated as a Distinguished Fellow of 2001 by Language Typology Research Center, La Trobe University, Melbourne, Australia. Nominated honorary member of Linguistic Society of America. At present, one of the members of Advisory Board of Terralingua, and advisor to UNESCO on language issues. Received Rashtriya Lokbhasha Samman 2003 for her contribution towards tribal languages of India.

Prof. Peter Austin, BA (AS) Hons, PhD (ANU) Department of Linguistics (Marit Rausing Chair in Field Linguistics) School of Oriental and African Studies University of London

Specialized in: Typology, morpho-syntax, language documentation and description, historical linguistics, Lexical-Functional grammar, computer-aided linguistic analysis, Austronesian languages, Australian Aboriginal languages.

Teaching: theory and practice of language documentation, including Technology and Documentation, and Applied Documentation and Description, as well as courses in descriptive and theoretical linguistics such as Advanced Syntax, Typology, Historical Linguistics, Austronesian Languages, and Australian Aboriginal Languages. Supervises students working on languages from the Pacific, Australia, India, Mexico, and Nigeria. 2008-9, teaching Technology and Language Documentation, Advanced Syntax, and Historical Linguistics.

Programmes Convened: PhD in Field Linguistics

Courses Taught: Advanced Syntax, Historical Linguistics, Historical Linguistics (Masters), Syntactic Structure and Semantic Interpretation.

Research: Research interests cover descriptive, theoretical and applied linguistics. Extensive fieldwork experience on Australian Aboriginal languages (northern New South Wales, northern South Australia, and north-west Western Australia) and co-authored with David Nathan first fully page-formatted hypertext dictionary on World Wide Web, bilingual dictionary of Gamilaraay (Kamilaroi), northern New South Wales, as well as publishing seven bilingual dictionaries of Aboriginal languages.

Since 1995, carrying out research on Sasak and Sumbawan, Austronesian languages spoken on Lombok and Sumbawa islands, eastern Indonesia, in collaboration with colleagues at Mataram University and Frankfurt University. Theoretical research mainly on syntax and focuses on Lexical Functional Grammar, morpho-syntactic typology, computer-aided lexicography and multi-media for endangered languages. Also published on historical and comparative linguistics, typology, and Aboriginal history and biography. Currently has research grant from British Academy to work with native-speaker scholar Eli Timan on Jewish Iraqi language, including recording oldest generation of speakers talking about traditional practices and memories of life in Iraq. This work being done with diaspora community in London, Canada and Israel. For more details and list of recent publications see HRELP web page.

Publications: Austin , Peter, ed. (2008) *1000 languages. The worldwide history of living and lost tongues.* London: Thames & Hudson, Austin, Peter K. and Bond,

Oliver and Nathan, David, eds. (2007) *Proceedings of Conference on Language Documentation & Linguistic Theory.* London, UK: Department of Linguistics, SOAS.

Chapter in Book, Austin , Peter (2008) 'Survival of Language.' In: Shuckburgh, E., (ed.), *Survival.* The Darwin College lectures. Cambridge University Press, pp. 80-98.

Austin, Peter K. and Bond, Oliver and Nathan, David (2007) 'Introduction.' In: Austin, Peter K. and Bond, Oliver and Nathan, David, (eds.), *Proceedings of Conference on Language Documentation & Linguistic Theory.* London, UK: Department of Linguistics, SOAS, pp. 1-2.

Austin , Peter (2006) 'Data and Language Documentation.' In: Gippert, J. and Himmelmann, N.P. and Mosel, U., (eds.), *Essentials of Language Documentation.* Mouton de Gruyter, pp. 87-112.

Austin , Peter (2006) 'Content Questions in Sasak, Eastern Indonesia: An Optimality Theoric Syntax Account.' In: Schulze, F. and Warnk, H., (eds.), *Insular Southeast Asia. Linguistic and Cultural Studies in Honour of Bernd Nothofer.* Harrassowitz, pp. 1-

Prof. Udaya Kumar Chakraborty
Department of Bengali & Coordinator Bhasacharya Suniti Kumar Chatterji Centre for Language Studies Jadavpur University Calcutta

B.A. Hons. & M.A., Bengali, first in university in both. Worked on Bengali Generative Grammar and awarded Ph. D. degree, 1986, Jadavpur University.

At present, member of Grant In Aid committee, CIIL, Mysore. Member of B.O.S. of Bengali Department, Sambalpur University, Netaji Open University and Jadavpur University. Member of Faculty Council of Arts in Jadavpur University. Member of Academic Committee of School of Languages, Jadavpur University. Ex member, Advisory Board of Lokasiksha Parishad of Ramakrishna Mission, Narendrapur, W.B.

Principal Investigator of the Project entitled **"Preparation of Teaching Materials in Minor and Smaller Languages"** under the financial assistance of CIIL, Mysore. Principal Investigator: U.G.C. Major Research Project: **'Orally Performed Literature of the Painters of Southern Bengal: Video Recording, Digitalizing and to Find-out its Linguistic Features of Orality.** Co-Investigator: Smt. Sonia Sahoo.

Department of English, J.U. Working on 'Ethno culture **of Tibeto-Burman & Austro-Asiatic Endangered speech communities of West Bengal:** field work, digitalization and documentation' under DRS programme, Bengali Department, J.U.

Participated as a Faculty Resource person at the Neo **Linguistic Survey** of India [NLSI] Summer Camp organized by CIIL (from 21st May 2007 to 10th June 2007) at Mysore.

Supervising Ph. D. works [Awarded: 23, Submitted: 03, Ongoing: 05, Adjudicated: 09] and M. Phil dissertation [Awarded: 19, Ongoing:1, Adjudicated: 07].

Published papers and articles on Linguistics and Literature in Bengali (more than 70). Published Books (11) such as, *'âdhunik kavi: kavitâr Sailî'* (Style of the **Modern Poetry** and Modern Poets) (1997), *'vâKglâ padaguccher saKgathan'* (Structure of Bengali **Phrases**) (2nd ed. 2004), *'vâKglâ saKvartani byakaran'* (Bengali Transformational Grammar), (1998), *'Narir bhasa o anyanya prabandha'* (Women's Dialect and other Articles) (2006) etc.

Creative writings: Novels (in book form 3, in journals 4), Poems (in book form 1, in Journals more than 150), Short stories (in Journals 10). Novels *'oggara bhattâ athavâ pitritîrther jal* (Boiled Rice or The Funeral Water) (1996), *atha soham carit kathâ* (Biography of Soaham (I am the Almighty)) (2002), *' nânak'* (The Biography of Guru Nânak) (1999) etc.

Paper presented, Chair, and Commentator of papers in several Seminars and Workshops. Worked as a resource person in UGC sponsored Refresher Courses (12).

Dr. Gail Coelho (Ph. D. University of Texas at Austin, 2003)
Reader, Department of Linguisticsn
University of Delhi.

Dr Coelho's research interests: documentation of adivasi languages of India, particularly those in Dravidian and Austroasiatic language families. Engaged for several years in documenting Betta Kurumba, South Dravidian language spoken by adivasi group living in Nilgiris, Tamil Nadu. Recently made short trip to Great Nicobar island for preliminary investigation of speech of Shompen and Nicobarese communities. Current plans to document Munda (sub-group of Austroasiatic) language of Koraput district, Orissa, while continuing with documentation of adivasi languages in Nilgiris.

Joy Dasgupta
Secretary, Greater Himalayan Bio-cultural Society, Shillong, Meghalaya

Anthropologist working on issues of Bio-cultural diversity in the Eastern Himalayas. Worked with a host of organizations like the Ashoka Trust for Ecology and Environment, the International Centre for Integrated Mountain Development. Currently involved in setting up an NGO called the Greater Himalayan Bio-cultural Society of which he is one of the co-founders. Has many presentations at international conferences and publications on a host of topics ranging from tenurial control of landscapes to legal issues with reference to natural resource management in the Eastern Himalayas.

Prof. Ganesh Devy
Founder Director Bhasha Research and Publication Centre, Ahmedabad

Professor G. N. Devy is a literary scholar and cultural activist, writes in three languages Marathi, Gujarati and English, and has received prestigious literary awards for his works in all three languages.

Established and edited several literary periodicals including Setu (in English and Gujarati), Dhol (in eleven different adivasi languages), Budhan (an activist journal in English) and Bol (a childrens magazine in Gujarati). Was Series-Editor for Sahitya Akademi's project on Indian Literature in Oral Taditions and Tribal Languages.

Founder of Bhasha Research and Publication Centre for the conservation of Adivasi languages, Adivasi Academy devoted to education and development, Denotified and Nomadic Rights Action Group, human rights campaign, and Himlok: An Institute for the Study of Himalayan Communities and Culture.

Community development work with the adivasi villages in western India has resulted in massive network of micro-enterprise self-help-groups, food-grain banks, water-harvesting cooperatives, informal learning centres and organic agriculture spread over twelve hundred villages.

Major publications in English include In Another Tongue (1993), Tradition and Modernity (1997), Painted Words (2002), Indian Literary Criticism: Theory and Interpretation (2002), A Nomad Called Thief: Reflections on Adivasi Voice and Silence (2006) and Indigeniety: Ex-pression and Representation, co-edited with Geoffrey V. Davis and K. K.Charkavarty (2008). The G. N. Devy Reader

(Orient Blackswan) containing four of his book length essays was launched in early 2009.

Tshering Dorje - Lahaul Himachal Pradesh

Born 1936 in village Guskyar, Lahul & Spiti district of Himachal Pradesh.

Studied in Local High School of Kyelang up to matriculation. Also Studied Bhoti language in local monastery Bokar. Received preliminary teachings and initiation of Dzog chen of Nyingma tradition from late Dzog chen master ven: Tulshug Lingpa Rinpoche. Received Dzog chen teachings of Bon tradition from ven: Sangye Tanzia Jongdong, abbot of Manri Bon Monastery.

Ventured into the seasonal wool and salt trade, according to tradition, with western Tibet, now Ngari prefecture, under China. Worked as Assistant Public Relations Officer for the Himachal Pradesh Government. After retirement, researching on his mother-tongue, Zhang zhung, and the early Bon religion, and has published several articles in Hindi, English and Bhoti languages.

Lisa Lomdak - Assistant Professor, Arunachal Institute of Tribal Studies, Rajiv Gandhi University

B.A (HON) in English – Fergusson College, Pune, Maharashtra (2002), M.A (HON) in Linguistics – Jawaharlal Nehru University, New Delhi (2004), M.Phil in Linguistics - Jawaharlal Nehru University, New Delhi (2006), pursuing PhD in Linguistics, Jawaharlal Nehru University, New Delhi (2006 onwards)

Academic Appointments: Course Incharge, (Winter Semester,2007) B.A (Optional), Introduction to Linguistics, Centre For Linguistics, School of Language, Literature and Culture Studies, JNU, New Delhi

Lecturer (*ad hoc*), July-August 2008, English Department, Jesus and Mary College, New Delhi

Assistant Professor of Linguistics, September 2008 to present, Arunachal Institute Of Tribal studies, Rajiv Gandhi University, Arunachal Pradesh.

Other Appointments/Responsibilities: Course Incharge – Language Package Course, Arunachal Institute of Tribal Studies.

Prof. Ajit Mohanty - Professor of Psychology, Former Chairperson, Zakir Husain Centre for Educational Studies Jawaharlal Nehru University New Delhi

Professor Mohanty has published over 100 papers in the areas of psycholinguistics, multilingualism and multilingual education focusing on education, poverty and disadvantage among linguistic minorities. Professor, since 1983, and Chairperson at Centre of Advanced Study in Psychology, Utkal University and President of National Academy of Psychology, India (1997). 2007-2008 Fulbright Visiting Professor in Columbia University, New York; taught course on Multilingual Education. Earlier Fulbright Senior Scholar (University of Wisconsin, Madison), Killam Scholar (University of Alberta), Senior Fellow (Central Institute of Indian Languages), Visiting Scholar (Universities of Geneva and Chicago). Recent book Multilingual Education for Social Justice (Mohanty, Panda, Phillipson & Skutnabb-Kangas: editors) published by Orient Blackswan with special international edition by Multilingual Matters, UK. Other books include: Bilingualism in a Multilingual Society, Psychology of Poverty and Disadvantage (co-editor: G. Misra) and Perspectives on Indigenous Psychology (co-editor: G. Misra). Written chapters on Language Acquisition and Bilingualism (co-author: Christian Perregaux) in Handbook of Cross-Cultural Psychology (second edition) and on Multilingual Education in India in Encyclopedia of Language and Education (Editors: J.Cummins & N.H. Hornberger). On Editorial Boards of International Journal of Multilingualism, Language Policy and Psychological Studies. Teaches M.Phil. level course on Multilingualism and Education in India; directs two International Projects From Mother Tongue to Other Tongue and National Resource Centre for Multilingual Education (www.nmrc-jnu.org) at JNU. Completed assignment as International Consultant to Governments of Finland and Nepal for Developing Multilingual Education Policy and Strategy document for Nepal. Keynote Speaker at International Congress of Applied Psychology, Madrid, Spain (1994), International Conference on Multilingualism, South Africa Applied Linguistics Association (2004), International Conference on Multilingualism and Third Language Acquisition (2007), University of Stirling, UK, Special Speaker at International Symposium on Imagining Multilingual Schools, Teachers College, Columbia University (2004) and Cornell Conference on Language and Poverty (2005).

Prof. Panchanan Mohanty, Centre of Applied Lingustics and Translation Studies, University of Hyderabad

Though he studied both literature and linguistics, Panchanan Mohanty decided to make his career in linguistics. Taught some years in Orissa Educational Service and Berhampur University in Orissa; joined Centre for Applied Linguistics and Translation Studies at University Hyderabad in 1990, now professor of applied linguistics. In last twenty-five years: taught various subjects in linguistics and applied linguistics, published more than 100 papers in journals such as, General Linguistics, Language Policy, Language Problems and Language Planning, Professional and Academic English, Mother Tongue, Indian Linguistics, International Journal of Dravidian Linguistics, Indian Journal of Linguistics, etc. and in different anthologies published from India and abroad on language teaching, psycholinguistics, sociolinguistics, ethnolinguistics, translation studies, computational linguistics, quantitative linguistics besides phonology and morphology that were topics of his doctoral thesis. Also written and edited 18 books in English and Oriya besides translating four books into Oriya. een associated with different linguistic associations and journals. President, Dravidian Linguistics Association, chief editor, Indian Linguistics, journal of Linguistic Society of India, deputy editor of International Journal of Dravidian Linguistics, journal of Dravidian Linguistics Association, academic editor of The Asian ESP Journal, published from Korea and BVI, and member of editorial boards of various linguistic journals. Also been visiting professor to number of universities in India and abroad. Head, Centre for Applied Linguistics and Translation Studies, Dean of Students' Welfare, University of Hyderabad, member of many language technology projects sanctioned by Ministry of Information Technology, Govt. of India. So far supervised 15 Ph. D. and 24 M. Phil. students from India and abroad, and ten Indian and overseas students are working with him for their Ph. D. degree at the moment.

Christopher Moseley - Editor-in-Chief, UNESCO Atlas of the World's Languages in Danger, 2009 School of Slavonic and East European Studies, University College, London University

Christopher Moseley specializes in the Baltic languages and is the editor of *Ogmios*, the journal of the Foundation for Endangered Languages. After leaving the BBC in 2005, he edited the Encyclopedia of the World's Endangered Languages (Routledge 2007) and co-edited the Atlas of the World's Languages (Routledge 2007, 1st edition 1994), prior to editing the UNESCO Atlas of the World's Languages in Danger (2009).

Puran Singh Negi Loktus - I.A.S. (Retd) Agri – Horticultural Farmer Shimla-171 002

M.A. (Social Work) Delhi University, M.A. (Criminology) Keele University, England

Postings in The IAS & constitutional assignments held: Principal Secretary (Culture, Art & Language) to the Government of Himachal Pradesh, Principal Secretary (Environment & Forests; Revenue; Health Services; Town & Country Planning; Education and held additionally the charge of Vice-Chancellor, H.P. University (1993-94 academic session), Member Secretary of the National Scheduled Areas and Scheduled Tribes Commission, Ministry of Tribal Affairs, GOI at Secretary level to the Government of India (July 2002 to September, 2004)

Worked as UN/FAO Project Consultant on three projects, assigned to China (1991-92).

Officially visited 28 countries-headed a number of teams of experts sponsored by the Commerce Ministry, GOI, STC India, HPMC & the State Government of H.P.

Membership of associations and NGOs, Life Member of INTACH, Convenor of the Trans Himalayan – Kinnaur, Lahul & Spiti Chapter (H.P.) of INTACH, President of Green Himalayas – an Ecological Society

Publications: Author of two books published, conducted study recording and documentation of the Cultural Heritage of the Trans Himalaya funded by Ministry of Culture, GOI which is under publication with the IGNCA, New Delhi.

Dr. Jean Robert Opgenort - University of Leiden, Netherlands

Doctorate: Leiden University, Date 6 June 2002 (Cum Laude), Supervisor Prof. Dr. G.L. van Driem, Title of thesis The Wâmbule Language

Conducted linguistic field research in Nepal and native province of Limburg since 1996 and produced several grammars of Kiranti languages and historical comparative studies. Since 2002, participated in the European research programme Languages and Genes of the Greater Himalayan Region. Committed to the recognition, protection and promotion of minority languages. Built dynamic websites with on-line dictionaries and audiovisual content on language communities. At Leiden University, taught Nepali and linguistics.

Since 2006, worked as project manager and e-Learning consultant. In 2008 and 2009, involved in UNESCO's activities for safeguarding endangered languages. Contributed to 3rd revised and updated edition of UNESCO Atlas of the World's Languages in Danger, in capacity of Regional Editor.

Selected publications: Opgenort, Jean Robert. 2006. 'About Chaurasia', in Roland Bielmeier and Felix Haller, eds., Himalayan Linguistics and Beyond. Berlin: Mouton de Gruyter.

Opgenort, Jean Robert. 2005. A Grammar of Jero. With a Historical Comparative Study of the Kiranti Languages. Languages of the Greater Himalayan Region, Vol. 3. Leiden: Koninklijke Brill.

Opgenort, Jean Robert. 2004 b. A Grammar of Wambule. Grammar, Lexicon, Texts and Cultural Survey of a Kiranti Tribe of Eastern Nepal (xxix + 900 = 929 pp., 16 illus.). Languages of the Greater Himalayan Region, Vol. 2. Leiden: Koninklijke Brill.

Opgenort, Jean Robert. 2004 a. 'Implosive and preglottalized stops in Kiranti', in Linguistics of the Tibeto-Burman Area, Volume 27.1 (pp. 1-27).

Opgenort, Jean Robert. 2002. The Wâmbule Language. Grammar, Lexicon, Texts and Cultural Survey of a Kiranti Tribe of Eastern Nepal (xxix + 615 = 644 pp., 39 illus.). Amsterdam: Jean Robert Opgenort [Leiden University doctoral dissertation, 6 June 2002].

Prof. Ramakrishna Reddy - Professor of Linguistics (Retd.) Former Dean School of Language Development, P.S. Telugu University

M.A. in Hindi Language & Literature (1966), I Class, S.V. University, Certificate in Linguistics (1967), I Class, Annamalai University, M. A. in Linguistics (1970), I Class, University of Poona, Ph.D. in Linguistics (1976), University of Edinburgh, United Kingdom. (Ph.D. topic: Localist Studies in Telugu Syntax).

Teaching and Research positions held: Tutor in Hindi, Annamalai University, (1966-68), Research Assistant in Linguistics, C.I.I.L., Mysore (1970-72), Lecturer in Linguistics, Central Hindi Institute, Agra(1976-77), Lecturer, Reader and Professor of Linguistics, Osmania University, Hyderabad (1977-90), Professor and Dean, School of Lg. Devlpt, P.S. Telugu University, Hyderabad (1990-98), Registrar, Dravidian University, Kuppam (1998-2002), Principal Investigator, FOSSILS, Trivandrum (2002-03), Chief Resource Person, LIS-India, CIIL, Mysore (2003-04), Professor of Linguistics, Taiz University, Taiz, Republic of Yemen (2004-05).

Teaching & Research experience: Teaching : 25 years, Research : 35 years, Post-doctoral research : 28 years, Research guidance : 25 years (12 Ph.D.s and 10 M.Phil.s awarded, 3 more Ph.D.s yet to be awarded)

Areas of specialization in research: Dravidian linguistics, General linguistics (grammar, semantics and typology), Sociolinguistics: Language contact and convergence, ethno linguistics and literacy, Field linguistics (with focus on tribal and endangered languages & literatures).

Books published, 12: Research papers published: 32, Guest Lectures given: 35.
Field Work and Research on Tribal Languages: 9
Knowledge of Languages: Telugu, English, Hindi, Kuvi, Manda, Tamil, Kannada, Oriya, Marathi, Kui and Pengo.

Dr. Nicholas Reid - Senior Lecturer school of Behavioural, Cognitive and Social Sciences, University of New England, Australia

Dr. Reid's main linguistic specialization over last three decades has been study of Australian Aboriginal languages. Has written grammar of two Northern Territory languages, Ngan'gikurunggurr and Ngen'giwumirri; recently completed Ngan'gi Dictionary, covering both these languages, with help of Patricia Marrfurra MacTaggart.

His descriptive work has fuelled other research interests, primarily within areas of morphological and syntactic typology, especially systems of nominal and verbal classification. Co-edited book on nominal classification in Australian languages.

Has strong commitment to preservation of linguistic diversity, actively involved in various language maintenance initiatives in Daly River region, including heritage work on endangered song-language traditions in Wadeye community. Also undertaken teacher training for NSW language maintenance programmes, run workshops for NSW Education Department's Board of Studies on writing NSW indigenous languages, acts in advisory capacity for local language re-awakening projects.

Teaching: Degree coordinator of University of New England's highly successful online Master of Arts (Applied Linguistics), actively involved in course development and teaching in external mode for students based around world, developed extensive multimedia teaching resources, including online units and CD ROM-based resources for teaching phonetics. Early adopter of online audio and video delivery, enhanced podcasting and web-based assessment at UNE.

Prof. Rajesh Sachdeva - Director in Charge, CIIL Mysore.

Commenced his research at CIIL with a doctoral dissertation on the speech of Punjabi-Hindi bilinguals in Delhi. The framework evolved by him to deal with forms of bilingual grammar was later applied in producing bi-literacy models for bilingual education of Wagdi speaking Bhil tribes in Rajasthan where tribal languages were introduced on experimental basis. He was actively associated with the National Literacy Mission as a Resource Person and contributed several articles on the use of spoken languages in literacy and adult education programmes. He worked actively with the tribes of the Northeast during his fifteen year tenure as an Associate Professor with the North Eastern Hill University both at Nagaland and Meghalaya. He contributed a monograph on language policy in education for Nagaland and also brought out a book on Language education in Nagaland: Sociolinguistic dimensions. He taught various courses in the University including Introduction to Linguistics, Sociolinguistics, Historical Linguistics, Semantics, Language Planning & Language education. On return to CIIL as a Professor he has been involved with the commencement of NELD-North East Language Development programme. Over 30 research projects involving several young tribal researchers belonging to all seven states have become functional. Professor Sachdeva dreams of producing at least one informed linguist from each speech community and takes the position that 'the destiny of man is inextricably linked to the destiny of language'. He is also actively involved with scholars in India and Europe to chalk out the forms of Multilingual education with solid foundations in Mother tongue and thereby develop models for cultural diversity and sustainable development.

Dr. Asha Sarangi - Associate Professor, Centre for Political Studies Jawaharlal Nehru University, New Delhi

Main areas of interest are political and cultural economy of development in modern India, identity and politics in South Asia and more specifically politics of linguistic nationalism in modern India. Most recent publication: edited volume, Language and Politics in India, published by Oxford University Press, 2009. Also published several articles in journals and edited volumes on this theme. Selected list of publications include: Languages as Women: The Feminisation of Linguistic Discourses in Colonial North India in *Gender and History*, Vol 21, #2, 2009

(Blackwell Publication Limited), pp. 287-304, Tribal Languages and the Cultural Politics in Contemporary India in *Moving Worlds: A Journal of Transcultural Writings* 9:1:2009. University of Leeds, U.K. (special issue on Chotro: Adivasi Voices and Stories), States Reorganisation: Contemporary Concerns in esocialsciences, January 2009, Language(s), Culture(s) and Region(s): Identity Politics in Independent India in N.K.Das and V.R.Rao (ed), *Identity, Cultural Pluralism and State in South Asia* (Macmillan India Publication, New Delhi, 2009, Ambedkar and the Linguistic States: A Case for Maharashtra in *Economic and Political Weekly*, January 14, 2006, Ritual of Political Rhetoric in *Seminar*, July 2004, Bernard S Cohn: Historian of the Future in *Economic and Political Weekly*, June 5, 2004, and Language as a Marker of Religious Difference in Imtiaz Ahmad and Helmut Reifeld (ed) *Lived Islam in South Asia: Adaptation, Accomodation and Conflict* (Delhi: Social Science Press, 2004).

Link to some of her published works are:
Bernard S Cohn: Historian of the future
http://www.epw.org.in/epw//uploads/articles/7697.pdf

Ritual of Political Rhetoric : Mandate for Change
http://www.india-seminar.com/semframe.html

Ambedkar and linguistic states : A case for Maharashtra
http://www.epw.org.in/epw//uploads/articles/1590.pdf

Language and Politics in India (New Delhi: OUP, 2009)
http://www.oup.co.in/search_detail.php?id=144696

States Reorganisation: Contemporary Concerns
http://www.esocialsciences.com/articles/displayArticles.asp?Article_ID=1839

Dr. G.D.P Shastry - Reader-cum-Research Officer, Head, Centre for Tribal and Endangered Languages Centre for Speech Sciences and Central Institute of Indian Languages

Worked extensively on the Tibeto-Burman languages of India, especially Arunachal Pradesh and Manipur, and the Pahari group in Himachal Pradesh.

Published works include a Grammar, Phonetic Reader, Dictionary and Adult Literacy Primer of Mishmi, spoken in Arunachal Pradesh; Mising Grammar (Edited and Revised).

Prof. Udaya Narayana Singh - Tagore Professor Rabindra Bhavan and Director of Indira Gandhi Centre for National Integration Visva-Bharati

Professor Singh was formerly Director of the Central Institute of Indian Languages (CIIL) - Dec 2000 to June 10, 2009.

Honors in Linguistics at Calcutta 1969-1972 (designated Eshan Scholar), Master's at the University of Delhi 1972-74 (awarded Uggarsain Memorial Gold Medal), a semester at the University of Illinois at Urbana-Champaign, USA in 1978, Ph.D. in Linguistics from Delhi in 1979 in Syntax and Semantics.

Reputed poet, playwright and essayist in Bangla and Maithili, Udaya Narayana Singh has published 6 collections of poems and 11 plays, 6 books of literary essays, besides translating 6 books. In addition, he has authored over 150 research papers in Linguistics and edited about 10 books.

Taught Linguistics, Translation Studies, Comparative Literature and Anthropology as Professor of Linguistics and Founder-Head, Centre for Applied Linguistics and Translation Studies at the University of Hyderabad: (1987-2000). Earlier, he was Visiting Lecturer (Delhi, 1979), Lecturer at MSU- Baroda (1979-81), Reader at Surat (1981-85) and Delhi (1985-87).

Was founder-head of CALTS (Centre for Applied Linguistics & Translation Studies) at the University of Hyderabad; as Director, also set up internationally acclaimed 'Study India Programme' and Centre for Distance Education.

Supervised several major research projects on Language Movement, NLP, Digital Documentation, Machine Translation, and Linguistic Data Consortium in Indian Languages (LDCIL), 14 doctoral and 21 M.Phil. level research works in Applied Linguistics, Translation Studies, ELT, Child Bilingualism, Lexicography and Literary Theory.

Chief Editor of 'Indian Linguistics, 1988-1990', (with P.P.Giridhar as Co-Editor) of Translation Today, Visiting Professor at the IIAS-Shimla (1989).

Visited and lectured in Bangladesh, Caribbean Islands, China, France, Germany, Iceland, Italy, Mauritius, Nepal, Pakistan, Russia, Singapore, Sri Lanka, Sweden, Thailand, U.K. & USA; received several grants and honours. Led Indian cultural delegation to China 2007-08; was Poet-Invitee at Frankfurt Book fair (2006), and London Book Fair 2009 – 'India Through Fresh Eyes'.

Dr. M. Sreenathan - Associate Professor, Department of Dravidian & Computational Linguistics, Dravidian University, Andhra Pradesh

Dr Sreenathan formerly held research position in the Anthropological Survey of India, Ministry of Culture, Government of India. His research and publications focus mainly on language and culture of tribal communities in India. Apart from research done in Andaman & Nicobar Islands and central and south India been published in leading journals on tribal language and culture. A faculty member in the International School of Anthropology. Authored six books, including Dravidian Tribes and Languages (2008), Languages of Kerala (2005), Jarawa Language and Culture (2001). Areas of interest: anthropological linguistics, eco-linguistics, linguistic paleontology, and language and genetics.

Dr. Lotika Varadarajan - Scholar, Ethnologist, Historian, Delhi

1962, M.A. History, University of Cambridge, U.K.; 1965, Ph. d. University of Bombay

Senior Fellowship, University Grants Commission (1969-1971); Fellowship, Indian Council of Historical Research (1972-75); Homi Bhabha Fellow, (1976-78).

Membershipof Learned Societies: Asiatic Society, Bombay; Société Asiatique, Paris; Centre International d'Étude des Textiles Anciens, CIETA, Lyon; Royal Asiatic Society, London, Academia de Marinha, Section of Maritime History, Lisbon.

Publications: 64 articles (on textiles, crafts, history etc.), 8 books (of which one book comprises 4 volumes)including: *India of the Seventeenth Century, Memoirs of François Martin (1670-1694)*1985, *South Indian Traditions of Kalamkari*, Perennial Press, Bombay, 1982, *Tradition and Transmission, Current Trends in French Ethnology, The Relevance for India,* New Delhi, 2003 with Dennis Chevalier Ed., *Of Fibre and Loom, The Indian Tradition*, National Institute of Design – Manohar, with Krishna Patel, forthcoming etc.

Delivered endowment lectures, travelled widely and delivered lectures worldwide, knows English, French, Hindi, Bengali, working knowledge Portuguese.

Dr. (Mrs) Kapila Vatsyayan - Member of Parliament, Rajya Sabha

Formerly: Secretary, Department of Arts, Ministry of HRD, Academic Director, Indira Gandhi National Centre for the Arts; President, India International Centre; and Member, UNESCO Executive Board.

Presently Chairperson, IIC-Asia Project, India International Centre;
B. A. (Hons.) and M. A. (English Literature), University of Delhi;
M.A. (Education), University of Michigan, Ann Arbor, USA;
Ph. D., Banaras Hindu University, Varanasi.

D. Litt. (Honoris Causa) from Banaras Hindu University; Mount Holyoke College, USA; Manipur University; Rabindra Bharati University, Kolkata; University of Michigan, Ann Arbor, USA.

'Vacaspati' of Rashtriya Sanskrit Vidyapeetham, Tirupati and 'Vakyapati' of Central Institute of Higher Tibetan Studies, Sarnath.

Has taught at the Universities of Delhi and Banaras. Has been a Visiting Professor in the University of Pennsylvania, Philadelphia and Regents Professor in the University of California (Santa Cruz).

Recognized internationally for her outstanding work in the diverse fields of Culture and the Arts. Spearheaded policy framework for programmes of art history, education, Sanskrit, Buddhist and Pali Studies. Responsible for establishing many cultural and educational institutions, such as the Central Institute of Higher Tibetan Studies. Was responsible for the Departments of Archaeology, Anthropology, Archives, Museums and other heritage institutions. Has been actively involved in and has initiated many conservation programmes. She was the architect of the conceptual plan of the Indira Gandhi National Centre for the Arts.

Author of over 15 books and many research papers and monographs, some specifically on environment, Indian myth and ecology, etc. Her writings have been internationally acknowledged for their universal vision, multi-disciplinary approach and as instances of a new and more appropriate paradigms of understanding the cultural fabric of India extended to Asia.

Widely travelled in India and abroad, received several recognition/honours, nationally and internationally. Fellow of the Russian Academy of Sciences and French Academy of the Study of Asian Civilizations. Fellow, Sangeet Natak Akademi and Lalit Kala Akademi

Recipient of many awards., including Rajiv Gandhi National Sadbhavana Award 2000; 'Akhil Bharatiya Sanskrit Sahitya Sewa Samman' for services to Sanskrit by Delhi Sanskrit Academy, Delhi Government; and Lifetime Achievement Award from the Sahitya Kala Parishad of the Government of NCT of Delhi for her significant contribution to enriching the lives of people and institutions.

Dr. Tomasz Wicherkiewicz - Adjunct Professor, Chair of Oriental Studies, Head of the Dept. of Language Policy & Minority Studies, Adam Mickiewicz University, Poznań / Poland

Member of scholarly institutes:

Kashubian Institute in Gdańsk, Kashubian Language Board in Gduńsk/ Gdańsk, Foundation for Endangered Languages, Bath/London, Fryske Akademy in Ljouwert/Leeuwarden, International Institute of Ethnolinguistic & Oriental Studies in Stêszew Member of Board of the European Bureau for Lesser-Used Languages, Dublin-Brussels Member of editorial boards: Journal of Multilingual and Multicultural Development, Linguistic and Oriental Studies from Poznań, Cassubia Slavica.

Studies abroad & Fellowships:

- TEMPUS Programme – Rijksuniversiteit Groningen & Fryske Akademy in Leeuwarden, the Netherlands (1992-1993)
- Xunta de Galicia – Universidad de Santiago de Compostela, Spain (1994)
- Alexander von Humboldt-Stiftung, Roman Herzog-Stipendium – Universität Bielefeld, Germany (1998-2000)

Field work projects among the minority communities in Poland, Austria, Belgium, China, Estonia, France, Georgia, Germany, Italy, Latvia, Lithuania, Mexico, Netherlands, Russia, Slovakia, Slovenia, South Africa, Spain, Switzerland, Ukraine.

Expert for the Council of Europe, Polish Ministry of Interior and Administration, *MERCATOR*-Network on minority language policy in Poland, European Commissions' Project *EuroMosaic III* on regional or minority languages in Europe, Council of Europe's Project *Valeur* on the foreign language policy in Europe (Graz, Austria).

Organizer of four International Conferences on regional and minority languages, and ethnolinguistics ca. 60 publications in minority studies, ethnolinguistics, language policy, and typology of minority language situations in Europe and Asia.

APPENDIX

(The following items are abstracts and power point presentation of seminar speakers whose papers are not available.)

Prof. Rajesh Sachdeva
Director in Charge
Central Institute of Indian Languages
Mysore

Abstract

Ecology of Endangered languages: Language planning in education

This paper examines the idea of an endangered language in an ecological perspective with a historical dimension. Specific examples from diverse settings in India are analyzed to understand how demographic factors interact with social and economic factors to change the forms of multilingualism and communication patterns, which lead to dispossession of language or loss in cultural transmission. It also takes the view that the UNESCO reports about several endangered languages should be seriously reviewed but cautions about false alarms being raised. The role of language policy in the context of language endangerment is critically reviewed. It is reasoned that conscious intervention with community involvement may be required in the domain of education to create favourable conditions for the survival of endangered languages. The government's possible action plan to counter the situation- Bharat Bhasha Vikas Yojna- may be discussed to ensure a successful outcome.

Dr. G.D.P Shastry
Reader-cum-Research Officer
Head, Centre for Tribal and Endangered Languages
Head, Centre for Speech Sciences
Central Institute of Indian Languages
Mysore

Abstract

The UNESCO Atlas lists 196 Indian languages as endangered. We, however, cannot accept this in toto for the following reasons.

- A number of names are not recognized as languages vide Census 2001. The Census lists only 100 as non Schedule languages of which 93 are tribal languages.
- Some languages in the Census list of tribal languages which are endangered as per our own research reports do not figure in the UNESCO list.
- Some of the languages are classified as mother tongues under a language.
- As a matter of policy, the Government does not publicize the figures of languages with population below 10000; hence some of the names from the UNESCO Atlas may not figure in the Census list.

From our own research and resources, we cannot fully agree with the mandate of UNESCO that '196 languages' are endangered. The term endangerment is new to the Indian ethos given the multilingual, multiethnic and multicultural nature of Indian society. Given the language tolerance and accommodation which exists in India, societies are encouraged to preserve their languages. Endangerment is a feature of the US, Canadian and Australian scenario where dominant monolingualism has led to mass extinction of smaller languages over the last two centuries.

Having said this, one should acknowledge that a majority of tribal languages, especially with small populations, are facing threats from within and sometimes from without. In order to sustain the small languages and develop them to a level where they will be stable, Government of India has taken many steps.

- Bodo and Manipuri have already been declared as languages under the 8th Schedule and are being used as media of instruction.
- Many of the 'endangered' languages are official languages of the states in which they are spoken and are used for administration, education and elsewhere – Mizo, Khasi, Garo, Kokborok.
- 16 languages spoken in Nagaland are used in schools as languages and media of instruction.

- The CIIL has been working on the smaller languages of India under the Centre for Tribal and Endangered Languages (erstwhile Tribal and Border Languages Unit). grammars, dictionaries, phonetic readers have been produced in many tribal languages. In addition, the Institute has also produced school and preschool primers, bilingual primers, primers for adult literacy, pictorial glossaries and other materials in many of these languages.
- The North East Development Programme has been in place for the past 5 years where work on 42 languages of the north east is under varying degrees of completion. 42 completed reports are under review.
- The Institute has proposed conducting workshops in 12 states with predominant tribal populations to study the viability of small languages and bring out a White Paper on Endangerment and Viability of Minor Languages which could form the basis for further language-specific work.
- Bharat Bhasha Vikas Yojana, a project aimed at preserving and developing tribal and minor languages of India, is under the active consideration of the Government.
- Under Cultural Documentation, we have produced 22 documentaries on culture and languages of Sikkim and West Bengal. 20 more are being taken up this year focusing on Arunachal Pradesh and Manipur.
- Under LIS India Project, linguistic and cultural profiles of 17 non scheduled languages are being put on the web.

Dr. Asha Sarangi
Associate Professor
Centre for Political Studies
Jawaharlal Nehru University
New Delhi

Abstract

Language and Power: A Long View

The question of endangered languages needs to be situated within the domains of power at various levels, i.e., social, cultural, political, economic, historical and ideological. In this context, a culturally and linguistically plural and complex society like India needs to engage with multiple forms of power expressed over time both institutionally and discursively. In this paper, I focus on two aspects of this relationship in the following manner:

1) What have been the institutional safeguards provided by the Indian State through protective measures in a variety of ways both constitutionally and extra-constitutionally?
2) What have been the responses from various linguistic communities and groups towards such protectionist measures?

I suggest that we need to map out the second aspect more carefully in order to make sense of various policies and programmes pursued by the State in the last sixty years after independence. In the past few years, various language communities have voiced their concerns to include their language in the Eighth Schedule of the Indian Constitution. Such a demand also ensures the administrative, legal, educational, political and social survival of their languages which may otherwise soon fall out of the domains of social and cultural capital and resources of power. Within this context, a number of linguistic-cultural movements have emerged questioning the primacy and dominance of a few languages over others in the fields of administration, education, economy and politics. These movements have called into question, very significantly, the dominant paradigm of caste and class alliances on the one hand, and have brought into focus the categories of language, region and culture central to modern concepts of power, hegemony and state on the other. This compels us to think about the inter-linkages existing among these various hierarchies of both traditional and modern forms of juridical and social power whose effects have shaped the political order of contemporary India.

It is important to see how the interface between power of languages and languages of power works itself out in various ways. The questions central to such an inquiry are of the following kinds. What can be the best possible way to understand this process of empowerment of languages? Can empowerment of some kind ensure their survival? Can the question of 'language rights' be more than simply a constitutional measure enshrined within the fundamental rights or directive principles of the state policy? If so, how do we reconcile the questions of representation, recognition and redistribution centered around the primacy accorded to language communities, their linguistic rights and resources in the same manner, if not differently, as we have dealt with the question of religious and caste communities? In what ways, has the cultural secularization process affected the domains of language and power and its impact on the larger phenomenon of the endangerment of languages in our times? What should be the criteria to formulate a more comprehensive and sustainable language policy of the country?

LANGUAGE REVIVALISM: MLE AND CRITICAL PEDAGOGY

Dr. Minati Panda,
Associate Professor,
Zakir Hussein Centre for Educational Studies, JNU
22 October, 2009

Whose Language is Endangered???

Roughly 3000 Languages in India, 3-400 being major Languages

196 languages are declared endangered. Most of these languages are spoken mostly by ethnic minority communities.

9 languages are already extinct, all of which are tribal languages

Is Revival Possible or Desirable - Best Practices

- Language Revivalism is Necessary, **But it Shouldn't be an Exclusionary Process.**
- Most Endangered Languages in Orissa are unwritten tribal languages
- So we decided to achieve the goal of revivalism of languages through education

The Biggest Challenge We had in front of us were

- First, finding an official Space to intervene
- Second, the Choice of a Paradigm for Education that doesn't make the language revivalism process an exclusionary and divisive process

- Decision to Implement Experimental MLE programme in Orissa provided us that space
- We (Prof. Ajit K. Mohanty and myself) decided to support MLE programmes in tribal area schools through our MLE+ initiatives
- What helped us most is my previous ethnographic work on mathematical and science practices in Saora areas of Gajapati District, Orissa and development of *Yerai Yerai* book (with Ramakant Agnihotri and Mahendra Mishra) in Saora language where a lot of local stories, songs and science practices were documented and used.
- And Prof. Mohanty's last three decades work in Kondh area in Orissa, his work and vision in Multilingual Education

Choice of Paradigm

- Critical Theory Perspective to inform all our intervention work
- Why Critical Theory Perspective??
- No universal truth, no absolutism, or universal reason
- It asks New questions:

– Whose world view is it?
– How is singular and group cultural identity constructed?
– How is knowledge transmitted?
– How many ways do people learn?
– Can there be any one form of knowledge?
– How many realities are there?

Contn.

- Critical post modern political project shifts the locus of power to the underprivileged, the marginalized and the oppressed.
- It is about real people struggling in the everyday world within their multi-shaped identities and subjectivities.
- It is about social and cultural injustice, emphasizing heterogeneity.
- Supports critical literacy over traditional literacy
- A Critical Pedagogue always seeks just and fair ways to alter a system

Traditional Literacy Versus Critical Literacy

- For whom and why the decisions are made?
- Why would I need an alternative teaching methodology?
- Why would I use children's authentic local stories, songs and experiences?
- Am I reinforcing stereotypes?
- Am I reproducing inequalities?
- What forms of alternative testing don't track students?
- How do I enhance quality of living among children...race, religion, caste, political interests etc.

A Major Value Shift

- Deviance Versus Resistance
- Deskilling Versus Reskilling
- Multiculturalism Versus Similarity Within Difference
- Individualism Versus Critical Individuality
- Negative Competition Versus Positive Competition
- Control Versus Democracy
- Authoritarianism Versus Authority
- Traditional Empowerment Versus Critical Empowerment
- Traditional Literacy Versus Critical Literacy

Documentation and Printing of Stories

- Story Books in Saora and Kui Languages (under MLE+ Programme)
- *Yerai Yerai*
- Documentation of Stories Through Srujan Programme (State Government Programme)
- Big books, small books etc (under state MLE programme)
- Library Programme in Community

Movement from Loka Katha to Saora and Kui Sahitya

ସରା ଜୁଲ୍‌ଜୁଲ୍ କାତାବିର୍- I

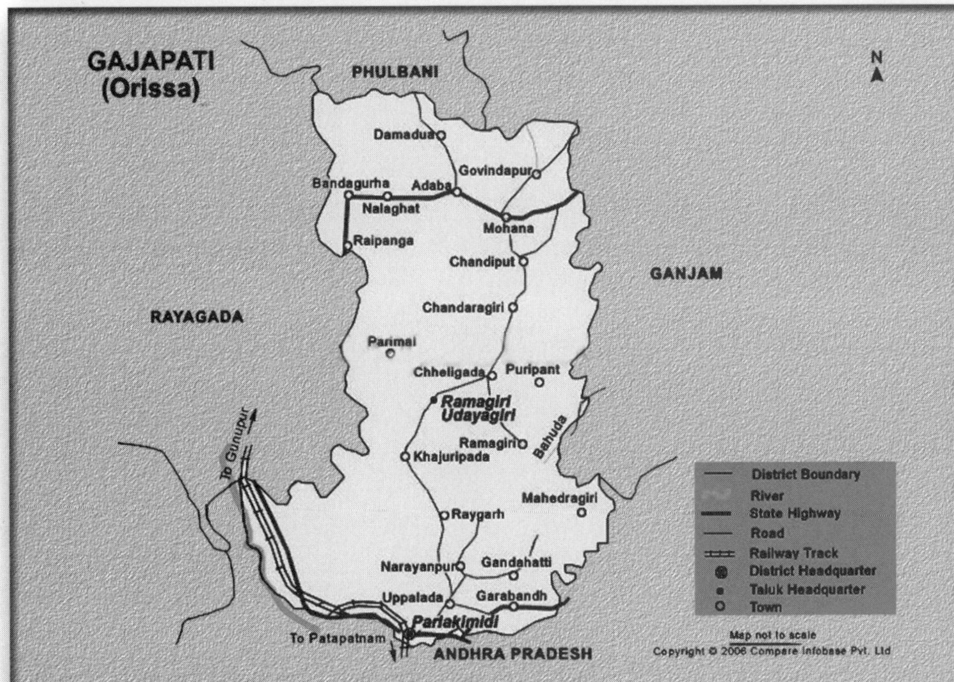
GAJAPATI
(Orissa)
PHULBANI
GANJAM
RAYAGADA
ANDHRA PRADESH
N
Damadua
Govindapur
Bandagurha
Adaba
Nalaghat
Mohana
Raipanga
Chandiput
Chandaragiri
Parimal
Chheligada
Puripant
Ramagiri
Udayagiri
Bahuda
Ramagiri
Khajuripada
Mahedragiri
Raygarh
Narayanpur
Gandahatti
Uppalada
Garabandh
Paralakimidi
To Gunupur
To Patapatnam
District Boundary
River
State Highway
Road
Railway Track
District Headquarter
Taluk Headquarter
Town
Map not to scale
Copyright © 2006 Compare Infobase Pvt. Ltd

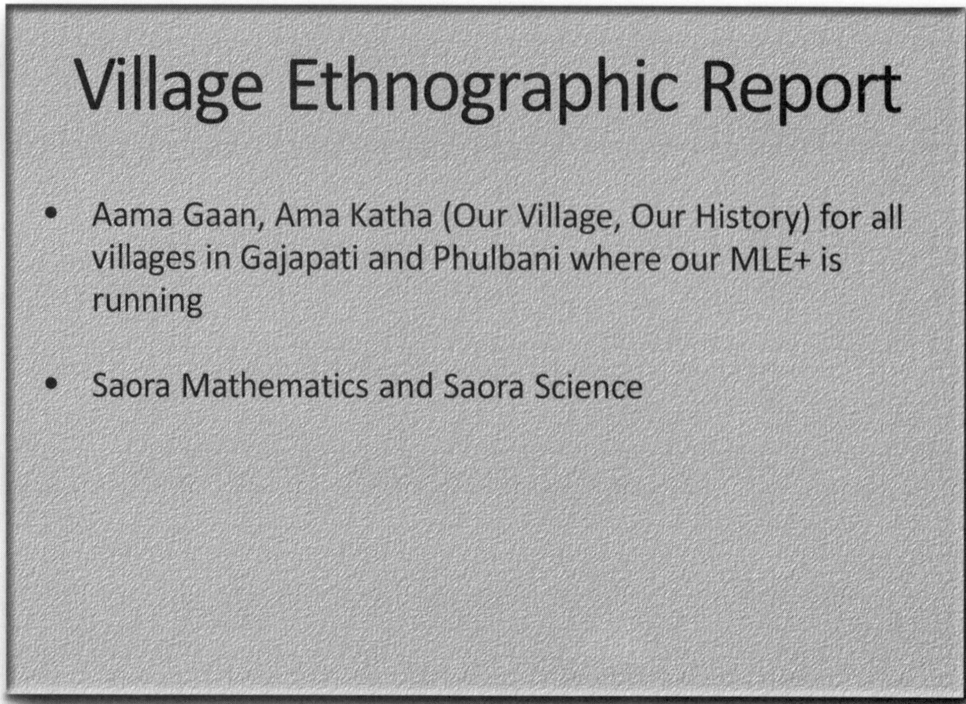
Village Ethnographic Report
• Aama Gaan, Ama Katha (Our Village, Our History) for all villages in Gajapati and Phulbani where our MLE+ is running
• Saora Mathematics and Saora Science

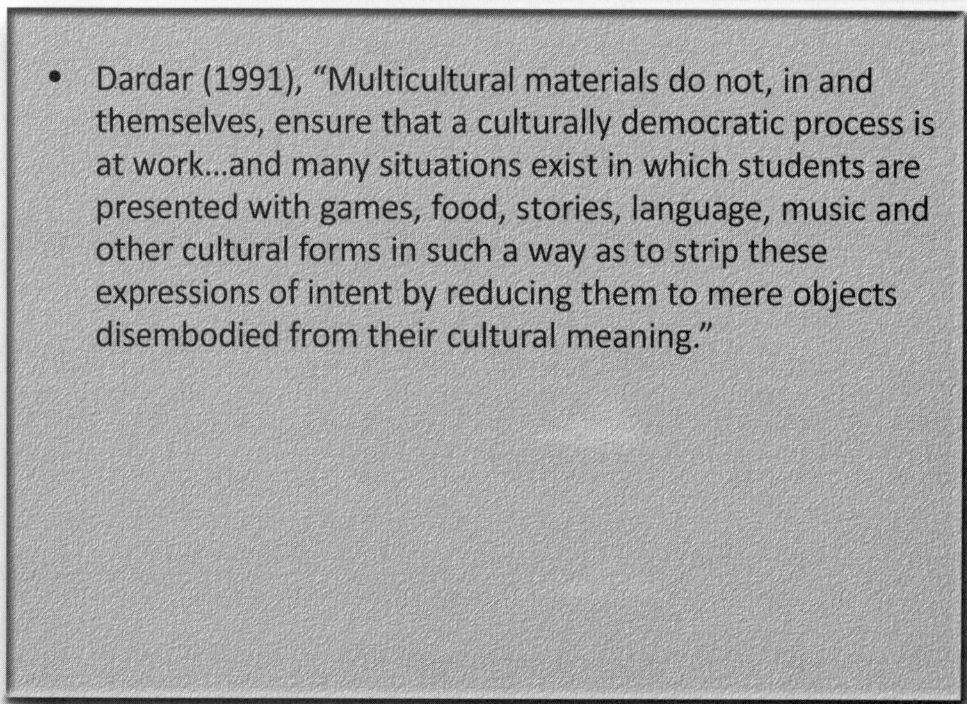
• Dardar (1991), "Multicultural materials do not, in and themselves, ensure that a culturally democratic process is at work…and many situations exist in which students are presented with games, food, stories, language, music and other cultural forms in such a way as to strip these expressions of intent by reducing them to mere objects disembodied from their cultural meaning."

Sample page from English-Great Andamanese Dictionary by Prof. Anvita Abbi (Refer page 72)

crow, one eyed bobulu बोबूलू N. *काना कौआ SD: Birds.*

crush rok रोक V. *कुचलना; रौंदना* **crush it.** it-bi-rok-e ईतबीरोके *कुचल दो इसे।*

cry ŋol डोल *Var:* ŋɔl डौल *Var:* ŋɔlɔ डौलौ *Var:* ŋolɔm डोलौम V. *रोना* **child cries.** tʰire ŋɔl-o-b-ɔm थीरे डौलो बौम *बच्चा रोता है।* **why are you crying?** ŋo-tʰi-bi-ŋolɔm डोठीबीडोलौम *तुम क्यों रो रहे हो?* **I am weeping.** tʰu-ŋɔlɔbɔm ठूडौलौबौम *मैं रो रहा हूं।*

- ɔŋɔrlo औडौरलो N. *रोना SD: Psychological Predicates.*

cry, of lizard eɲɔkom एञौकोम [SM] N. *छिपकली की आवाज SD: Insects.*

cuckoo cɛreo चैरेओ *Var:* cereo चेरेओ N. *एक प्रकार की कोयल SD: Birds.* Male is black and female is brownish-red coloured bird.

Cuculus Micropetrus koi कोई *Var:* kɔi कौई *Var:* kɔe कौए *Var:* kol कोल N. *एक प्रकार का कठफोड़वा SD: Birds.* It knocks on the branches and trunk so that worms come out for its feed.

Cuculus Saturatus ceṭale चेटाले N. *एक प्रकार का छोटा पक्षी SD: Birds.* This bird lifts its plume when calls. When this bird cries, it is good to go for hunting.

cunt ara : ttayfu आराऽत्तायफू *Morph:* ara : -ttayfu. [SM] N. *योनी SD: Body Part Terms.*

current cor चोर N. *प्रवाह SD: Natural Environment.*

- taracɔr₁ ताराचौर *Morph:* tara-cɔr. N. *धारा; बिजली SD: Natural Environment.*

curry erkʰera एरखेरा *Morph:* er-kʰera. N. *तरी SD: Edible Items.*

curvy coṭɔ चोटौ ADJ. *घुमावदार* **curvy road.** ɲɔrto-coṭɔ ञौरतो चोटौ *घुमावदार सड़क SD: Attributes.*

cut etpʰo एत्फो *Morph:* et-pʰo. *Var:* it-pʰu ईत्फू V. *काटना* Cut something like beatle-nut.

- ɛkopʰo ऐकोफो *Morph:* ɛ-kopʰo. V. *काटना* **don't cut trees.** ŋo-ṭɔkʰo-be-kopʰom डोटौखोबेकोफोम *पेड़ मत काटो।*

- ɛwo : r ऐवोऽर [SM] V. *काटना; कटाव*
- ibeliŋ ईबेलींग *Morph:* i-beliŋ. *Var:* ibeviŋ ईबेवीड V. *काटना (सब्जी आदि को) छोटे चाकू से* **she cut herself.** ŋum beliŋ डूम बेलीड *उसने अपनेआप को काट लिया।* **chop the potato.** mino-bi-beliŋe मीनोबी बेलीडे *आलू काटो।* Cut something like vegetables.
- sɛrɛp सैरैप *Var:* sěrep शैरेप V. *काटना* **Lico is making me cut the wood.** lico tʰi aṭ-bi sɛrɛ-bi-liwo लीचो ठी आटबीलीवो *लीचो मुझसे लकड़ी कटवा रही है।* *See:* cut utsěrep ऊत्शेरेप *काटना*
- utsěrep ऊत्शेरेप *Morph:* ut-sěrep. V. *काटना* **he cuts tree.** o ṭɔŋe sěrep ओ टौडे शेरेप *वो पेड़ काटता है।* **I am cutting.** tʰɔ-e-sěre-bɔm ठौए शेरे बौम *मैं काट रहा हूं।* *See:* hit; attack; cut sɛrɛp सैरैप *मारना; प्रहार करना; काटना* Cut something like green coconut.

cut a long piece into small pieces ikkubeliŋ ईक्कूबेलीड *Morph:* ikku-beliŋ. V. *लंबी वस्तु को छोटे टुकड़ों में काटना* **to cut clothes.** julu biko beliŋ जूलू बीको बेलीड *कपड़ा काटना।*

cut a very small piece okkokata ओक्कोकाता *Morph:* okko-kata. V. *बहुत छोटा टुकड़ा काटना*

cut grass cɔl चौल V. *घास काटना* **he cut the grass.** cɛ mil tɛc bi cɔlo चै मील तैच बी चौलो *उसने घास काटी।* **Cut the grass fast.** ŋaram-kalemu-e-cɔle डाराम कालेमू एचौले *घास जल्दी जल्दी काटो।*

- tɛccɔbejukʰ तैच्चौबेजूख *Morph:* tɛc-cɔbe-jukʰ. *Var:* tɛc-belim-tot-calo तैच्बेलीम्तोत्चालो ADJ. *कटी हुई घास SD: Attributes.*

cut in big pieces ṭowoke टोवोके *Morph:* ṭowo-k-e. V. *बड़े टुकड़ो में काटना (चप्पू या नांव बनाने के लिए)* **make the centre of the boat (by scooping it).** rowo-katrao-ṭowo-ke रोवो कात्राओ टोवोके *नांव का बीच का हिस्सा बनाना (खोदकर)* **before the boat was made, he finished cooking turtle.** ṭowo-tut-tɛmo-cokbi-bi-banom-arališuko टोवो तूत तैमो चोक्बीबी बानोम आरालीशूको *नांव बनने से पहले, उसने कछुआ पका लिया।*

Language Culture and Bio-diversity: A critique of the formal legal systems of North-East India

Joy Dasgupta
Secretary, Greater Himalayan Bio-Cultural Society,
Shillong, Meghalaya

(The author did not present his paper at the seminar. He was an observer)

This paper explores the narratives of international discourse on the protection and preservation of Traditional Knowledge Systems (TKS) in particular the linkages between Language, Culture and Biodiversity and looks at how this discourse has evolved in the context of north east India.

The International discourse about the need to protect biodiversity-based traditional knowledge (TK) is epitomized by a host of International Conventions and treaties most notably Article 8(j) of the Convention on Biological Diversity. The overarching discourse at the international level has been to recognise the importance of TKS and the contributions made by traditional/indigenous people; and their importance as major actors in the conservation of biodiversity is highlighted in article 8(j) of the CBD. However in the context of north east India, there has been a very paternalistic acknowledgement of the importance of TK by the emerging state institutions in the field of biodiversity management. The emerging formal legal structures have tended not to take into consideration the complex linkages between the transmission of oral knowledge and the specialised role played by the languages of the region which help to transmit, enrich and add value to these knowledge systems. This is quite unbelievable given the fact that the North East is a major bio-cultural hotspot and a part of the linguistically and culturally rich greater Himalayan region. In fact the Greater Himalayan region, of which the north eastern region is very much a part, has over 400 languages spoken by less than 100,000 speakers. The paper argues that it is critically important for the formal legal systems to evolve a nuanced understanding of these interlinkages and in particular the links between language, culture and bio-diversity . The approach should move beyond mere documentation of TKS and a more holistic approach which takes the bio-cultural approach rather than a traditional biodiversity centric approach.

Introduction:

Biological diversity as a conceptual construct emerged in the latter part of the 20th century. The transition from wild life conservation to the conservation of biological diversity took place during this period. The passage of the Convention on Biological Diversity in 1992 and the widespread acceptance of the Convention signalled the emergence of the discourse of conservation and sustainable utilization of Biodiversity at the international level. Subsequently the importance of cultural diversity also has been widely recognized as an intrinsic chord in promoting biodiversity conservation and the bedrock for the development and transmission of traditional ecological knowledge. This bio-cultural diversity is not uniformly distributed and most of it is concentrated in the humid and semi-arid tropical and subtropical regions concentrated around 34 major biological diversity hotspots which account for over 90% of the world's biological and cultural diversity (Conservation International 2007). There is a tremendous overlap between the hotspots of biological and cultural diversity throughout the tropical and sub-tropical regions. It also has been widely recognized that mountains are home to most of the planet's bio-cultural diversity and it is important to develop a nuanced approach to address these realities (Stepp et al 2005 & Turin 2005).

The Emergence of the Global Biodiversity Conservation Regime.

Bio-diversity Conservation in the formal western sense started probably with the establishment of the Yellowstone National Park, though conservation of wildlife has been an age–old phenomenon. The transition to a holistic bio-diversity approach started with the passage of the Convention on Biological Diversity in 1992. The three pillars of the CBD are the conservation, sustainable usage of biodiversity and the fair and equitable sharing of benefits from access to biodiversity/ biodiversity based knowledge. The CBD is important for it recognizes the rights of indigenous people over their knowledge, innovations and practices and calls upon parties to the convention to respect, preserve and maintain such knowledge, innovations and practices relevant for the conservation and sustainable use of biological diversity. Article 8j of the CBD focuses on benefit sharing provisions and stipulates that benefit sharing can be accomplished through the utilization of knowledge, innovations and practices of indigenous and local communities. These articles (8(j), 10© 11 and 15) talk about the importance of indigenous/ local communities and their knowledge systems along with the need to incorporate these knowledge systems into the management of biological resources and promulgate a system of access to and benefit sharing from biodiversity based knowledge.(CBD 2007). There was also an acknowledgement and understanding of linguistic diversity which is reflected in the preamble to the CBD and also in the post CBD documents that have outlined the linkages between linguistic and bio-logical diversity (CBD 2004). Thus at the international level there is not only an increasing recognition but traditional and indigenous communities are being increasingly looked on as equal partners in the quest for a world where the values of bio-cultural diversity have more meaning along with an understanding about the tenurial linkages of biodiversity based TKS.

Profile of North East India:

North east India comprises of Arunachal Pradesh, Assam, Manipur, Meghalaya, Mizoram, Nagaland, Sikkim and Assam. Mountains and hills cover most of Arunachal Pradesh, Mizoram, Nagaland, Meghalaya, Sikkim and about half of Tripura, one-fifth of Assam and nine-tenths of Manipur. The northern part of the region is a part of the eastern Himalayan region but the rest of the region comprises of a series of hill ranges, which merge into the Arakan Yoma.

According to the 2001 census, the total population of the North East is 39 million (3.75 percent of the country) with 88% living in rural areas and 12 % in urban centers. Overall, tribals account for over 30% of the total population of this region. However, in Arunachal Pradesh, Manipur, Meghalaya, Mizoram and Nagaland, scheduled tribes comprise more than 60% of the population. This gives these states a predominantly tribal character.

The primary mode of subsistence is shifting cultivation, a land use practice that is in many ways one of the major reasons for the maintenance of the mosaic landscapes of forests interspersed with *Jhum* (swidden) i.e shifting cultivation fallows. The area also is extremely rich in faunal resources and houses representative fauna from the Indian, Malayan & Palearctic realms, that are also critically endangered (Chatterjee 2006).

North-east India is linked to the rest of India through a very narrow 21 km long corridor called the chicken's neck which passes through West Bengal in eastern India. The region is ethnically distinct from the rest of India with swidden cultivation being the primary land use. This region was by and large lightly administered in the colonial era, especially in the hill states, which resulted in a geographical and political isolation from the rest of colonial India. Thus, just after India's Independence, as the rule of the central government was strengthened, the result was that many isolated hill communities became involved in separatist movements. This forced the central government to address the social, political and economic grievances and the real difference that exists between the so-called mainland and this region. The process followed was through amendments to the Indian Constitution such as the creation of the Sixth Schedule and the incorporation of Article 371. This process covered the whole gamut of natural resource management, but remained largely a paper exercise and thus failed to meet the aspirations of the people of the region (Hazarika 1996).

Bio-cultural Diversity of North–East India:

This region is arguably the richest among all the different parts of India. It is a part of two major bio-diversity hotspots namely the Himalayan and the Indo-Burma (Conservation International 2008). It is also a part of the Himalayan hotspot of linguistic diversity .(Turin 2007 & Ved 2007). In fact it is believed that north east India has over 325 languages and dialects. As linguistic diversity is a well accepted proxy indicator for cultural diversity one can very well imagine the scale of cultural diversity that is being talked about here.

Biodiversity Governance Systems of North East India.

The biodiversity governance systems are inherently different from the rest of India and as stated above have also survived the onslaught of colonial rule as this area was comparatively lightly administered. In many ways it is a bridge between south and south east Asia and thus these land use systems have a lot of affinity with the land use systems of south east Asia.

The primary land owner ship structure in the North East has from time immemorial been community owned land; there are numerous examples of community based ownership in the region ranging across all the hill states. The following examples from many of the states in the region testify to this fact:

Community lands, including forest areas, have a number of uses, which are reflected in their names. In the Khasi and Jaintia hills of Meghalaya, the functions and purposes of most forests are based on village administration and religious perceptions. Community forests are known as *Law Kyntang, Law Adong, Law Lyngdoh, Law Shnong, Law Raij, Law Sumar, Law Kur*, etc., denoting the usages to which they are supposed to be put (H.J. Symlieh, personal communication). Land tenure was not disturbed by the colonial presence in these areas, as only a few areas were acquired outright by the British colonizers, while most of the smaller territories were treated as though they were beyond the borders of colonial India (Simon, 1996). After independence, the prevailing land tenure and practices were recognized and maintained in the district council legislation.

Most land in the Garo hills is forested and belongs to a specific clan. These lands are known as *A'king* lands and are theoretically controlled by the community through the *Nokma*. However, the *Nokma* is a woman, and actual control of *A'king* land lies with her husband (Dutta 2001).

There are no sacred forests in the *Garo* hills, but the people believe that the spirits of the dead reside in thick forests. *Garo* forests are used for slash-and-burn agriculture with adequate return cycles, and other traditions are still followed, in spite of the many changes that have taken place (Dutta 2001). In the case of Mizoram there are a lot of forests registered as village safety and supply reserves which in many cases predate the colonial presence in Mizoram(Singh 1996). In the case of Nagaland there are village forests, clan Forests, Community Wildlife Sanctuaries (Charles Chasie personal communication & Choudhary 1998). In Arunachal Pradesh there are a host of community managed areas like the Sacred forests of the *Nishis*, the *Anchal* Reserve Forests across the state, monastery forests of Bomdila and Tawang (Sudipto Chatterjee personal communication).

The Biodiversity Legal Framework in India.

In India forest and wildlife are a part of the concurrent list of the Indian constitution. The oldest law in force with reference to the question of ownership over biodiversity/forests/ wildlife is the forest act of 1927. There has been a host of subsequent legislation since including the Wildlife Protection Act 1972 along with its amendments in 2002, the forest conservation act of 1980, the Biodiversity act of 2004 and Forest Rights Act 0f 2006. These legislations by and large espouse a very strong guns and guards approach to biodiversity conservation. The overall thrust is to protect bio-diversity from the people and not with the people; though of late things are changing and there are quite a few sections in the Biodiversity act (Section 41 and the rules framed under the Forests Right act) which are a testimony to this changing mindset (adapted from Choudhary 2006, MOTF 2006, NBA 2005, Upadhaya 2002).

The constitution also acknowledges the different notions of forest ownership and governance structures in Mizoram and Nagaland through article 371 and also confers the ownership and management responsibility of land and forest resources other than reserved forests to autonomous district councils established under the sixth schedule in the states of Meghalaya, Assam, Mizoram. (MOLJ 2007).

Discussion: These laws by and large have not been drafted looking at the diverse linkages and actions that are required for the conservation of bio-diversity. They have put forth a very narrow understanding of the notions of biodiversity conservation , and a very poor understanding of the linkages between language culture and bio-diversity conservation.

These issues are outlined in the paragraphs below:

The issue of cultural diversity, which is the bedrock of the entire benefit-sharing scenario, is of critical importance. As already stated, the entire Himalayan region is a hot spot of cultural diversity and it is more so in the context of the eastern Himalayas of which north east India is an intrinsic part; over 400 languages are spoken throughout the Himalayas with most of the speakers numbering less than 100,000 (Turin 2007); the legal regimes while they acknowledge the importance of this diversity do not really address it, though it is language which carries the knowledge associated with its speakers.

There is no special provision for the protection of endangered languages and in some cases the different arms of the state pursue different policies. A good example is the current scenario in Arunachal Pradesh. Today, as a part of 'nation building', Hindi the Indian national language has been aggressively promoted in this state. The end result is that Hindi is becoming the *lingua franca* and the local tribal languages are beginning to have less speakers. In the long run, this means a loss of biodiversity-based knowledge, as the children of today fail to pick up language-based knowledge from their forefathers (Moji Riba personal communication). This issue is not being looked at both by the Arunachal State Biodiversity Board or the National Biodiversity Authority. Their approach is that the answer to these issues is documentation of TK, but in many ways it is a museum approach as TK is a dynamic system. These laws also see the role of local communities to basically being documenters of TK rather than active managers of natural resources and associated TK. A very good example in this regard is the Indian Biodiversity Act and the associated rules which look at the role of the biodiversity management committees only as documenters of TK and very marginally as managers. Though some of the laws do recognize the rights over TKS the tendency to impose a sense of hierarchical importance *vis a vis* the formal systems of knowledge cannot be ruled out. This means that though the rhetoric of rights for traditional / indigenous communities is adhered to in line with international prescriptions, the reality on the ground may be very different. The following example will highlight the point. Section 41 (1) of the Indian Biodiversity Act provides the space for local communities to manage and conserve local varieties. It may provide an important incentive for defending and adding value to different forms of swidden (slash and burn or *jhum*) agriculture. However, if one looks at the actual prescriptions of the state governments in the north eastern region where this is the dominant form of land use, the tenor is very much to replace it with commercial agriculture.

Thus one can see that the discourse on TK has by and large remained highly rhetorical and a very state centric one where the knowledge is deemed to be important but not the resources that sustain this knowledge. In north east India where the state does not control in most cases the access to these resources, the battle lines have been drawn. While on the one hand the government reiterates its commitment to protect TKS, on the other hand there are a host of attempts being made to assert control over community controlled biodiversity rich landscapes. There is also no understanding of how to ensure that these bio-diversity based TKS would be transmitted to the next generation. It is only through the medium of language that this transmission takes place. The state needs to develop a legal regime that addresses this reality may be through an integration of existing legal prescriptions that deal with language loss and also develop a regime of fiscal incentives to enable the transmission of bio-diversity based knowledge systems to the next generation.

References:

- **Chatterjee S. 2006**. The review of Biodiversity in North- East India. Unpublished Document.

- **Conservation International 2007**: Biodiversity Hotspots of the world/ Himalaya.: available at (http://www.biodiversityhotspots.org/xp/Hotspots/)

- **Convention on Biological Diversity 2004**. Indicators for assessing progress towards the 2010 target:status and trends of linguistic diversity and numbers of speakers of indigenous languages available at.(https://www.cbd.int/doc/meetings/ind/tegind-01/information/tegind-01-01-inf-07-en.pdf.)
Montreal: Secretariat of the Convention on Biological Diversity.

- **Convention on Biological Diversity (2007)**: Phase two of the composite report on the status and trends regarding the knowledge, innovations and practices of indigenous and local communities relevant to the conservation and sustainable use of biological diversity. Available at http://www.cbd.int/doc/meetings/tk/wg8j-05/official/wg8j-05-03-en.doc.Montreal: Secretariat of the Convention on Biological Diversity

- **Convention on Biological Diversity (2007)**: Plan of action for the retention of traditional knowledge research on and implementation of mechanisms and measures to address the underlying causes of the decline of traditional knowledge, innovations and practices. Available at http://www.cbd.int/doc/meetings/tk/wg8j-05/official/wg8j-05-03-add1-en.doc. Accessed on 29.11.2007.Montreal: Secretariat of the Convention on Biological Diversity.

- **Choudhary D. 1998**: Conservation by Local Communities in north east India in Kothari A. Pathak N. Anuradha R . Taneja B eds Communities and Conservation: Natural resource management in South and Central Asia. Sage , New Delhi , India.

- **Choudhary R. 2006** . Law of Forests in India. Orient Publishing Company. New Delhi, India.

- **Dutta, R.** 2001. *Community Managed forests in Meghalaya.* Socio-Legal Information Centre, India.

- **Hazarika S. 1996:** Strangers of the Mist, tales of war and peace from India's North-east. Penguin Publications, New Delhi, India.

- **MOLJ 2007.** The Constitution of the Republic of India. Available at http://lawmin.nic.in/coi.htm. Ministry Of Law and Justice . New Delhi , India..

- **MOTAF 2006.** Scheduled Tribes and other Traditional Forest Dwellers (Recognition of Forest Rights) Act, 2006. New Delhi, Ministry of Tribal Affairs, Government of India. Available at http://tribal.nic.in/actTA06.pdf.

- (**MOTAF 2007**). Draft Rules of the Scheduled Tribes and other Traditional Forest Dwellers (Recognition of Forest Rights) Act, 2006. New Delhi, Ministry of Tribal Affairs, Government of India. Available at http://tribal.nic.in/rules-190607.pdf.

- **NBA 2005:** The Biological Diversity Act 2002 and the Biological Diversity Rules 2004.
  Chennai: National Biodiversity Authority, Ministry of Environment and Forests, Government of India.

- **Simon, I.M. 1996.** Gazetteer of India, Meghalaya District Gazetteer – Khasi Hills. Shillong, India, Directorate of Arts and Culture, Government of Meghalaya.

- **Simon, I.M. 1996.** Gazetteer of India, Meghalaya District Gazetteer – Garo Hills. Shillong, India, Directorate ofArts and Culture, Government of Meghalaya.

- **Singh D.1996.** The last frontier: land, forests and people a case study of Mizoram. India, Tata Energy Research Institute.

- **Stepp J.R , Castaneda H. & Cervone S 2005**. : Mountains and bio-cultural diversity. Mountain Research and Development volume 25, number 3, August 2005 pp-223-227. United Nations University & the International Mountain Society. Berne, Switzerland.

- **Turin M 2005**. Language Endangerment and Linguistic rights in the Himalayas: A case study from Nepal. Mountain Research and Development volume 25, number 1, February 2005 pp-4-9. United Nations University & the International Mountain Society. Berne, Switzerland.

- **Turin M 2007**: Mapping Linguistic Diversity: An Atlas of Minority Languages in the Himalayan region. International Centre for Integrated Mountain Development, Kathmandu, Nepal. AVAILABLE at http//icimodbooksonline.org.

- **Upadhaya S& Upadhaya V 2002**. Handbook of Indian Environmental Law. Butterworth London, U.K

- **Ved P 2007**. Encyclopedia of North-East India, 5 Volumes. Saujanya Books, Delhi, India

List of Participants

Prof. Anvita Abbi
Professor of Linguistics,
Jawaharlal Nehru University
New Delhi – 110 067, INDIA
Mobile No. 9810627835
Office No.: 011-26704234
Residence No. 26742401
E-mail id.: anvitaabbi@gmail.com

Prof. Ramakant Agnihotri
Department of Linguistics
Faculty of Arts
University of Delhi
New Delhi – 110 007
E-mail id.: agniirk@yahoo.com

Prof. Peter K. Austin
Marit Rausing Chair in Field Linguistics
Director, Endangered Languages Academic Programme
Department of Linguistics, SOAS
Thornhaugh Street, Russell Square
London WC1H 0XG, United Kingdom
E-mail id.: pa2@soas.ac.uk

Prof. Udaya Kumar Chakraborty
M-4/13, Jadavpur University Teachers Quarters,
J.U. Campus, Kolkata 32, West Bengal
E-mail id.: udayachakra@gmail.com

Dr. Gail Coelho
Associate Professor, Department of Linguistics
Rm. 229, Arts Faculty Extension Bldg,
University of Delhi,
New Delhi – 110 007
Campus Phone: 27666676, ext. 112
Fax: 27666390
E-mail: gailcoelho@gmail.com /
gailcoelho@yahoo.com

Joy Dasgupta
C/o Dr L.Cajee,
"Shalom", Mawlai -Mawroh.
Shillong-793008.
Meghalaya.
E-mail:ghbsociety@gmail.com.

Prof. Ganesh Devy
Founder Director, Bhasha Trust
Mobile No.: 09879019130
Ph No.: 0265-2331968
E-mail id.: ganesh_devy@yahoo.com

Tshering Dorje
E-mail id.: tshering_dorje@hotmail.com
Mobile No. 09418356466
Tel No.: 019100222648
Fax No.: 011 91 11 2461 1290

H.E. Prof. Piotr Klodkowski
Ambassador of Poland
The Embassy of the Republic of Poland
50-M, Shantipath,
Chanakyapuri
New Delhi – 110 021

Prof. Krishna Kumar
Director, NCERT
National Council of Education Research & Training
Sri. Aurobindo Marg
New Delhi-110016
E-mail id.: director.ncert@nic.in
Office No.: 011-26964712/ 26519154

Lisa Lomdak
Arunachal Institute Of Tribal studies,
Rajiv Gandhi University,
Rono Hills , Doimukh,
Arunachal Pradesh-791113
Telephone: 0360-2277372
Fax: 0360-2277372
Mobile- 09612311935
E-Mail: lisa.lomdak@gmail.com

Prof. Ajit Mohanty
Professor, Zakir Hussain Centre for
Educational Studies
Jawaharlal Nehru University
New Delhi – 110 067
E-mail id.: ajitmohanty@gmail.com
Mobile No.: 9818447909
Phone No.: 011-26704419 (O) / 011-26741247 (R)

Prof. Panchanan Mohanty
Centre for Applied Linguistics
& Translation Studies
University of Hyderabad
Hyderabad – 500 046
Office No.: +91 40 23012068 (Home)
Telefax: +91 40 23010161 (Work)
E-mail id.: panchanan_mohanty@yahoo.com

Christopher Mosley
Editor in Chief
World Atlas of Endangered Languages
UNESCO
Research Fellow
University College London
Gower Street London – WC1E6BT
Phone No.: +44(0) 207679200
E-mail id.: chrismoseley50@yahoo.com

P.S. Loktus Negi (IAS Retd.)
Loktus Villa
Ravensdale
Shimla – 171 002
Mobile No. 09418020925
Office No. 0177-2620925
E-mail id.: negi_loktus@yahoo.co.in

Dr. Jean Robert Opgenort
University of Leiden
P.O. Box – 9500
2300RA Leiden
Netherlands
E-mail id.: jeanrobert@opgenort.nl

Prof. Minoti Panda
Assistant Professor
School of Social Sciences
Zakir Hussain Centre for
Education Studies, JNU
New Mehrauli Road
New Delhi – 110 067
E-mail id.: minotip@gmail.com

Prof. B. Ramakrishna Reddy
Professor of Linguistics (Retd)
Flat No.114, Gayatri Towers,
Street No.1, Tarnaka,
Secunderabad – 500 017
Mobile No.: 09849660355 / +91-40-27017613
E-mail id.: brkrin@yahoo.com

Dr. Nick Reid
Senior Lecturer
Programme Director, Master of Arts (Applied Linguistics)
School of Behavioural, Cognitive and Social Sciences
University of New England
Armidale NSW 2351
Australia
Phone No.: +61 2 6773 3400
Fax No.: +61 2 6773 3748
E-mail id.: nreid@une.educ.au
Webpage: www.une.edu.au/staff/nreid.php

Prof. Rajesh Sachdeva
Director I/C
Central Institute of Indian Languages
Manasagangotri,
Mysore -570 006 INDIA
Tel.No. +91 0821 - 2345020 (O), 2303529 (R)
Fax : 0821 - 2515032 (O)
Email : rajeshnehu@rediffmail.com /
rajesh@ciil.stpmy.soft.net

Dr. Asha Sarangi
Associate Professor
Centre for Political Studies,
School of Social Sciences,
Jawaharlal Nehru University
New Delhi 110 067, India.
Office No.: 011-26704413
E mail: ashasarangi@mail.jnu.ac.in

Dr. G.D.P. Shastry
Reader-Cum-Research Officer
Head, Centre for Tribal & Endangered Languages
CIIL, Mysore – 570 006
Phone No.: 0821-2345094 (O) / 0821 -2478049 ®
Mobile No.: 09980764094
E-mail id.: devi1953@yahoo.co.uk

Prof. Udaya Narayana Singh
Professor, Rabindra Bhavana
Visva-Bharati (University)
Santiniketan – 731 235
West Bengal
Telphone No.: (O) 94340-50218; (03463)262566 (RB)
E-mail id.: unsciil@yahoo.com

Dr. M. Sreenathan
Associate Professor
Dravidian University
Dept. of Dravidian
Srinivasa Vanam Kuppam-517 425,
Chittoor Dist. (A.P.)
E-mail id.: sreenathan.ansi@yahoo.com
Mobile No.: 09959172551

Dr. Kapila Vatsyayan
E-mail id.: asiaprojectiic@yahoo.com
India International Centre
40, Max Mueller Marg,
New Delhi – 110 003
Telephone No.: 24619431
Fax No.: 24627751

Dr. Lotika Varadarajan
4A Girdhar Apartments
28 Ferozeshah Road
New Delhi – 110 001
Telephone, Fax: (00 91 11) 371 3137, 371252;
fax: 323 1095
E-mail id.: lotika.varadarajan@gmail.com /
l_varad@hotmail.com

Dr. Tomasz Wicherkiewicz
Adam Mickiewicz University
Dept. for Language Policy & Minority Studies
PoznaA,,, Poland
Telephone No.: +48 606635571
E-mail id.: wicher@amu.edu.pl

Index of Languages and Scripts